PHILOSOPHY OF RELIGION

Towards a More Humane Approach

Religious belief is not just about abstract intellectual argument; it also impinges on all aspects of human life. John Cottingham's *Philosophy of Religion* opens up fresh perspectives on the nature and basis of the religious outlook, arguing that the detached neutrality of much of contemporary philosophizing may be counterproductive – hardening us against the receptivity required for certain kinds of important evidence to become salient. This book covers the traditional areas of the subject, including the meaning of religious claims, the existence of God, and the relation between religion and morality, as well as the role of spiritual praxis and how religious belief affects questions about the meaning of life, human suffering, and mortality. While preserving the clarity and rigour that are rightly prized in the analytic tradition, the book also draws on insights from literary and other sources, and aims to engage a wide readership.

John Cottingham is Professor Emeritus of Philosophy at the University of Reading; Professorial Research Fellow at Heythrop College, University of London; and an Honorary Fellow of St John's College, Oxford. He has served as Chairman of the British Society for the History of Philosophy, President of the Mind Association, President of the Aristotelian Society, and President of the British Society for the Philosophy of Religion. He was also editor of *Ratio*, the international journal of analytic philosophy, from 1993 to 2012. Professor Cottingham's books include *Descartes* (1986); *The Rationalists* (1988); *Reason, Will and Sensation* (1994); *Western Philosophy: An Anthology* (2nd edition, 2007); *Philosophy and the Good Life: Reason and the Passions in Greek, Cartesian and Psychoanalytic Ethics* (Cambridge, 1998); *On the Meaning of Life* (2003); *The Spiritual Dimension* (2005); *Cartesian Reflections* (2008); and *Why Believe?* (2009). He is co-translator of the standard three-volume Cambridge edition of *The Philosophical Writings of Descartes* (1985–1991). *The Moral Life*, a collection of essays honouring his work on moral philosophy and philosophy of religion, was published in 2008.

Cambridge Studies in Religion, Philosophy, and Society

Series Editors

PAUL MOSER, *Loyola University Chicago*
CHAD MEISTER, *Bethel College*

Philosophy of Religion: Towards a More Humane Approach, John Cottingham

Already published
Roger Trigg *Religious Diversity: Philosophical and Political Dimensions*

PHILOSOPHY OF RELIGION
Towards a More Humane Approach

JOHN COTTINGHAM
University of Reading
and
Heythrop College, University of London

CAMBRIDGE
UNIVERSITY PRESS

CAMBRIDGE
UNIVERSITY PRESS

32 Avenue of the Americas, New York, NY 10013-2473, USA

Cambridge University Press is part of the University of Cambridge.

It furthers the University's mission by disseminating knowledge in the pursuit of education, learning, and research at the highest international levels of excellence.

www.cambridge.org
Information on this title: www.cambridge.org/9781107695184

© John Cottingham 2014

First published 2014

Printed in the United States of America

A catalog record for this publication is available from the British Library.

Library of Congress Cataloging in Publication Data
Cottingham, John, 1943–
Philosophy of religion : towards a more humane approach / John Cottingham, University of Reading.
pages cm. – (Cambridge studies in religion, philosophy, and society)
Includes bibliographical references and index.
ISBN 978-1-107-01943-0 (hardback-13) – ISBN 978-1-107-69518-4 (pbk.-13)
1. Religion – Philosophy. I. Title.
BL51.C6785 2014
210–dc23 2014016074

ISBN 978-1-107-01943-0 Hardback
ISBN 978-1-107-69518-4 Paperback

Cambridge University Press has no responsibility for the persistence or accuracy of URLs for external or third-party Internet Web sites referred to in this publication and does not guarantee that any content on such Web sites is, or will remain, accurate or appropriate.

For JTW and HJC

CONTENTS

CONTENTS

PREFACE AND
ACKNOWLEDGEMENTS

The philosophy of religion is a growing and flourishing field, as may be seen from the increasing numbers of textbooks, anthologies, and companions now available in the area. This book certainly does not try to cover all the topics that have been included under the heading 'philosophy of religion', though it aims to discuss those I take to be the most central. It is primarily a work of philosophy, as opposed to philosophical theology, and does not include detailed discussion of doctrines like the Trinity or the Incarnation that have received attention from philosophers (often very fruitfully and interestingly) in recent years. Nor, apart from one or two brief passing references, does it venture into comparative world religion, which has become a vast and fascinating academic field in its own right. All philosophizing (whether its practitioners acknowledge it or not) is inevitably conducted within a given cultural and historical context, and this book is no exception, being primarily informed by the philosophical tradition going back to Plato and Aristotle, and the religious tradition whose roots go back to the Judaeo-Christian scriptures. The audience at which the book is aimed includes colleagues and students working in the philosophy of religion, but I have tried to make the philosophy accessible to as wide a readership as possible. Many of the topics are inevitably complex, but I have endeavoured to avoid technical jargon, and for the most part I have avoided engaging with the minutiae of the debates in the recent academic literature.

It will be apparent that while much of the discussion in the following chapters falls broadly within the 'mainstream' of contemporary philosophy of religion, the approach taken sometimes diverges in some respects from that which has become prevalent in the anglophone philosophical world. My aim in developing this approach is certainly not to disparage the prevailing model, and nothing I say here is intended to cast doubt on its value. I think there are many possible ways of approaching the subject, and it should not be assumed that they are necessarily incompatible or that they must somehow be in competition. One of my aims in what follows is to open up what I take to be enriched modes of philosophical understanding, which seem to me especially fruitful in the philosophy of religion (and for that matter in a number of other branches of philosophy), without compromising the standards of clarity and precision that are so rightly prized in the anglophone philosophical world. I shall be happy if at least some of my readers take away from this book a sense of the conviction that has motivated me to write it: that philosophizing about religion is no mere academic exercise but something that engages every part of us, and impinges in the closest possible way on who we are and how we lead our lives.

In various places I have drawn on material from the following previously published articles, and my thanks are due to the respective editors and publishers for allowing me to make use of it here: (in Chapter 3) 'Human Nature and the Transcendent', in Constantine Sandis and M. J. Cain (eds.), *Human Nature*, Royal Institute of Philosophy supplement 70 (Cambridge: Cambridge University Press, 2012), pp. 233–254; (in Chapter 4) 'Confronting the Cosmos: Scientific Rationality and Human Understanding', *Proceedings of the ACPA* (Philosophy Documentation Center), Vol. 85 (2011), pp. 27–42; (in Chapter 6) 'The Question of Ageing', *Philosophical Papers* 41:3 (2012), pp. 371–396; 'Meaningful Life', in Paul K. Moser and Michael T. McFall (eds.), *The Wisdom of the Christian Faith* (Cambridge University Press, 2012), pp. 175–196; and 'Meaningfulness, Eternity, Theism', in Beatrix Himmelmann (ed.), *Meaning in Life* (Berlin: De Gruyter, 2013); (in Chapter 7) 'Philosophy and Self-improvement: Continuity and Change in Philosophy's Self-conception from the Classical to the Early-modern Era', in Michael Chase, Stephen Clark, and Michael McGhee (eds.), *Philosophy as a Way of Life: Ancients and Moderns* (Oxford: Blackwell, 2013), pp. 148–166; 'Spirituality', in C. Taliaferro, V. Harrison, and S. Goetz (eds.), *The Routledge Companion to Theism* (New York: Routledge, 2013), ch. 50, pp. 654–665; and 'Conversion, Self-Discovery and Moral Change', in Ingolf Dalferth and Michael Rogers (eds.), *Conversion.*

Claremont Studies in the Philosophy of Religion (Tübingen: Mohr Siebeck, 2013), pp. 211–229.

A word about the reference system used in the footnotes. I have made a point of *not* using the increasingly prevalent 'Harvard' system, which refers to texts by giving only the author and date. Though it may be suitable for the sciences, where priority of discovery is important, this system is singularly inept for the humanities. Expressions like 'Kant 1958' or 'Aquinas 1990' are not just an affront to chronology; they are pedagogically uninformative (students and others are deprived of being told or reminded when the work originally appeared); they are tiresome (the reader will constantly have to leaf back to the bibliography to discover which title is being referred to); and they are unhelpful, since they often simply reflect the edition the writer happened to have on his or her shelves when writing, and do nothing to enable readers to find the relevant passage, unless they happen by chance to have the self-same edition at their disposal. With this in mind, when citing sources in the footnotes, I have always given the title of the work referred to, and, at the first mention, the original date when it appeared (and, where appropriate, the original title). Also, wherever possible, and especially with canonical philosophical and literary texts, I have referred to passages by *part, chapter,* or *section numbers,* which are common to all editions and translations and thus enable the reader to find the passage in whichever edition they are using. In the case of passages quoted from non-English texts, the English renderings supplied are generally my own; but for the convenience of the reader details of widely available English editions are given in the Bibliography.

Some of the materials included here have been presented in one form or another at various conferences and discussion groups around the world, including at the following institutions: Bristol University, Cape Breton University, Central European University Budapest, Claremont Graduate University, Durham University, Erasmus University Rotterdam, Fordham University, Heythrop College University of London, Oxford Brookes University, Peking University, Rhodes University, St Francis Xavier University, University of Johannesburg, University of Oxford, Thomas More Institute London, University of Stirling, and the University of Utrecht; I am indebted to the many participants on those occasions for their stimulating comments and questions. I am grateful to the many friends and colleagues who by their writings and in conversation have enriched my understanding of many of the topics discussed here, including Julian Baggini, Guy Bennett-Hunter, Rachel Blass, Vincent Brummer, Clare Carlisle, Tim Chappell, Beverley Clack, Sarah Coakley, David Cooper, Ingolf Dalferth, Max De Gaynesford, Modesto Gomez, Fiona Ellis, Peter Hacker, Christopher Hamilton, John Hare, Victoria Harrison, Douglas Hedley, Beatrix Himmelmann, Johannes Hoff, Jonathan Jacobs, Ward Jones, John Kekes, Ian Kidd, Stephen Law, Michael Lacewing, David Leal, Tim Mawson, Iain McGilchrist, Thad Metz, Adrian Moore, Stephen Mulhall, David Oderberg, Herman Philipse, Andrew Pinsent, Roger Scruton, Severin Schroeder, Jim Stone, Eleonore Stump, Richard Swinburne, Pedro Tabensky, Samantha Vice, Keith Ward, William Wood, and Mark Wynn. I am grateful to Myra Cottingham for helpful discussion and advice on many points. My particular thanks are due to the series editors, Paul Moser and Chad Meister, for encouraging me to undertake this project, and to David McPherson, who most kindly read the entire typescript, picking up many errors and offering a host of helpful comments. My greatest debt, as always, is to my family for their sustaining love and support; the book is dedicated to its two youngest members, both born in the past two years during which this book was written.

West Berkshire, England
November 2013

I

METHOD

Legoito d'an hikanōs ei kata tēn hypokeimenēn hylēn diasaphētheiē.
('Our discussion will be on the right lines if it illuminates things in a
way that is appropriate to the subject-matter in question.')
Aristotle[1]

I. THE NATURE OF THE SUBJECT

The philosophy of religion has unique attractions. At a time when academic philosophizing has become increasingly fragmented, separated
off into a host of specialisms preoccupied with narrow programmes of
'research',[2] the philosophical study of religion has a stimulatingly wide
purview and necessarily connects us with a whole spectrum of inquiries.
It embraces practical moral questions (about how we should live our
lives), as well as more theoretical moral issues about the objectivity of
morality and the source of moral value; it takes us into the philosophy
of mind – questions about the nature of the self and consciousness,
and the extent to which we are ultimately responsible for our character
and actions; and it delves into cosmological questions about the ultimate source of our world and of human existence. But perhaps most
strikingly, it is concerned with our overall view of the nature of reality.

1 Aristotle, *Nicomachean Ethics* [c. 325 BC], Bk. I, Ch. 3, ed. T. Irwin (Indianapolis, IN:
Hackett, 1985).
2 Although the term 'research' has become unavoidable for those seeking funding in the
humanities, it is in many ways a misleading label for the work done in the humane disciplines. See further J. Cottingham, "What Is Humane Philosophy and Why Is It at Risk?",
in A. O'Hear (ed.), *Conceptions of Philosophy* (Cambridge: Cambridge University Press,
2009).

Hence, it necessarily resists division into hermetically sealed subdisciplines, and instead keeps alive the traditional grand vision of philosophy as the attempt to achieve a comprehensive 'synoptic' vision of things – one that endeavours to discern how (or how far) the different areas of our human understanding fit together.

These grand holistic questions are ones that many contemporary analytic philosophers are wary of; understandably enough, the needs of gaining a doctoral qualification and making one's career in a competitive academic world are apt to lead people to retreat into specialized niches where they can gain a respected expertise in a narrow area. There is surely nothing wrong with this specialisation as such – indeed, it can yield significant scholarly dividends. But for all that, I suspect that many people still retain something of the drive that led them to philosophy in the first place: an urge to deepen their understanding of what meaning, if any, their lives as a whole may have, or what kind of overall vision of reality may be possible. And sooner or later, this quest, the quest that has always been at the heart of the philosophical enterprise, is likely to draw us into the grand questions tackled by philosophy of religion.

This does not of course mean that all philosophers should become philosophers of religion, nor does it mean that philosophers of religion cannot themselves develop specialized expertise in particular texts or problems. But if we feel the pull of the ancient Socratic slogan, 'the unexamined life is not worth living for a human being',[3] then seeing whether we can achieve a framework for understanding our lives as a whole will be a task that we cannot put off for ever. At least 'once in our life' (*semel in vita*), as René Descartes remarked in one of the founding texts of modern philosophy,[4] most of us will be called to tackle this task. To be sure, we may not as a result decide to embrace a theistic worldview; an increasing number of philosophers today have opted for some form of 'naturalistic' alternative ('naturalism' is a highly problematic term, but has come to mean, roughly, the view that there are no ultimate constituents of reality apart from those studied by the physical sciences). But the question of whether theism or naturalism constitutes a more coherent and compelling outlook is itself one of the

---

3 Plato, *Apology* [c. 395 BC], 38a.
4 René Descartes, *Meditations on First Philosophy* [1641], First Meditation, first paragraph.

grand synoptic questions of which we are speaking, and one that is central to the philosophy of religion.

As well as its unique attractions, philosophy of religion also presents unique problems. Almost any philosophical question may from time to time keep us awake at night, because of the intricate and demanding nature of the concepts and arguments involved; and philosophy of religion is no exception. But aside from that, there is a special aspect to the philosophical study of religion, namely, that the issues are ones in which practitioners generally have a strong personal stake, and which may even affect their entire sense of who they are and what kind of world they inhabit. In other areas of philosophy (in the case of a shift from foundationalism to coherentism in the philosophy of knowledge, for instance), there may well be a considerable intellectual struggle, but for the most part it is not one that has an impact on people's deepest commitments, or that pervasively affects their understanding of themselves and the direction of their lives. Religious belief, by contrast, is something that touches our most profound sense of who and what we are; and hence debating the validity of the theistic outlook can never be something about which the believer feels entirely detached. And similarly, the atheistic outlook is also one that implies deeply held beliefs about the nature of human life and the world we inhabit, beliefs in which the subject often has a significant personal involvement (for example, they may have been forged in the heat of a fierce struggle to break away from views inherited from parents or teachers); so here again, detached dispassionate evaluation is seldom the whole story.

These issues of commitment and involvement that are so often bound up with the practice of philosophy of religion might at first seem to suggest that there is something suspect about the philosophical credentials of the subject. Can philosophy of religion really be practised in that calm, dispassionate, purely rational spirit that is supposed to be the hallmark of proper philosophical inquiry? One possible response to this challenge is a 'neutralist' response: the philosophical student of religion should set aside his or her personal commitments and try to adopt the impartial perspective of, say, a judge in a law court. One should listen to the arguments, evaluate the evidence, and draw the appropriate conclusion; and if the results of this process are unpalatable to one's prior convictions, so be it – the obligations of impartial rationality should be paramount. We should, on this view, model ourselves on the professionalism of a presiding judge in a law court, who might reach his decision somewhat as follows: 'as a property-owner myself, I might be emotionally inclined to side with the landlord in this dispute, but, given the evidence presented to the court, and the statute and case law on this issue, the correct legal judgment must be in favour of the tenant.'

Unfortunately, this analogy doesn't quite work. In the first place, if a judge finds herself too personally involved in a case, then the proper course is for her to decline to hear it and pass it on to a colleague. But in the momentous choices connected with religious belief, there is no way the questions can be declined or delegated. As Blaise Pascal, one of Western philosophy's most insightful writers on religion, put it: 'you must choose'.[5] This may seem a little overstated: perhaps after due consideration the right response might be some kind of agnosticism. But simply stepping aside from the question altogether is just not an option.

In the second place, the neutral model of decision making seems in certain contexts to be unstable. This instability is wittily exposed in the piquant address of the Usher to the jury in Gilbert and Sullivan's comic opera *Trial by Jury*:

> Now jurymen hear my advice
> All kinds of vulgar prejudice
> I pray you set aside:
> With stern judicial frame of mind
> From bias free of every kind
> This trial must be tried
>
> Oh, listen to the plaintiff's case:
> Observe the features of her face
> The broken-hearted bride.
> Condole with her distress of mind:
> From bias free of every kind
> This trial must be tried![6]

Even those trained to be detached and impartial can and should recognize that there are cases where their personal commitments or emotional responses are simply too deeply entrenched for them to be confident that

---

5 'Il faut choisir.' Blaise Pascal, *Pensées* ('Thoughts') [1670], ed. L. Lafuma (Paris: Seuil, 1962), no. 418. Compare William James on 'forced options', in *The Will to Believe* [1896] (Cranston, RI: Anglenook, 2012), §1.
6 First performed 1875; libretto by W. S. Gilbert.

they can be set aside. More serious still, emotional commitments may operate at a subconscious level, exerting a subtle and not fully detected influence on which pieces of evidence appear particularly salient, or which arguments seem particularly persuasive. Religion is hardly the only field in which these points are applicable, but given the pivotal importance of the religious outlook (or its absence) in our lives, and the role played here by personal commitment, it seems worth spending a little more time at the start of our inquiry thinking about the pros and cons of the 'neutralist' model, and the implications for the appropriate methodology to be adopted in the philosophy of religion.

2. DETACHMENT AND RATIONALITY

'Arguments seldom work on men of wit and learning when they have once engaged themselves in a contrary opinion'; so wrote Thomas Hobbes in the mid-seventeenth century.[7] His contemporary Descartes vividly warned against the power of preconceived opinions (*praejudicia*) to cloud the 'natural light' of rationality.[8] Now clearly philosophy is, and should be, committed to the principles of rational argument, which means, most importantly, maintaining consistency and coherence in our thinking. We should, as Socrates famously said, 'follow the argument where it leads'.[9] In our own time, the prevailing way of philosophizing in the anglophone world that is known as 'analytic philosophy' (though that term is problematic in several respects) is rightly committed to upholding high standards of clarity and rigour – and let me make it quite clear at the outset that I subscribe wholeheartedly to those values – the values of the philosophical tradition in which I was trained. But in the way a considerable number of analytic philosophers tend to work, there is an additional dimension that seems more questionable.

This is the implicit assumption that the truth is, as it were, 'flat', and that we reach the best results in philosophy by eliminating all ambiguity

---

7 Thomas Hobbes, *The Questions concerning Liberty and Necessity and Chance* [1654], in *English Works of Thomas Hobbes*, ed. W. Molesworth (London: Bohn, 1841), Vol. V, no. 38, Postscript, p. 435. By 'wit', Hobbes means intelligence.
8 See Descartes, *Meditations*, Synopsis, first paragraph; and *Search for Truth* [*La recherche de la vérité*, c. 1641], first two paragraphs.
9 Plato, *Republic* [c. 375 BC], 394d.

from our discourse and striving to emulate the austere, pared-down language of modern science. Increasing numbers of philosophers appear to subscribe to this kind of view; Brian Leiter, for example, has spoken admiringly of the recent 'naturalistic revolution' in philosophy which holds that philosophy should 'adopt and emulate the methods of successful sciences'.[10] But a leading contemporary philosopher of religion, Eleonore Stump, has recently voiced a growing disquiet about this trend in analytic philosophy, particularly in areas, such as moral philosophy and philosophy of religion, which are specially concerned with the significance of the human predicament and our responses to the deep moral and spiritual challenges of our lives. While fully supporting the precision and discipline for which the analytic tradition is rightly prized, Stump deplores its 'cognitive *hemianopia*' – its blindness to the kinds of insights associated with the right cerebral hemisphere, and its unwarranted tendency to 'suppose that left-brain skills alone will reveal to us all that is philosophically interesting about the world'.[11] The reference here is to recent studies in neurophysiology and psychology, which suggest that the left hemisphere of the brain plays a major role in the exercise of our logical and conceptual abilities, while the right hemisphere is associated with more intuitive, imaginative, and holistic forms of awareness. Some possible implications of this have been developed by Iain McGilchrist:

There are two ways of being in the world, both of which are essential. One is to allow things to be *present* to us in all their embodied particularity, with all their changeability and impermanence and their interconnectedness, as part of a whole which is forever in flux. In this world we, too, feel connected to what we experience, part of that whole, not confined in subjective isolation from a world that is viewed as objective. The other is to step outside the flow of experience and 'experience' our experience in a special way: to *re-present* the world in a form that is less truthful, but apparently clearer, and therefore cast in a form which is more useful for manipulation of the world and one another. This world is explicitly abstracted, compartmentalised, fragmented,

10 Brian Leiter, *The Future for Philosophy* (Oxford: Clarendon Press, 2004), Editor's Introduction, pp. 2–3.
11 Eleonore Stump, *Wandering in Darkness* (Oxford: Oxford University Press, 2010), pp. 24–25.

static (though its 'bits' can be set in motion, like a machine), essentially lifeless. From this world we feel detached, but in relation to it we are powerful.[12]

This kind of distinction between two distinct but equally vital modes of cognition raises complex questions about human awareness that deserve more attention from philosophers generally than they have hitherto received. But with respect to the philosophy of religion in particular, at least one important lesson suggests itself. For many of the issues that arise in the subject, for example, the problems connected with human suffering, sin, evil, repentance, conversion, and redemption, and religious experience generally, even though technically expert argument no doubt has its place, we are also going to need additional resources.

What might these resources be? Eleonore Stump, in her recent study of the problem of evil, refers in particular to those arising from our manifold responses to the multiple resonances of literary, and scriptural, narrative. This chimes in with calls for a certain kind of narrative or literary turn in philosophy, powerfully advocated in the widely admired work of Martha Nussbaum. Nussbaum argues that in learning to appreciate a great literary text we have to allow ourselves to be receptive and 'porous', knowing when to yield instead of maintaining constant critical detachment.[13] Somewhat analogously, Stump insists that literary narratives cannot be used as mere illustrative tools for philosophical arguments – that would be to 'demean' the role of narrative to that of a mere picture or example. She proposes instead an 'antiphonal' structure, where the narrative is considered in its 'disorderly richness', so that subsequent philosophical reflection can operate in a more deeply informed way, enlightened to aspects of reality to which it might otherwise have been blind.[14]

---

12 Iain McGilchrist, *The Master and His Emissary* (New Haven: Yale University Press, 2009), p. 93 (slightly adapted). It should be added that associating these two modes of awareness with the right and left hemispheres, respectively, is something of a schematic approximation, as McGilchrist himself stresses. There is evidence to suggest that in most people the respective functions do broadly correlate with neural activity in the relevant halves of the brain, but in normal subjects there is constant interaction between the halves.

13 Martha Nussbaum, *Love's Knowledge* (Oxford: Oxford University Press, 1990), pp. 281–282.

14 Stump, *Wandering in Darkness*, pp. 26–27.

Reflection on these points suggests that the appropriate style for philosophy of religion may be somewhat different from that which dominates the contemporary literature. This need not mean constantly bombarding the reader with quotations from scripture or poetry; but it might allow scope for a more generous deployment of scriptural and literary sources when these seem relevant to the arguments being discussed and when our understanding of the issues seems likely to be thereby enriched. The key point here is that much religious discourse is *multilayered* – it carries a rich charge of symbolic significance that resonates with us on many different levels of understanding, not all of them, perhaps, fully grasped by the reflective, analytic mind. Any plausible account of the human condition must make space for the crucial role of imaginative, symbolic, and poetic forms of understanding in deepening our awareness of ourselves and the reality we inhabit. And for this reason it may be a serious error to try to reduce all religious thinking to a bald set of factual assertions whose literal propositional content is then to be clinically isolated and assessed. Some philosophers may suppose that any departure from complete analytical detachment would involve a loss of philosophical integrity; and certainly there is need for philosophical caution whenever our imaginative and emotional resources are made use of. But equally, if we insist on maintaining a detached analytical stance at all times, this may be less a sign of intellectual integrity than what Nussbaum calls 'a stratagem of flight' – a refusal of the openness and receptivity that is prepared to acknowledge all the dimensions of our humanity.[15] The task, after all, is to enrich our philosophical understanding of religious thought and experience, and there is no reason to suppose that achieving such understanding always has to be a comfortable, detached, purely 'academic' matter. We might instead want to take on board Aristotle's reminder that in philosophy one's methods have to be suited to the subject matter under investigation.[16] And we may also want to reflect on Andrew Louth's observation that in the sphere of religion, true understanding characteristically involves a 'growth in experience [which] is not primarily an increase in knowledge of this or that situation, but rather an escape from what had deceived us and held us captive. It is learning

---

15 Nussbaum, *Love's Knowledge* (Oxford: Oxford University Press, 1990), p. 268.
16 See the epigraph at the start of the present chapter.

by suffering, suffering in the process of undeception, which is usually painful'.[17]

3. WAYS OF PHILOSOPHIZING ABOUT RELIGIOUS BELIEF

The points just made about the methods and language appropriate to the philosophical discussion of religious belief inevitably raise questions about the way in which philosophy of religion is currently practised. As standardly taught in university courses, a large part of the subject focuses on the domain of so-called natural theology – the examination of 'pure' rational demonstrations or probabilistic arguments about God's existence, which are intended to appeal to any rational inquirer, irrespective of their personal commitments or religious beliefs (or lack thereof). The aim is an impartial investigation of questions about the existence and nature of God that can be tackled by intellectual argument alone. But from what has been said in the previous section, it may already be clear that there is a certain cost to be paid if philosophy of religion is entirely or even mainly restricted to these kinds of inquiry. It is not that there is anything wrong with the careful analysis and critical discussion of arguments of this sort; on the contrary, such work can be philosophically valuable in all sorts of ways. But philosophy is about more than skill in evaluating arguments, or the accumulation of knowledge about the various moves and countermoves in an intellectual debate. At its deepest and most rewarding level it has always aimed not so much at increasing our *knowledge* (in the way that is true of many primarily empirical and scientific disciplines), but rather at enriching our *understanding*. As Anthony Kenny has aptly put it, 'Philosophy is not a matter of expanding knowledge, of acquiring new truths about the world; the philosopher is not in possession of information that is denied to others. Philosophy is not a matter of knowledge, it is a matter of understanding, that is to say, of organizing what is known'.[18] And the more one thinks about understanding, the clearer it becomes that it cannot operate just analytically but needs to work holistically, or synthetically, achieving, at its fullest, a 'synoptic' view of how far the various elements of our world fit together.

17 Andrew Louth, *Discerning the Mystery* (Oxford: Clarendon Press, 1983), p. 37.
18 Anthony Kenny, *What I Believe* (London: Continuum, 2006), p. 14.

Now the phrase 'our world', in this context, could be taken to mean simply a collection of facts, rather like a collection of atoms, expressible as the set of all true propositions. This very scientifically oriented conception was essentially the one Ludwig Wittgenstein held in his early work, the *Tractatus*: 'the world is everything that is the case'.[19] But even in that early work, Wittgenstein allowed that there were things that could not be said, on this austere model of language, but which might somehow be 'shown'.[20] Moreover, Wittgenstein's view of the nature of language and meaning underwent significant developments between the publication of the *Tractatus* and the composition of his other great masterpiece, the *Philosophical Investigations*; and these developments have important implications for the question of how we should approach religious language. Wittgenstein came to think that there is no general form of language; rather, if we are interested in the meaning of linguistic utterances we should think about their *use* in a particular practice or activity – in a 'language game'. The term 'language-game' is meant to bring into prominence the fact that the speaking of a language is 'part of an activity, or of a form of life'.[21] The lesson to be drawn from Wittgenstein's later philosophy is that if we wish to understand any type of language, including religious language, we have to look at how it operates as part of the culture in which it is embedded. Wittgenstein's interest in 'forms of life' (*Lebensformen*) was in some respects a 'holistic' reaction against the atomistic approach to meaning he had espoused in the *Tractatus* (where an individual proposition was taken to be a 'picture of reality').[22] Our language games, he later came to see, are interwoven with a web of nonlinguistic activities and cannot be understood apart from the context that gives them life.

The Wittgensteinian approach to religion may have problems of its own,[23] and the present book is not especially committed to defending the value of such an approach in general. (For example, in many

---

19 Ludwig Wittgenstein, *Tractatus Logico-Philosophicus* [1921], trans. D. F. Pears and B. F. McGuinness (London: Routledge, 1961), §1.
20 Wittgenstein, *Tractatus*, §6.522.
21 Ludwig Wittgenstein, *Philosophical Investigations* [*Philosophische Untersuchungen*, 1953], trans. G. E. M. Anscombe (New York: Macmillan, 1958), Part I, §23.
22 Wittgenstein, *Tractatus*, §4.01.
23 See further J. Cottingham, 'Wittgenstein's Philosophy of Religion', in H.-J. Glock and J. Hyman (eds.), *A Companion to Wittgenstein* (Oxford: Wiley, forthcoming).

quarters Wittgenstein has come to be linked, rightly or wrongly, to a 'noncognitivist' approach to religion, which this book certainly does not subscribe to.)[24] But there is nonetheless an important methodological lesson to be learned from Wittgenstein's insights about language being embedded in a 'form of life'. If we want to understand and evaluate religious belief we need to do more than analyse and dissect the truth claims involved: we need to make a serious attempt to understand the context of culture and praxis that gives life to those claims. If we apply this insight to the typical university course on philosophy of religion, with its standard syllabus that works through the various traditional arguments for and against God's existence, we cannot but notice that these take us into a very abstract domain that is often far removed from religion as it actually operates in the life of the believer. It is rather as if the philosophy of music were to confine itself to the abstract theories and arguments of musicologists, without any attention being paid to the transforming power of music in the lives of those who experience it. So without in any way disparaging the enterprise of natural theology (and we shall certainly from time to time have occasion to refer to the traditional arguments and counterarguments concerning God), our overall aim will be to develop a more 'humane' model for philosophy of religion: one that preserves the virtues of a critical philosophical methodology, but connects the subject more closely with the moral and spiritual sensibilities that have shaped religious belief over the centuries, and which continue to inform the lives of believers today.

4. THE HEART HAS ITS REASONS

How does the 'humane' model for philosophy of religion that we are beginning to sketch out match up when set against the long Western tradition of philosophical reflection about God? At first sight, it might appear to be radically out of tune with that tradition, since the tradition is often interpreted by philosophers in a very abstract and intellectualistic way. Descartes, for example, is often presented as the 'arch-rationalist', deploying purely intellectual arguments about God's existence that are intended to be accessible to, and assessable by, any

24 See some of the essays in D. Z. Phillips (ed.), *Religion and Understanding* (Oxford: Blackwell, 1967).

rational inquirer. One has to admit that Descartes himself often spoke in ways that encourage this detached and abstract model for philosophy of religion. 'I have written my philosophy', he reportedly observed, 'in such a way as to make it acceptable anywhere – even among the Turks'.[25] By the 'Turks', he had in mind the followers of Islam, and in general those outside the Christian faith; and indeed he clearly intended his writings to have force even for sceptics and atheists.[26] So Descartes's position often appears to be that the pure light of reason, relying simply on the 'clear and distinct' intuitions of the intellect, will be enough to yield the desired conclusions about the nature and existence of God.[27]

But even in the 'arch-rationalist' Descartes, we find, perhaps surprisingly, language that seems designed to appeal to much more than the calm and dispassionate intellect. Having gone through a complex logical demonstration of God's existence, in the Third Meditation, the meditator pours out his joyful affirmation of the truth just discovered in a passage that can only be described as devotional: 'Here let me pause for a while, and gaze at, wonder at, and adore the beauty of this immense light, in so far as the eye of my darkened intellect can bear it'.[28] Such passages are often skipped over, or studiously ignored, in today's typical university lectures. But in fact they follow a long tradition of philosophizing about God, going back to Anselm in the eleventh century, and even harking right back to Augustine at the close of the Roman empire – a tradition that intermingles philosophical reflection with expressions of religious commitment and awe.

But some might ask: could not we just filter out these devotional elements, on the grounds that they interfere with the 'purity' of our philosophical assessments? Such a strategy turns out to be highly dubious, not just because it often involves a cavalier attitude to the style

25 Descartes, *Conversation with Burman* [1648], AT V 159: CSMK 342. AT refers to C. Adam and P. Tannery, *Œuvres de Descartes*, 12 vols., revised ed. (Paris: Vrin/CNRS, 1964–76); CSM to J. Cottingham, R. Stoothoff, and D. Murdoch, *The Philosophical Writings of Descartes*, vols. I and II (Cambridge: Cambridge University Press, 1985), and CSMK to vol. III, The Correspondence, by the same translators and A. Kenny (Cambridge: Cambridge University Press, 1991).

26 See Descartes, *Meditations*, Dedicatory Letter to the Sorbonne (AT VII 6: CSM II 6).

27 Hence, there is very little reference to revelation or Scripture in Descartes's philosophy of religion: he was wary of discussing such matters, remarking that 'we must leave these to the theologians to explain.' *Conversation with Burman* (AT V 178: CSMK 353).

28 Descartes, *Meditations*, Third Meditation, final paragraph.

and composition of the texts we are supposed to be studying, but also because it involves a blindness to the actual character of the arguments deployed. Thus Descartes's Third Meditation, for all the careful intricacy of the reasoning, also takes us on an intensely personal meditation, in which the weak and finite mind of the meditator is brought into contact with something that wholly exceeds its power fully to encompass. The key to this is Descartes's awareness of his own creaturely imperfection, which plays a pivotal role in his reaching for God. 'How could I understand that I... lacked something, and that I was not wholly perfect, unless there were in me some idea of a more perfect being which enabled me to recognise my own defects by comparison?' The phrasing echoes very closely indeed that of the medieval Franciscan St Bonaventure, in his *Journey of the Mind towards God*, written four centuries earlier.[29] My awareness of my weakness and finitude carries with it, for Descartes, as for St Bonaventure, an implicit and immediate sense of something other than, and infinitely beyond, myself, which necessarily eludes my full mental grasp.

So even a cursory look at how Descartes philosophizes about God seems to show that more is going on than detached, impersonal evaluation of arguments and evidence. As one commentator has put it,

what Descartes is reporting is not a step in a deductive reasoning, but a profound religious experience, an experience which might be described as the experience of a *fissure*, of a confrontation with something that disrupted all his categories. On this reading, Descartes is not so much proving something as *acknowledging* something, acknowledging a Reality that he could not have constructed, a Reality which proves its own existence by the very fact that its presence in my mind turns out to be a phenomenological impossibility.[30]

Interpreting the Third Meditation as a kind of personal 'confrontation' would be consistent with the general character of the *Meditations*,

29 Third Meditation (AT VII 46: CSM II 31). Cf. St Bonaventure, *Itinerarium mentis in Deum* [1259] ('Journey of the Mind towards God'), in *Opera Omnia* (Collegium S. Bonaventurae: Quaracchi, 1891), Part III, §3: 'How would the intellect know it was defective and incomplete if it had no awareness of a being free from all defect'?
30 Hilary Putnam, 'Levinas and Judaism', in S. Critchley and R. Bernasconi (eds.), *The Cambridge Companion to Levinas* (Cambridge: Cambridge University Press, 1986), pp. 33–70, at p. 42. Putnam is here expounding the interpretation of Descartes put forward by Emmanuel Levinas in *Ethique et infini* [1982], trans. as *Ethics and Infinity* (Pittsburgh: Duquesne University Press, 1985), 91ff.

which Descartes himself suggested were not a set of formal arguments but a kind of individual journey that has be undertaken by each of us.[31] It is, to be sure, a journey that follows a precisely structured path, based on the 'clear and distinct' ideas that are the very hallmark of the Cartesian system. But nevertheless the phrasing used in the *Meditations* unmistakably reflects a kind of submission to the divine – a humble acknowledgement that the idea of God cannot be fully encompassed by my finite intellect. Just as we find in St Anselm of Canterbury, many centuries earlier, the impetus of the argument stems from individual reflection on what happens when the finite creature attempts to confront its infinite creator – when, as Anselm put it, the 'wretched mind' is 'stirred up to contemplation of God'.[32] And just as in Anselm, and also in the 'journey of the mind towards God' later described by Bonaventure, the journey of the Cartesian meditator is, unavoidably, a religious as well as an intellectual quest.[33]

If we cannot properly study Descartes's philosophizing about God without being prepared to acknowledge these religious elements, it is nonetheless true that he steers clear of the 'revealed' elements of religion – for example, doctrines such as the Incarnation or the Resurrection or other elements of the specifically Christian tradition to which he belonged (he was brought up as a Catholic and remained so all his life). But when we turn instead to Descartes's contemporary, Blaise Pascal, we find an altogether more forthright espousal of that specifically Christian perspective. From the point of view of our present discussion about the appropriate methods to be followed in philosophy of religion, it is important to notice how Pascal dissociates himself not just from the typical modern academic stance of a pure detached inquirer into theistic claims, but even from the stance of those who restrict themselves to

---

31 Descartes, *Meditations*, Preface to the Reader: 'I would not urge anyone to read this book except those who are able and willing to meditate along with me' (AT VII 9: CSM II 8).

32 St Anselm of Canterbury *Proslogion* [1077], ch. 1 I have elsewhere called this interpretation of what Descartes's meditator is doing the 'cognitive confrontation' view. See further J. Cottingham, 'The Desecularization of Descartes', in Nathan Jacobs and Chris Firestone (eds.), *The Persistence of the Sacred in Modern Thought* (Notre Dame, IN: Notre Dame University Press, 2012), pp. 15–37.

33 For more on this, see J. Cottingham, 'Sceptical Detachment or Loving Submission to the Good: Reason, Faith and the Passions in Descartes', *Faith and Philosophy*, 28:1 (January 2011), 44–53.

'natural' as opposed to revealed theology. In stark contrast to Descartes, we find woven into Pascal's writings abundant references to Jesus, to the Church, to the Sacraments, to grace and redemption. He writes not as an observer or detached evaluator, but as someone steeped in a specific religious culture. And not only does he unashamedly philosophize from this standpoint, but he explicitly repudiates the kind of abstract inquiry that is concerned with the 'God of the philosophers and intellectuals', as he put it. The God he invites us to consider instead is the 'God of Abraham, Isaac and Jacob' – the God addressed in a living tradition of faith.[34]

Alongside this explicitly committed stance, Pascal famously defended an approach to these matters that underlines the role of the emotions. This is not just a 'concession' – as if one were reluctantly or indulgently to accept that some emotional decoration is permissible; on the contrary, the emotions are, for Pascal, a vital part of the cognitive apparatus whereby humans come to awareness of God. *C'est le coeur qui sent Dieu, et non la raison*: it is our heart that senses God, not our reason.[35] In saying this, moreover, Pascal does not rule out the possibility that the perceptions of the heart can *complement* the deliverances of reason. Just as the eventual conclusion reached by McGilchrist (see previous section) is that *both* kinds of cognition, those broadly associated with the right and left hemispheres, need to work together to facilitate proper understanding, so Pascal went on to allow that rational and emotional awareness can cooperate in bringing us to the truth: *nous connaissons la vérité non seulement par la raison, mais encore par le cœur* ('we know the truth not only by reason, but also by the heart').[36]

In our own time, there have been some striking developments in anglophone philosophy of religion that are in many ways reminiscent of what might broadly be called a 'Pascalian' epistemic framework. Paul Moser, in two recent books, expresses a very Pascalian concern about the value of the abstract intellectual arguments of natural theology. The demand made by 'skeptics and philosophers' that God should provide

---

34 Blaise Pascal, *Pensées* [1670], ed. L. Lafuma (Paris: Seuil, 1962), no. 913.

35 Pascal, *Pensées*, ed. Lafuma, no. 424. For a highly illuminating study of the role of the emotions in religious understanding, see Mark Wynn, *Emotional Experience and Religious Understanding* (Cambridge: Cambridge University Press, 2005).

36 Pascal, *Pensées*, ed. Lafuma, no. 110.

us with 'spectator evidence' of divine reality misses, for Moser, what would be the main redemptive aim of the Jewish and Christian God, by allowing the topic of divine reality to become a matter for casual speculative discussion, and thereby in a certain sense trivializing it.[37] Though Moser does not quite put it this way, one could say that knowledge of God is all too often assimilated to the kind of knowledge science seeks to achieve – to some kind of abstract explanatory hypothesis about how the cosmos came into being, or about the origins of human life – whereas, if the overwhelming evidence of scripture is any guide, it must primarily be understood in the context of our urgent need to change our lives, and of our human confrontation with an authoritative call towards moral transformation and redemption.

Again in broadly Pascalian spirit, Moser proposes a reconceived model of theology, a *kardiatheology*, as he calls it, which is aimed 'primarily at one's motivational heart, including one's will, rather than just at one's mind or one's emotions'.[38] It is significant that the notion of the 'heart' is glossed here in a way that develops and amplifies the original Pascalian suggestion that 'it is the heart that senses God': being able to direct one's mind towards God is not just a matter of a change in our feelings but requires a change in motivation or will. And this connects crucially with the question of evidence. On any plausible understanding of the nature of a God worthy of worship, 'divine self-revelation and its corresponding evidence . . . would seek to transform humans *motivationally*, and not just intellectually, towards perfect love and its required volitional cooperation with God'. It follows from this, Moser argues, that the traditional methods and arguments of natural theology suffer from a 'debilitating flaw': they offer 'no evidence whatever' of a living personal God who is worthy of worship and seeks fellowship with humans'.[39]

So this recent work, linking back to the approach found in Pascal in the seventeenth century, and partly discernible even in his more 'austere' contemporary Descartes, proposes in effect that we should

---

37 Paul Moser, *The Elusive God: Reorienting Religious Epistemology* (Cambridge: Cambridge University Press, 2008), p. 47. See also Paul Moser, *The Evidence for God* (Cambridge: Cambridge University Press, 2010).
38 Moser, *The Evidence for God*, p. 26.
39 Moser, *The Evidence for God*, pp. 26 and 158.

tackle the philosophy of religion in a way that draws on all the resources of the human mind. And indeed one could trace the roots of this idea back much further, at least as far as St Augustine, whose philosophical quest for the truth about God cannot entirely be separated from the intimations and yearnings of what he called the 'restless heart'.[40] Such an approach, to use the terminology of Eleonore Stump that we touched on earlier, in effect warns us against 'cognitive hemianopia' – the exclusive privileging of the analytic part of the mind, to the point of blindness to the whole rich range of volitional and affective mental activity that shapes our awareness of reality.

5. THE QUESTION OF EVIDENCE

Any serious evaluation of what we have as a convenient shorthand been calling the 'Pascalian' approach to the philosophy of religion will need to examine the *kind of evidence* that it takes to be relevant to religious belief. To be sure, Pascal himself did not always write from within the framework of personal commitment – in his famous 'wager' argument, he offers considerations designed to appeal to the nonbeliever;[41] but for the most part, including when he talks of 'reasons of the heart', it seems clear that a large part of the evidence he relies on appeals to his personal experience of divine transformative power. That might initially suggest a very individual and subjective orientation, of the kind made famous by Søren Kierkegaard in the nineteenth century – a purely faith-based or 'fideistic' stance (from the Latin *fides*, faith), which appeals to the need to trust oneself to the salvific power of God either without rational support, or even in the face of reason. Faith for Kierkegaard is 'the infinite passion of the individual's inwardness [in the face of] objective uncertainty'.[42] If that were the direction in which the 'Pascalian' approach takes us, there would be a serious price to be paid: we would risk putting religious belief beyond rational evaluation,

---

40 St Augustine of Hippo, *Confessions* [*Confessiones*, c. 398], Bk. I, ch. 1: 'You have made us for yourself, and our heart is restless [*inquietum*] until it finds repose in you.'
41 Pascal, *Pensées*, ed. Lafuma, no. 418.
42 Søren Kierkegaard, *Concluding Unscientific Postscript* [*Afsluttende Uvidenskabelig Efterskrift*, 1846], trans. D. F. Swenson (Princeton, NJ: Princeton University Press, 1941), p. 182.

and insulating it from any questions about evidence or indications for or against its truth.

A possible response to this is to argue that there is indeed genuine evidence available, but that it is evidence that only has force for those whose motivational lives are already being transformed by (what is taken to be) divine grace. The evidence, in other words, involves not some impersonally accessible body of data but something that becomes (as Moser puts it) 'salient to me, as I, myself, am increasingly willing to become such evidence – that is evidence of God's reality'.[43] The stress on *willingness* here is worth thinking about, since further reflection shows it is a feature that arises in all sort of contexts, not just religious ones. In the first place, getting oneself into a position where evidence will become salient often takes a lot of work: even in scientific cases, one often has to invest time, energy, and commitment (for example, in the determination to design an experiment and persevere with it), in order for the relevant evidence to come to light.[44] But in the second place, there are some cases where it may also require a certain attitude of 'willing receptivity', of 'porousness', to use Nussbaum's term, for the evidence supporting a certain picture to start to take hold.[45]

Does this lead us into a kind of 'internalism' where the claims of religion can only be discussed and evaluated *within* a given faith tradition? Some philosophers have seemed to move in this direction. For example, discussing his notion of a 'properly basic belief', Alvin Plantinga writes: 'The criteria for proper basicality must be . . . argued to and tested by a relevant set of examples. But there is no reason to assume, in advance, that everyone will agree on the examples. . . . Must my criteria [for a properly basic belief] or those of the Christian community conform to [the examples of atheists]? Surely not. The Christian community is

43 Moser, *The Evidence for God*, p. 172.
44 The component of commitment is underlined in the work of Bas van Fraassen, who argues that when the scientist accepts a theory there is 'a commitment to the further confrontation of new phenomena within the framework of that theory, a commitment to a research programme, and a wager that all relevant phenomena can be accounted for without giving up that theory.' *The Scientific Image* (Oxford: Oxford University Press, 1980), p. 88.
45 For Nussbaum, see note 12 earlier. Compare also Ward E. Jones, 'Being Moved by a Way the World Is Not', *Synthèse* DOI 10.1007/s11229–009–9522-z, published online 9 April 2009.

responsible to *its* set of examples not to theirs'.[46] But one worry with this kind of approach is that it could seem to take us down the path to a kind of 'epistemological relativism', where each system of thought carries its own standards and methods of knowledge acquisition, which do not recognize the authority of those from any other system.

The waxing and waning of relativism is a recurring feature of the shifting philosophical landscape in each generation. In the twentieth century, thinkers like Richard Rorty (in turn owing much to the work of Thomas Kuhn) gave it articulate voice. One of the examples discussed by Rorty is the dispute between Galileo and Cardinal Bellarmine in the seventeenth century over whether the planetary system was sun-centred or earth-centred. Rorty suggests that the two protagonists simply had different epistemological standards as to what counted as authoritative data or evidence – one relying on telescopic observation of the heavens, the other relying on scriptural authority. And if their standards were different, then, so the argument runs, there is no neutral set of rules or procedures that could settle the dispute between them.[47] This in turn would lead us towards the view that a given belief system operates according to its own internal epistemic standards and so is insulated against critical evaluation from outside.

But there seem to be strong reasons for resisting such a radically relativistic conclusion. There are, to be sure, many different ways of viewing and interpreting the world, but on reflection it seems very doubtful whether there really are incommensurable epistemic standards – radically different criteria for what counts as knowledge. Rorty's argument depends on supposing that Cardinal Bellarmine in his dispute with Galileo adhered to different epistemic principles (such as that empirical observation must always give way to Holy Scripture); but the role of sensory observation seems so fundamental to human life that it must be highly questionable that the Cardinal held, or indeed that any human being has ever seriously proposed, that the results of observation can be just *discarded*. Admittedly, what counts as empirical evidence is not a

---

46 A. Plantinga, 'Reason and Belief in God', in A. Plantinga and N. Wolterstorff (eds.), *Faith and Rationality* (Notre Dame, IN: University of Notre Dame Press, 1983), pp. 16–93, at p. 77.
47 Richard Rorty, *Philosophy and the Mirror of Nature* (Princeton, NJ: Princeton University Press, 1981), pp. 328ff.

straightforward matter, and our observational 'data' are always to some extent mediated by the theories we hold (this is one of Thomas Kuhn's chief points).[48] But for all that, Bellarmine had to give *some* weight to Galileo's reported sightings of all the phases of Venus: perhaps they were a bit of trickery, an optical illusion, or explicable in some other way compatible with the Ptolemaic system that Bellarmine favoured; but they could not simply be *set aside*. The idea of ordinary observation as one of the principal sources of knowledge is not just a feature of one particular system or culture, but is a basic human resource without which we could not function at all. And the same holds for fundamental logical principles, like the principle of noncontradiction – implicit in such judgements as 'Venus cannot *both* exhibit a full set of phases *and* only ever exhibit a crescent phase'. To be sure, logic, as modern theorists have taught us, is not immutable in all respects: there may be 'deviant' systems of logic where one or more of the standardly accepted axioms are modified or even deleted. But for any system in which our beliefs are to have any intelligible content, they must be logically constrained by the fundamental rules of consistency or inconsistency. In short, there are universal constraints to which all human knowledge must conform.[49]

The upshot of this discussion of knowledge and epistemic standards is that a 'Pascalian' approach to the evidence for God does not necessarily imply that philosophy of religion has to be conducted within a 'believer's fortress', where one is closed off from input from other faiths, or from scientific or secular systems of thought. In the case of Pascal himself, even when he is writing and thinking firmly within the point of view of a committed Christian, he still has not abandoned fundamental epistemic ideas like that of 'evidence': it is important for his position that there is indeed evidence of the grace of God at work. Admittedly, he does not think that such evidence can be appealed to in advance, to convince the detached sceptic; rather it is evidence that comes to light *further down the line*, as it were, once the prospective convert has made the decision

---

48 See Thomas S. Kuhn, *The Structure of Scientific Revolutions* [1962], 2nd ed. (Chicago: University of Chicago Press, 1970).

49 For acute discussion of some of these issues, see Paul Boghossian, *Fear of Knowledge: against Relativism and Constructivism* (Oxford: Oxford University Press, 2009).

to embark on a certain kind of spiritual journey.[50] We might say, linking up with our earlier discussion, that it is evidence that requires certain personal transformations in order to be accessed.[51]

It is important to realize that the notion of a kind of interplay between a change in the subject and the resulting availability of evidence is not in itself an unusual or unorthodox idea. Something analogous can been seen in the account given by that most dry and dispassionate of philosophers of religion, Thomas Aquinas, in his discussion of the way in which divine grace operates so as to accomplish someone's moral and spiritual regeneration. Only when a person ceases to cling to past wrong-doing, only when their resistant will becomes quiescent, will there be space for an infusion of divine grace. So the salvific action of God, on this view, is not something straightforwardly 'out there', like the power of gravity; rather, some degree of voluntary change on the part of the subject is necessary for grace to do its further work.[52]

But the idea of radical change linked to evidence that is subject to individual 'accessibility conditions' is by no means confined to instances involving religious belief.[53] In case anyone should think that there is something philosophically suspect about the kind of evidence involved in these religious examples, it is worth remembering that a whole range of our ordinary human beliefs – the beliefs two friends hold about the state of their relationship, for instance, or the beliefs a professional musician has about whether a certain composition works – will crucially depend for their validation on the occurrence of certain internal experiences and responses and transformations. Of course such experiences are not infallible: as with any support for our beliefs, the evidence of my own responses may need to be carefully scrutinized – for example, to see if it is compatible with other parts of my belief system, including, to be sure, evidence derived from science. (Some may be inclined

50 See Ward E. Jones, 'Religious Conversion, Self-Deception and Pascal's Wager', *Journal of the History of Philosophy* 36:2 (April 1998), 167–188.
51 Compare Moser, *The Evidence for God*, p. 172.
52 For a compelling account of this process, see Stump, *Wandering in Darkness* (Oxford: Oxford University Press, 2010), pp. 165–167, drawing on Aquinas, *Summa theologiae* [1266–1273], IaIIae (First Part of Second Part), Qu. 9.
53 See J. Cottingham, *Why Believe?* (London: Continuum, 2009), ch. 5, §2; see also *The Spiritual Dimension* (Cambridge: Cambridge University Press, 2005), ch. 5.

to insist in advance that the results of science must necessarily exclude the possibility of a theistic interpretation of my experience. But such an insistence is of course not itself a scientific result.)[54] What is more, other relevant evidence from the responses and the transformations experienced by other people may be called upon to support my confidence in the validity of my own reactions; so we are not dealing with something entirely within the unsupported domain of private subjectivity. At all events, there are clearly whole swathes of our human cognition where the beliefs we have will depend on evidence drawn from the nature of our own experience – from what is made strongly manifest to our consciousness with an authenticity and power that we cannot in integrity deny.[55]

6. SOME CONCLUSIONS ABOUT METHOD

In asking about the appropriate methods to be employed in philosophy of religion, we have focused on the views and insights offered by a variety of thinkers. To sum up, we have seen that many of these views imply that we should be wary of applying a detached, neutral, quasi-scientific template to all philosophizing about religion. But it should also have emerged that it is possible to move away from strict adherence to the neutral model without thereby sliding into irrationalism or relativism. Thus, in the case of Wittgenstein and his emphasis on the importance of forms of life, one could at first be tempted to take this as implying that only if we completely and unreservedly enter a given form of life can we understand, and therefore evaluate, the claims involved. But the true Wittgensteinian lesson is a more modest and a more subtle one. We must indeed pay attention to tradition and context, for we cannot hope to fully grasp the significance of a set of assertions unless we know how they are embedded within a rich web of culture and practice. Yet developing such understanding need not mean that we have thereby lost any power of critical reflection, or that we have immersed ourselves so deeply into a system that we are somehow paralysed from examining its

---

54 Some of the issues concerning the compatibility of science and theism are taken up in Chapter 5, section 1, this volume.
55 See further J. Cottingham, 'Human Nature and the Transcendent', in Constantine Sandis and M. J. Cain (eds.), *Human Nature*. Royal Institute of Philosophy supplement 70 (Cambridge: Cambridge University Press, 2012), pp. 233–254.

coherence, or judging how far it speaks to our deepest intuitions about the human condition and the world we inhabit.

We might call this an *epistemology of involvement*, while adding the crucial rider that this should be clearly distinguished from an 'epistemology of submission' where all subsequent questioning is ruled out. Equally, as we have seen, an epistemology of involvement most emphatically need not be equated with an anarchic epistemology or an epistemology of radical relativism. And this fits in well with some of the other threads we have explored in this chapter. One of the lessons from the work of Martha Nussbaum is that we shut ourselves off from understanding if we always remain detached and critical; for we must to some extent open ourselves, be 'porous', to allow the significance of a given text or a given set of claims to reach us. Yet, once again, this need not imply that the philosopher of religion has to be so 'passive' as to lose all powers of rational discernment. The literary critic can be fully open to, and even be devoted to, a given novel or poem, while at the same time retaining a keen sense of those aspects that are problematic, or in tension with other aspects; and there seems no good reason why the same cannot be in principle true of the philosopher of religion. Finally, our emerging conclusions also seem to chime in with Pascal's claim about the central role of the emotions in awareness of God, which in turn finds an echo in Paul Moser's emphasis on 'kardiatheology' – an approach to the philosophy of religion that construes the question of evidence for God in the light of possible motivational transformations on the part of the subject. By engaging with these possibilities we do not suddenly cease to be proper philosophers, or become mindless devotees rather than rational evaluators. On the contrary, the job of philosophy is precisely to seek always to develop and enrich our understanding of what the search for truth involves, instead of resting content with rigidly defined blueprints for how philosophical inquiry must proceed.

For the truth of the matter is surely that our human cognitive situation is far more fluid than is implied by 'flat' scientific or crudely empiricist models. It is a complex interplay between commitment and withdrawal, affirmation and doubt, yielding and resisting. This continuing dynamic process of human learning and cognition is at the very core of rational inquiry, and there is no compromise to our rationality involved in giving ground, in trying out a position, in opening ourselves to new possibilities. Perhaps most importantly, the conclusions reached by our arguments in this chapter are *philosophical* conclusions. Some philosophers sometimes give the impression of believing that any departure from strictly scientific methods of knowledge acquisition, and any invoking of the affective or experiential resources of the human mind, must be a retreat from true philosophy and a descent into mere rhetoric, or even into 'apologetics', the enterprise of proselytizing for the faith (or for atheism). But in reality it is the job, the legitimate job, of the philosopher to probe the human epistemic condition, to investigate the nature and variety of human awareness, and, if necessary, to resist simplistic models that try to reduce all cognition to a single rigid template. There are many branches of philosophy where such points are applicable; and on any showing one of the most significant amongst them will be the philosophy of religion.

2

METAPHYSICS

Der Sinn der Welt muß außerhalb ihrer liegen.
('The sense of the world must lie outside of it.')
Wittgenstein[1]

I. ARGUING FOR GOD

The conclusions reached in the previous chapter suggest, amongst other things, that there may be reasons to be wary of wholly detached and neutralist models for philosophizing about religious belief. And this in turn has significant implications with respect to the established canon of philosophical arguments about the existence of God that bulks so large in the philosophy of religion as commonly practised. Countless textbooks take the standard arguments for God as their starting point, beginning with Anselm's famous 'ontological argument' put forward in the eleventh century, and moving on to the celebrated 'Five Ways' of proving God's existence deployed by Thomas Aquinas in the thirteenth. As is well known, these two great Christian philosophers take contrasting approaches to their task. The Anselm argument proceeds purely a priori, without depending on observational evidence, and proposes that God, defined as 'that than which nothing greater can be thought', must exist not just in the mind but in reality. In contrast to this a priori approach, Thomas Aquinas starts from observation of the world around us, reasoning that five features found in the cosmos (motion, causality, contingency, perfection, and purposiveness) allow us to infer

1 Ludwig Wittgenstein, *Tractatus Logico-philosophicus* [1921], 6.41.

the existence of something 'which all men call God', which must be the ultimate source of these things, or that on which they depend.[2]

The terminology used to classify these various arguments is not as transparent as it might be. The label 'ontological', from the Greek word for 'being' or 'essence', is not Anselm's but was introduced much later by Kant; the idea is that the very essence or nature of an unsurpassably perfect being must entail its real existence. By contrast, the first three of the proofs provided by Aquinas are often grouped under the heading of 'cosmological' arguments, a term that has been employed quite widely to cover inferential moves from the existence of the cosmos to its supposed first principle or cause, as found both in Aquinas and also in earlier Islamic philosophers;[3] some of the latter developed the 'Kalam' version of the cosmological proof (from the Arabic *kalam*, meaning word, speech, or argument), which reasons that the universe must have had a beginning in time, and since nothing comes into existence without a cause, it must have a transcendent creator as its cause.[4] The label 'cosmological' is however also used in a more restricted sense, for arguments of the kind found in Aquinas's 'third way' that focus specifically on the contingency of the world and argue to a supposed necessary being on whom it depends. Amongst the most influential later versions of this latter type of argument is that of Gottfried Wilhelm Leibniz in the eighteenth century, who argued that a sufficient reason for the existence of something cannot be found merely in any one contingent thing, or even in the whole aggregate or series of things, and hence 'no matter how far we go back to earlier states, we will never discover in them a full reason why there should be a world at all'. Leibniz concluded that even if we suppose the world to be eternal, we cannot escape the 'ultimate extramundane reason of things', namely, God, or 'some one Being of metaphysical necessity'.[5]

2 Anselm of Canterbury, *Proslogion* [1077], ch. 2; Thomas Aquinas, *Summa theologiae* [1266–73], Part I, Qu. 2, art. 3.
3 Notably al Kindi [801–873], al Farabi [c. 872–950], and al Ghazali [1058–1111].
4 For an influential recent version of this, see William Lane Craig, 'The *Kalam* Cosmological Argument', in W. L. Craig and J. P. Moreland (eds.), *The Blackwell Companion to Natural Theology* (Oxford: Wiley-Blackwell, 2012).
5 G. W. Leibniz, 'On the Radical Origination of Things' [*De rerum originatione radicali*, 1697], in Leibniz, *Philosophical Writings*, ed. G. H. R. Parkinson (London: Dent, 1973), p. 137.

The various approaches just mentioned by no means exhaust the catalogue of philosophical arguments for God's existence that have been
developed down the ages. Amongst the most popular of the arguments
has been the argument for God as the principle of design or order in the
universe, which has roots in Aquinas's fifth way but received its most
famous expression from Archdeacon William Paley at the start of the
nineteenth century. Paley reasoned that if one came upon something
like a watch, whose parts are intricately ordered to function in a certain way, it would be rational to conclude that it was the product of
a designer. And yet 'every indication of contrivance, every manifestation of design . . . in the watch, exists in the works of nature'. Indeed,
continues Paley, 'the contrivances of nature surpass the contrivances of
art in the complexity, subtlety, and curiosity of the mechanism . . . yet
are . . . not less evidently accommodated to their end, or suited to their
office, than are the most perfect productions of human ingenuity'.[6]
Though David Hume, over half a century earlier, had raised serious
objections to this type of argument,[7] and though Charles Darwin, not
long afterwards, was to propose that intricate biological systems might
evolve without any intelligent design or intervention,[8] the argument
that the natural and especially biological world manifests an underlying intelligence is by no means extinct today.[9] Other widely discussed
arguments for God's existence include the argument for God as the
source of human conscience or moral sensibility, and arguments based
on the widespread phenomenon of religious experience.

As regards the status of these various arguments for God, many
were traditionally construed as *demonstrative* – that is to say, to be
logically watertight proofs, where the conclusion is supposed to follow
inevitably once the premises and definitions are granted. But since a
good many of the arguments involve inferences from various kinds
of supposed evidence, it is also possible to interpret them otherwise
than as strict demonstrations. In recent times, the main emphasis in
discussions of God's existence has been on inductive or *probabilistic* as
opposed to demonstrative forms of reasoning, with philosophers such

6 William Paley, *Natural Theology* [1802].
7 David Hume, *Dialogues concerning Natural Religion* [published posthumously, 1777],
 Part II.
8 Charles Darwin, *The Origin of Species* [1859].
9 See Chapter 5, section 1, this volume.

as Richard Swinburne arguing for God's existence as the most plausible hypothesis to account for certain features of the cosmos. These general features, according to Swinburne, 'include the universal operation of simple laws of nature . . . and the initial (or boundary) conditions of the universe being such as to bring about the existence of human bodies, and humans being conscious beings, open to a finite amount of suffering and having some ability to bear it or alleviate it'. In the light of these features, the hypothesis that the cosmos came into being as a result of being willed to exist by God is, according to Swinburne, the simplest and most probable explanation of its existence.[10]

2. HOW IMPORTANT ARE THE ARGUMENTS?

The preceding section provides a very brief overview of some of the main lines of reasoning about God that will be familiar to students from most introductory courses in the philosophy of religion. But how significant is this array of philosophical proofs or arguments for God in the all-important choice of whether one is to adopt a religious or theistic outlook? There are no doubt cases where people have become believers as a result of becoming intellectually convinced by one or more of the standard arguments, but it seems fair to say that most religious conversions occur for other reasons. Believers may perhaps find the traditional proofs reassuring as formal confirmation of the intellectual respectability of the religious outlook (or alternatively they may have doubts about the proofs' soundness); but they will often admit that other factors were of more immediate importance in making them turn to God – perhaps some deep crisis in their lives, perhaps something overwhelming or inspiring in their experience of the natural or the human world, or perhaps a growing sense that religious commitment satisfied some profound fundamental human need or yearning. Religious allegiance, it seems, does not typically hinge on intellectual evaluation of arguments – and it is doubtful whether, on reflection, most religious adherents would

---

10 Richard Swinburne, 'God as the Simplest Explanation of the Universe', in Anthony O'Hear (ed.), *Philosophy and Religion*, Royal Institute of Philosophy Supplement 68 (Cambridge: Cambridge University Press, 2011), pp. 3–24, at p. 11. See also Richard Swinburne, *The Existence of God* [1979], 2nd ed. (Oxford: Oxford University Press, 2004).

want it to work like that. Conversion that is merely a doxastic shift – a purely cognitive change in one's beliefs based on dispassionate logic or impartial scrutiny of data – would not have the right kind of religious significance to qualify as authentic.[11] On any plausible understanding of the religious outlook, conversion, though it no doubt involves a doxastic component, has to be integrally bound up with moral and spiritual change.[12]

All this, of course, is quite compatible with supposing that the traditional arguments are valid – or perhaps that they are in some other way illuminating. Stephen Evans has recently offered a kind of revamping or reinterpretation of three of the classical arguments for God's existence, proposing that they 'derive their force and enjoy whatever plausibility they possess from the *signs* that lie at their core'. Signs, as understood by Evans, do not conclusively or compellingly indicate the presence of what they point to, but nevertheless do carry a certain persuasive force, provided they are interpreted or 'read' properly. So behind the various forms of cosmological argument lies our human sense of 'cosmic wonder', which points us beyond the natural world to 'a reality that exists in some deeper and more secure way than the contingent beings of the natural world do'. Behind the 'teleological' or design argument lies the 'purposive order that can be observed in nature', which 'points to a designer of the natural world' (albeit one who appears to work via the mechanisms of evolution); and behind the moral arguments for God's existence lie two distinct natural signs for God: the sense of being bound by moral obligations, and the awareness that human beings have intrinsic worth or dignity.[13]

Such looser or more informal interpretations of the traditional arguments may possibly betray an anxiety that the arguments no longer command acceptance in the form in which they were originally proposed. But however the arguments are construed, it seems unlikely that they could ever succeed in convincing any rational inquirer 'cold', as it were, in the way in which, say, a geometrical proof in Euclid must

---

11 Compare James 2:18: 'You believe that there is one God. Splendid! Even the demons believe that, and shudder.'
12 For more on the kind of 'moral and spiritual' change involved here, see Chapter 7.
13 C. Stephen Evans, *Natural Signs and Knowledge of God* (Oxford: Oxford University Press, 2010), pp. 2, 74, 149.

convince any attentive reader who carefully follows the axioms and deductions, or even in the way in which a proof of the solubility of gold in hydrochloric acid must be accepted by any reasonable observer who carefully examines the experimental evidence.

The question of how obvious God's existence is, or ought to be, to any rational inquirer who considers the matter is a complex and long debated issue. A notable passage in Paul's letter to the Romans (1:20) declares that 'ever since the creation of the world God's eternal power and divine nature, invisible though they are, have been understood and seen through the things he has made'. The thought is a recapitulation of earlier ideas, found, for example, in The Wisdom of Solomon (13:1): 'Surely vain are all men by nature who are ignorant of God, and could not, out of the good things that are seen, know him that is; neither by considering the works did they acknowledge the master craftsman'. This suggests that the inference to God is a straightforward one that everyone can make, and indeed *ought* to make – for Paul goes on to declare that those who fail to recognize the divine authorship of the world and in consequence fail to give him thanks are 'without excuse', recapitulating the warning in Wisdom that they are 'not to be pardoned'. Citing the passage from Paul, and summarizing a long tradition of Catholic philosophical thought, the First Vatican Council of 1870 laid it down that 'God, the beginning and end of all things, can be known, from created things, by the light of natural human reason'.[14]

But actually, things are not quite as simple as may at first appear. The Pauline passage, though affirming our knowledge of God on the basis of his works, makes it clear that the divine attributes themselves, God's power and divine nature, are beyond our ken, or as Paul puts it, *invisible*. This is in line with the frequent warnings in the Christian New Testament, prefigured in the Hebrew Bible, that God is not to be seen by human eyes: he dwells (as the letter to Timothy expresses it) 'in light inaccessible, whom no man hath seen or can see'; or, as the book of Exodus puts it, rather more dramatically, no man can see God and live.[15] Consistently with this, although the Five Ways of Aquinas

---

14 First Vatican Council, Dogmatic Constitution on the Catholic Faith (*Dei Filius*) [1870], ch. 2.

15 I Timothy 6:16. Cf. Colossians I:15: Christ, who has 'delivered us from the power of darkness' is the 'image of the invisible God'. See also I John 4:12 ('No man hath seen

patently aim to demonstrate God from his effects, the conception of God so arrived at is, in the words of one distinguished commentator, a very 'minimalist' one[16] – the proofs don't disclose the nature of the invisible God but simply allow us to infer the existence of an original, uncaused, unmoved *something*, an ultimate X, to which, as Aquinas puts it, we apply the label 'God' (the phrase 'and this we call God', or a similar clause, is found at the end of each of Aquinas's Five Ways). And finally, to come to the passage from the First Vatican Council document, although a place for natural reason is clearly affirmed, this affirmation occurs in a concessive clause, which immediately leads on to an emphasis on the role *not* of natural inference but of special divine revelation and faith – the main subject of the document in question. So the sense of the relevant passage is somewhat as follows: although the mysterious and invisible God *can* certainly be inferred by the natural light via created things, nevertheless the truths on which our salvation depends are those revealed to the eyes of faith. The text goes on to say 'this faith, which is the beginning of man's salvation, is a supernatural virtue, whereby . . . we believe that the things which he has revealed are true . . . *not* because of the intrinsic truth of the things, viewed by the natural light of reason.' And it concludes by quoting the definition of faith in the letter to the Hebrews (1:11): faith is 'the substance of things hoped for, the conviction of things *that appear not*'.[17]

So despite Paul's characterization of those who fail to infer God as 'inexcusable', and notwithstanding Vatican I's affirmation that there can be natural knowledge of God, the emerging picture from a closer reading of these texts is that there are limitations to how far the natural light can get us when it comes to knowing God. So even in what may be called mainstream Catholic Christianity, the results achievable by natural reason alone are somewhat circumscribed; and the Protestant tradition is for the most part even more sceptical about what reason alone can tell us of God – indeed in the twentieth century, Karl Barth

---

God at any time.'). For the Hebrew Bible ('no man can see God and live'), see Exodus 33:17, 20 (Moses) and 1 Kings 19:13 (Elijah).

16 Brian Davies, *Aquinas* (London: Continuum, 2002), p. 27.

17 *Dei Filius*, ch. 3. See further J. Cottingham, 'Confronting the Cosmos: Scientific Rationality and Human Understanding', *Proceedings of the ACPA* (Philosophy Documentation Center), Vol. 85 (2011), pp. 27–42. DOI: 10.5840/acpaproc20111854.

actually urged people to turn their back on the rational arguments of natural theology as 'a great temptation and source of error'.[18]

The project of arguing for God's existence using natural reason alone thus emerges under scrutiny as problematic or controversial in a number of respects. What is more, if we go back to some of the traditional arguments for God that are presented as proofs of his existence, it turns out on closer examination of the relevant texts that they are not always quite the 'cold' and neutral pieces of reasoning that they have subsequently been taken to be. Anselm, for example, was steeped in a meditative and contemplative tradition, stretching back to Augustine (in his *Confessions*), which intermingles philosophical reasoning with humble praise and worship.[19] The two elements may seem incompatible to the modern analytic mind, but they coexist happily in the tradition. It is noticeable for example (though to modern readers perhaps baffling) that Anselm actually *addresses* God, humbly prays to him, at the very moment he is about to embark on trying to prove his existence by deploying the famous ontological argument: 'I will not attempt, Lord, to reach your height, for my understanding falls so far short of it. But I desire to understand your truth just a little, the truth that my heart believes and loves'.[20]

Anselm's tone here is quite unlike that of the modern scientist or typical analytic philosopher, autonomously and confidently 'in charge', dispassionately scrutinizing the phenomenon to be examined, critically interrogating the data and the arguments. Instead, in his humble acknowledgement of his own cognitive inadequacy, he recapitulates Augustine, for whom God can never be brought wholly within the grasp of our human comprehension. If we supposed we had succeeded in this task, says Augustine, it would be the best indication that what was so grasped was not God: *[Deus] non est, si comprehendisti* – if you claim to have grasped him, what you have grasped is not God.[21] Similarly, for Anselm, God is precisely *not* the 'greatest conceivable

18 Karl Barth, *Nein!* [1934], trans. in Emil Brunner and Karl Barth, *Natural Theology* (Eugene, OR: Wipf and Stock, 2002), p. 75; cited in B. Davies, 'Is God beyond Reason?', *Philosophical Investigations* 32:4 (October 2009), 342.
19 Augustine of Hippo, *Confessiones* [397–401]; Anselm of Canterbury, *Proslogion* [1077–1078]; Bonaventure, *Itinerarium mentis in Deum* [1259]. See Chapter 1, section 4, this volume.
20 Anselm, *Proslogion*, chs. 1 and 2.
21 Augustine, *Sermones* [early fifth century] 52:16.

being' (as an account sometimes found in undergraduate essays inaccurately puts it); on the contrary, he always recedes beyond the horizon of our thinking – he is that *'than which* nothing greater can be thought'. Following Anselm's line several centuries later, in the so-called age of reason, Descartes stresses in several of his writings how far the human mind falls short in its grasp of the infinite. We should, he warns, not so much try to grasp the perfections of God as to be grasped by them – to surrender to them (*non tam capere quam capi*).[22] And in another place he wrote to a correspondent:

I say that I know [that God is the author of everything], not that I conceive it or grasp it; because it is possible to know that God is infinite and all powerful although our soul, being finite, cannot grasp or conceive him. In the same way we can touch a mountain with our hands but we cannot put our arms around it as we could put them around a tree or something else not too large for them. To grasp something is to embrace it in one's thought; to know something it is sufficient to touch it with one's thought.[23]

For Augustine and Anselm, and perhaps to some extent even for Descartes, intellectual argument about God is not a self-standing enterprise designed to constrain the assent of any rational inquirer, but is part of the activity of 'faith seeking understanding'. This last phrase (in Latin *fides quaerens intellectum*) is the subtitle of Anselm's *Proslogion*. His starting point is an unquestioned commitment to God, which he takes to be a prerequisite for embarking on the meditation that will establish God's existence by rational reflection; as he puts it, *credo ut intelligam* ('I believe in order that I may understand').[24] Anselm's approach here is unmistakeably indebted to St Augustine's reflections on a passage from Scripture, *nisi credideris, non intelliges* ('unless you have believed you will not understand'), based on the Septuagint (Greek) translation of a verse from the prophet Isaiah.[25]

---

22 Descartes, *Meditations*, First Replies (AT VII 114: CSM II 82).
23 Descartes, Letter to Mersenne of 27 May 1630 (AT I 151: CSMK 25).
24 Anselm, *Proslogion* [1077–8], ch. 1.
25 Augustine, *Against Faustus the Manichaean* [*Contra Faustum Manichaeum*, 400], Book IV. The text of Isaiah that Augustine was using was based on the Greek Septuagint translation, which diverges from the original Hebrew at this point; the Hebrew actually says 'unless you believe, you will not stand firm'. For a critical exposition of the 'faith seeks understanding' programme in Christian philosophical theology, see Paul Helm, *Faith and Understanding* (Edinburgh: Edinburgh University Press, 1997).

Some philosophers may have qualms about reading these celebrated philosophical texts by reference to the 'faith seeking understanding' tradition: they may harbour suspicions that this moves the debate away from philosophical argument about God's existence towards a murkier or less rational realm of discourse. But part of the philosopher of religion's task is surely to examine the true structure and character of religious belief, and of the language used to expound and evaluate it. And if that examination discloses that such belief has not traditionally been understood in purely intellectual terms (as the bald acceptance of conclusions supposedly following from self-evident or plausible premises), then so much the worse for a philosophy of religion that insists on over-intellectualizing the phenomenon it is supposed to be examining.

The various points canvassed during this section suggest that there may be something questionable about the way in which the standard arguments for God's existence are understood and examined in many contemporary philosophy of religion courses. This is not to deny that scrutinizing the traditional arguments can have considerable pedagogical and historical value, and indeed bring all sorts of other benefits (for example, in helping to counter the widespread idea that religious belief is a matter of 'blind faith'). Nevertheless, it seems that more thought needs to be given to the precise role and status of the standard arguments and exactly what they contribute to the philosophical understanding of religious belief. One possible suggestion, for instance, is that they are best understood not as ways in which any impartial inquirer can be rationally led to conclude that God exists, but rather as throwing light on the *content* of theistic faith. Such a construal of the arguments would be in broad harmony with the 'faith seeking understanding' tradition. Thus, the ontological argument would serve to underline the unsurpassable perfection of God; the various cosmological arguments would serve to emphasize God's role as creator on whom everything else depends; the design argument would point to how nature in its beauty and harmony reflects the creative action of God; and the moral argument would identify God as the ultimate source of goodness, meaning and value. Sceptics, or those who are for other reasons resistant to adopting a theistic outlook, are unlikely to be swayed by any of the traditional arguments; and even for those whose stance is neutral, it seems unlikely that the arguments could ever command universal rational acceptance as a matter of pure logic or inductive probability. But for those who already are committed or inclined towards theism, reflection on the arguments could succeed in deepening the reach of their faith and illuminating its object.

3. THE ENLIGHTENMENT CRITIQUE OF METAPHYSICS

Aside from the methodological and interpretative concerns discussed in the previous section, there is a further important philosophical issue that now needs to be addressed about the standard arguments for God, and this concerns the entire tradition of natural theology – the project of arguing for God's existence using natural reason alone. Modern philosophy, ever since the so-called Enlightenment inaugurated by Hume and Kant in the eighteenth century, has been wrestling with serious problems about the legitimacy of grand metaphysical speculation (philosophical theorizing about the ultimate destiny of mankind, or the ultimate causes of the cosmos); and as a result of this there are major doubts in the wider philosophical community about whether the type of reasoning found in the traditional 'proofs' of God could possibly be philosophically viable. Can philosophers really reason in a way that enables them move beyond the empirical domain and posit supernatural principles or causes that wholly transcend the natural world?

Notice that this potential worry applies irrespective of whether we are considering the various arguments as supposed demonstrative proofs, or instead as inductive or probabilistic, or indeed merely as pointers or signs of the existence or action of God, or even as ways of illuminating the content of a pre-existing faith. For however construed, the arguments aim to establish, or support, or clarify the content of, the theistic claim of an ultimate transcendent divine reality underlying the natural or empirical world. So the emphasis that modern philosophy of religion so often places on scrutiny of the traditional arguments for a transcendent God, according them pride of place in the subject, runs the risk of appearing to bracket off the Enlightenment revolution in philosophy pioneered by Hume and Kant, and proceeding as if grand metaphysical speculation about the ultimate principles of reality was still an unproblematic option. To be sure, the Enlightenment critique of metaphysics may be confused or mistaken; but it surely needs to be addressed more explicitly than is often done when the standard theistic arguments are being expounded and evaluated.

It is sometimes thought that the Enlightenment critique of metaphysics is nothing more than an early form of the verificationist philosophy known as logical positivism that flourished in the mid-twentieth century; and that the subsequent near-complete collapse of positivism means that we no longer have to take the Humean and Kantian critique seriously. One recent commentator, for example, though without explicitly mentioning the Enlightenment, writes optimistically that 'the heyday of logical positivism and forms of scientism have given way to a more pluralistic philosophical era', and hence 'we are no longer in an age of anxiety during which religious belief seems to face an unanswerable critique'.[26] It is certainly true that logical positivism was wedded to a crude verificationist theory of meaning that has since been thoroughly discredited; but it would be fallacious to argue that because positivism entailed the rejection of speculative metaphysics, and positivism is false, therefore speculative metaphysics is now acceptable (this would be the logical fallacy of 'denying the antecedent').[27] It is also true that in the contemporary philosophical academy, metaphysics now flourishes as a respectable discipline; but modern metaphysics turns out on examination either to be a form of conceptual analysis, or else to be an inquiry into the most general ways of classifying what exists in the world;[28] in neither case, for the most part, does it venture to speculate on a transcendent reality or a supposed ultimate cause of the cosmos. Finally, the collapse of verificationism has certainly not led to the demise of scientism – the view that nothing exists apart from the objects studied by empirical science, or the events and properties that depend on those objects. On the contrary, scientism and naturalism continue to flourish in various forms in today's philosophical climate, and

---

26 Charles Taliaferro, 'Religious Rites', in C. Taliaferro and C. Meister (eds.), *The Cambridge Companion to Christian Philosophical Theology* (New York: Cambridge University Press, 2010), pp. 183–200, at p. 185.

27 Let P mean '*positivism is correct*' and M mean '*speculative metaphysics is viable*': from 'P implies not M', and '*not P*', it is fallacious to infer '*therefore M*'. (To avoid misunderstanding, I am certainly not attributing any such fallacy to Taliaferro in the passage quoted.)

28 See Jonathan Lowe, *A Survey of Metaphysics* (Oxford: Oxford University Press, 2002).

indeed are arguably the default mode of thinking for the majority of philosophers.

Let us however focus more specifically on the Enlightenment and its critique of metaphysics. In different ways, both Hume and Kant were concerned with establishing the limits of speculative reason: our human minds cannot attain to knowledge that purports to transcend the phenomenal world. And since God, as understood in the standard theistic worldview, is by definition transcendent, speculative metaphysics is fruitless. The 'ultimate springs and principles of nature', as Hume graphically put it, 'must remain forever shut up from human curiosity and inquiry',[29] so any attempt to pronounce on such matters must be 'sophistry and illusion'.[30] In Hume, this conception of the limits of human knowledge is grounded in an empiricist account of our ideas and their origins. Ultimately, our ideas can only come from experience of the world around us, and the basic source for this must be the impressions of the senses. 'The existence ... of any being can only be proved by arguments from its cause or its effect; and these arguments are founded entirely on experience.'[31] But as for the ultimate causes of these causes, Hume insists, 'we should in vain attempt their discovery'.[32] Similarly in Kant, who was of course strongly influenced by Hume, whom he credited with rousing him from his 'dogmatic slumbers',[33] any attempt to prove or disprove matters that lie outside the limits of the 'phenomenal world' – the world described by empirical science – can only result in empty contradictions and paradoxes.[34] If we invoke transcendent ideas, ideas relating to objects that 'lie outside all possible experience', then, Kant argued, 'we are cut off from any reasons that could establish the possibility of such objects'.[35]

29 David Hume, *An Enquiry concerning Human Understanding* [1748], Section IV part 1.
30 Hume, *Enquiry concerning Human Understanding*, Section XII, part 3.
31 Hume, *Enquiry concerning Human Understanding*, Section XII, part 3.
32 Hume, *Enquiry concerning Human Understanding*, Section IV, part 1.
33 Immanuel Kant, *Prolegomena to any Future Metaphysic that will be able to present itself as a Science* [*Prolegomena zu einer jeden künftigen Metaphysik die als Wissenschaft wird auftreten können*, 1783], Preface.
34 Kant called these 'antinomies'; see especially the 'Fourth Antinomy', concerning whether or not there is an absolutely necessary being; Immanuel Kant, *Critique of Pure Reason* [*Kritik der reinen Vernunft*, 1781/1787], A452–3; B480–1, trans. N. Kemp Smith (New York: St. Martin's Press, 1965), p. 451ff.
35 Kant, *Critique of Pure Reason* A565, B593, trans. N. Kemp Smith, p. 484.

Does this Enlightenment position close the door to metaphysical claims about God? One of the metaphors Kant used was that of our phenomenal world as a kind of *island*, the 'land of truth', as he called it. Our reason, our knowledge, he insisted, can get a foothold only on this land. There is no point in launching out on the foggy ocean surrounding the island, in an attempt to reach some world of ultimate reality, the world of *noumena* or 'things in themselves'; for although 'our reason sees in its surroundings a space for the cognition of things in themselves', nevertheless, we can 'never have determinate concepts of them'.[36] The metaphor is an interesting one, since it implies that in the very act of specifying the limits of rational knowledge, the Kantian philosopher *still implicitly has some conception of a possible space outside those limits.* We may never be able fruitfully to enter that space, or describe what is in it – but even saying this much seems to imply that we are not in a position to declare it is empty. The limits of language may be the 'limits of my world', as Ludwig Wittgenstein was later to say;[37] but what reason have we to equate 'my world' with the whole of possible reality? How do we know that there are not what Tim Williamson has called 'elusive objects', lying beyond the boundary of the conceptual?[38] From this perspective it seems to follow that the mystery, which 'all men call God', though hidden from our sight, may nonetheless exist. And indeed Kant himself, who held fast to a belief in God, clearly aimed to make philosophical space for that belief, even though he insisted, for the reasons just indicated, that it could not be an object of knowledge: 'Ich musste das *Wissen* aufheben, um zum *Glauben* Platz zu bekommen' ('I had to abrogate *knowledge* in order to find a space for *belief*').[39]

It follows from the analysis just offered that the 'Enlightenment critique' of metaphysics may by no means be as devastating to the theistic outlook as is sometimes supposed. For the Humean and Kantian position, properly understood, appears to be an epistemological rather than an ontological one: it is about the limits of knowledge, not the limits of reality. Even in Hume, who from his aggressive comments on metaphysics in the final section of his First Inquiry is sometimes

---

36 Kant, *Prolegomena*, §352.
37 Wittgenstein, *Tractatus*, 5.62.
38 Tim Williamson, 'Past the Linguistic Turn', in B. Leiter (ed.), *The Future for Philosophy* (Oxford: Clarendon Press, 2004), pp. 109–110.
39 Kant, *Critique of Pure Reason*, B xxx.

interpreted as a kind of proto-positivist who would consign to the flames as nonsense all propositions not rooted in empirical reality,[40] it turns out that there is no basis for the kind of dogmatic naturalism that has become prevalent amongst quite a number of present-day philosophers – the insistence that the cosmos is, as it were, 'closed', and that no reality exists apart from what can in principle be described in the language of science, or which ultimately depends on objects that can be so described. As a good empiricist, Hume would never go as far as the modern dogmatic secularist and insist that science tells us the cosmos is closed. For how could science, if (as Hume thought) it is rooted in the phenomenal world, possibly tell us what does or does not lie beyond the limits of that world? It is much better to think of Hume as a certain kind of sceptic – and sceptics characteristically suspend judgement; they do not lay down the law about ultimate reality. Hume the sceptic is in no position to pronounce, nor does he, on whether or not there are, as he puts it, some 'ultimate springs and principles' of reality. Admittedly he himself rejected the theistic belief in an ultimate principle – the mysterious first cause which, as Aquinas put it, 'all men call God'; but Hume's very empiricism and scepticism means that he cannot logically rule it out. His point is that if there is any such principle, then given the limits of our knowledge, it must remain 'shut up from human curiosity and enquiry'.[41]

If the 'Enlightenment' outlook need not be inherently hostile to theism, it does nonetheless seem to close down the possibility of rational arguments establishing the existence of God. There may be something 'out there', so to speak, beyond the 'island' of empirically based truth, but the Humean and Kantian strictures suggest there could hardly be any method of arguing for its existence, or even bringing it within the domain of what is humanly conceivable. So it appears that by defusing one mistaken worry about Enlightenment philosophy (that it supposedly rules out the possibility of God) we do not avoid a further underlying worry, namely, that the reality the theist wants to believe in, though

---

40 'If we take in our hand any volume; of divinity or school metaphysics, for instance; let us ask, Does it contain any abstract reasoning concerning quantity or number? No. Does it contain any experimental reasoning concerning matters of fact and existence? No. Commit it then to the flames: for it can contain nothing but sophistry and illusion'. David Hume, *Enquiry concerning Human Understanding*, Section XII, part 3.

41 Hume, *Enquiry concerning Human Understanding*, Section XII, part 3.

not ontologically excluded, would be a reality about which nothing can be said. And this might seem to lead us back to the impasse expressed in Wittgenstein's famous dictum: 'what we cannot speak of, we must pass over in silence.'[42]

4. MYSTICISM AND THE APOPHATIC ROUTE

As we have just seen, the Enlightenment position entails that ultimate reality is ineffable: language must fall silent before the mystery of the transcendent. If this position is accepted, how serious a problem would it be for the believer? The answer, it seems, must hinge on what sort of believer we have in mind. For a believer who wishes to specify the nature and properties of a transcendent God in order to provide a quasi-scientific explanation for the existence and nature of the cosmos, conceding the ineffability of the divine will be a serious stumbling block. But if we look at what the majority of religious practitioners typically believe and say as opposed to what atheist critics like Richard Dawkins would *like* them to be saying, in order to make easy targets, things appear somewhat different. Dawkins speaks scathingly of the 'God hypothesis', as if the role of religious belief was to provide rival explanations to those found in science. But much religious language turns out, even on a cursory inspection, to have little to do with putting forward explanatory hypotheses for the cosmos, or indulging in metaphysical speculation; much of it is concerned instead in acknowledging with awe and wonder the profound mystery of existence. 'Thou has beset me behind and before', says the Psalmist (139:5–6), 'and laid thine hand upon me. Such knowledge is too wonderful for me; it is high and I cannot attain unto it'. As the Dominican writer Herbert McCabe once put it, to invoke God is not to clear up a puzzle; it is to draw attention to a mystery.[43] In many religious writers there is a sense of dependency and helplessness in the face of the stupendous enigma that is the existing cosmos, and there may be a case for saying that this primal human existential response – of vertigo, of terror, of wonder, of awe – is the well-spring of spirituality, the basis of the religious impulse.

---

42 Wittgenstein, *Tractatus*, final sentence.
43 Herbert McCabe, *God and Evil in the Philosophy of Thomas Aquinas* [1957] (London: Continuum, 2010), p. 128.

As T. S. Eliot put it in *Four Quartets*, the work that bears most clearly the stamp of his religious outlook,

> You are not here to verify,
> Instruct yourself, or inform curiosity,
> Or to carry report. You are here to kneel . . . [44]

As the verses from the Psalms quoted in the previous paragraph make clear, acknowledging the mysteriousness of ultimate reality is not a defensive ploy that modern thinkers have come up with under pressure from critics, but on the contrary is well within the mainstream of traditional religious thought. The hiddenness and mystery of God is a theme of many writers in the so-called apophatic tradition, such as Nicolas of Cusa in the fifteenth century, who advocates approaching God through *docta ignorantia* – a kind of 'learned ignorance'; or the anonymous author of a fourteenth-century English treatise who speaks of seeking God through a '*Cloud of Unknowing*'.[45] Blaise Pascal later made it central to his conception of religious belief that God has 'hidden himself from direct human knowledge', citing the name *Deus absconditus*, the 'hidden God', that is applied to God by the prophet Isaiah.[46] What is more, as we saw in the previous section, the incomprehensibility of God is stressed even in paradigmatically philosophical thinkers like Augustine, Anselm, and Descartes. Even Aquinas, whose name is almost synonymous with the most rational and analytic approach to philosophical theology, insists on the incomprehensibility of God: the philosopher is obliged to follow the *via negativa*, and is able merely to establish what God is *not*. Insofar as we can aspire to any more positive awareness of the divine nature, this can only be analogical: the predicates we venture to deploy of God are understood by analogy with properties drawn from the human world, which cannot be predicated of God in the strict sense.[47]

---

44 Eliot, 'Little Gidding' [1942], lines 43–45, in *Four Quartets* [1943] (London: Faber, 1959).
45 See further Denys Turner, *The Darkness of God* (Cambridge: Cambridge University Press, 1995), p. 19.
46 Pascal, *Pensées* [c. 1660], ed. Lafuma, no. 427; citing Isaiah 45:15. For more on the 'hiddenness' of God, see Daniel Howard-Snyder and Paul Moser (eds.), *Divine Hiddenness* (Cambridge: Cambridge University Press, 2002).
47 Aquinas, *Summa theologiae*, Ia, 13, 6.

An even more radical insistence on God's fundamental unknowability is found in a number of modern European philosophers and theologians: we always risk blasphemy, Jean-Luc Nancy remarks, if we 'baptize our abysses with the name of God'.[48] This problem, Hent De Vries observes, is as old as Western thought: 'Here, we encounter the unavoidable and, in a sense, transcendental illusion of all discourse.... The word... "god" is always accompanied by a dual temptation: the seduction to baptize all experiences of the limit of our world with a divine name, and the desire to protect this name and the obscurity of our experience from idolatry and superstition'.[49] The point has been put even more emphatically by the contemporary French philosopher and theologian Jean-Luc Marion:

God cannot be seen, not only because nothing finite can bear his glory without perishing, but above all because a God that could be conceptually comprehended would no longer bear the title 'God'.... God remains *God* only on condition that [our] ignorance be established and admitted definitively. Every thing in the world gains by being known – but God who is not of the world, gains by *not* being known conceptually. The idolatry of the concept is the same as that of the gaze, imagining oneself to have attained God and to be capable of maintaining him under our gaze, like a thing of the world. And the Revelation of God consists first of all in cleaning the slate of this illusion and its blasphemy.[50]

If the line variously taken by these thinkers is accepted, it would follow that authentic religious belief is not and cannot be about explanatory solutions, despite the tendency of a good many theistic philosophers, and also of their atheist critics, to write as if it was. When De Vries, for example, talks of '*the obscurity of our experience*', he is pointing to the fact that the cosmos confronts us with a deep mystery and

---

48 Jean-Luc Nancy, *Des lieux divins* (Mauvezin: Editions Trans-Europe Repress, 1987), trans. as *The Inoperative Community* (Minneapolis: University of Minnesota Press, 1991), p. 115.

49 Hent De Vries, '"Winke": Divine Topoi in Hölderlin, Heidegger, Nancy', in A. Rioretos (ed.), *The Solid Letter: New Readings of Friedrich Hölderlin* (Stanford, CA: Stanford University Press, 1999), p. 97.

50 Jean-Luc Marion, 'In the Name: How to Avoid Speaking of "Negative Theology"', in J. D. Caputo and M. J. Scanlon (eds.), *God, the Gift, and Postmodernism* (Bloomington: Indiana University Press, 1999), p. 34, emphasis supplied. Marion's point has a long ancestry: compare St Augustine's *Si comprehendis, non est Deus* ('If you grasp him, he is not God'), *Sermones* [392–430], 52, vi, 16 and 117, iii, 5.

seems to be suggesting in effect that it would be dishonest to pretend otherwise, let alone to claim that theism clears everything up. One is brought back here to the Enlightenment impasse: we cannot have knowledge of the transcendent, if indeed there is a transcendent. And to this, one might add the further point that if we try to circumvent this by construing claims about God in a plonkingly literalistic way, as some fundamentalist believers are apt to do, then this risks what De Vries and Marion call idolatry or superstition. It triumphantly claims knowledge at the severe price of making the object of that knowledge a crude invention of our own, not worth the title 'divine'.

5. A POSSIBLE WAY FORWARD?

The apophatic approach just outlined is, as we have seen, part of a long-standing and important tradition of thinking about God. Yet to rest content with this cannot, it seems, provide the resources for a viable or coherent theism. For too great a stress on incomprehensibility and ineffability leads to the challenge that was vividly posed by David Hume to mystical or apophatic theology. As Cleanthes, one of the characters in Hume's *Dialogues concerning Natural Religion*, tartly puts it: 'How do you mystics, who maintain the absolute incomprehensibility of the Deity, differ from sceptics or atheists, who assert that the first cause of all is unknown and unintelligible?'[51] If we examine what the mystics have to say, Hume goes on to suggest, we ought to conclude that there is so little genuine theistic content to their beliefs that they are in danger of turning out to be 'atheists without knowing it'.[52] A serious philosophical dilemma now seems to beset the ship of theism: it risks either running aground on the rock of fundamentalist idolatry and superstition or being sucked down into the whirlpool of apophatic mystification. Yet there may be a third way, as was perhaps hinted at by Kant, in the passage quoted earlier where he says he denies knowledge in order to make room for belief or faith. Talk of faith is often misunderstood, as if religious belief was about launching out blindly into the unfathomable depths in the way Søren Kierkegaard

---

51 David Hume, *Dialogues concerning Natural Religion* [c. 1755], Part IV, first paragraph, ed. H. D. Aiken (New York: Haffner, 1948), p. 31.
52 *Dialogues concerning Natural Religion*, Part IV, third paragraph (Aiken ed., p. 32).

described.[53] That again would be what some militant atheist critics might *like* it to be – something inherently irrational. But it is worth examining the possibility that there may an authentic kind of faith, a philosophically well-grounded faith.

One way towards this is to resist the temptation to suppose that 'well-grounded' must be construed in a purely intellectualist way, which invokes, for example, only the evidential standards and methodological rules of science, or the principles of abstract rational argument alone. But why should we exclude the other resources of the human mind? It is interesting that the mystic Nicolas of Cusa, mentioned in the previous section, canvassed the possibility of drawing on wider mental resources when he drew attention to the powers of the *imagination* as a kind of pole (*baculum*) which might enable us to vault over the abyss towards the unknown.[54] And Pascal, who spoke so eloquently of the 'hidden God', nevertheless argued that there are 'signs' that enable us to reach towards awareness of God – signs that are, however, available 'only to those who seek him *with all their heart*'.[55] If we suppose that there is a God, who desires humans to turn towards him, there is no a priori reason to suppose that the methods for such conversion will have to confine themselves exclusively to the resources of the analytic intellect.

By way of making this suggestion more vivid, let us conclude this chapter by taking a specific example of religious language, which is particularly suited to the present argument because it embodies both elements stressed by Pascal: the biblical idea of the 'unknown God', and the notion of religious awareness based on resources other than purely intellectual ideas. The example is taken from the opening verse of a fairly well-known hymn that will be familiar to some readers (and there are performances readily available online)[56]:

53 Søren Kierkegaard, *Concluding Unscientific Postscript* [*Afsluttende Uvidenskabelig Efterskrift*, 1846], trans. D. F. Swenson (Princeton, NJ: Princeton University Press, 1941), pp. 177–182.

54 Nicolas of Cusa, *Dialogus de deo abscondito* [1444], h 3 (Opuscula 1), n. 1, 4–12, cited in Johannes Hoff, 'Mystagogy beyond Onto-theology: Looking back to Post-modernity with Nicholas of Cusa', preliminary essay for J. Hoff, *The Analogical Turn. Re-thinking Modernity with Nicholas of Cusa* (Eerdmans, MI: Grand Rapids, 2013).

55 Pascal, *Pensées*, ed. Lafuma, no. 427.

56 For example, at http://www.youtube.com/watch?v=W2oYTtyBSxk or http://www.sms .cam.ac.uk/media/1195337.

All my hope on God is founded;
He doth still my trust renew,
Me through change and chance he guideth,
Only good and only true.
    God unknown,
    He alone
Calls my heart to be his own.

The lyrics are by the English poet Robert Bridges (who later became Poet Laureate), and were first published in Bridges's compilation, the *Yattendon Hymnal* (1899), named after the Berkshire village where he was living at the time; the words are based on the German hymn *Meiner Hoffnung stehet feste* by Joachim Neander (1650–1680), in turn inspired by a verse from Psalm 71:5, 'Thou art my hope, O Lord God: thou art my trust from my youth'. The popularity of the hymn in the English-speaking world steadily increased after a fine new tune, 'Michael', was written for it in 1936 by the celebrated English composer Herbert Howells.

Why are the hymn, and the historical details about its composition, philosophically relevant? In part, because they are an indication of how religious worship, as in the case of the quoted verse, is not just a matter of the assertion of propositional claims about God, but characteristically involves joyful acts of affirmation and trust. What is more, they make us aware of how such acts are not just isolated behaviour to be evaluated out of context, but on the contrary get their significance from a transmission history that is inseparable from the faith that is thereby embodied and developed. And finally, they illustrate how religious approaches to God often take us behind mundane language to resonances of meaning that defy literal reduction but somehow find expression, as here, in poetry and music. Thus there is a rhythmical power to the lyrics of this hymn, which matches the original German[57] – and indeed it was one of Bridges's explicit aims to preserve the metrical

---

57   *Meine Hoffnung stehet feste*
    Auf den lebendigen Gott;
    Er ist mir der allerbeste,
    Der mir beisteht in der Not:
        Er allein
        Soll es sein,
    Den ich nur von Herzen mein.

shape of the hymn texts he translated instead of altering them to the standard template of 'English common metre', as was usual at the time. But on top of that, in the precise phrasing that Bridges employs in order to translate Neander's sturdy but perhaps somewhat pedestrian German original, there is a special reverberation and eloquence that somehow takes us to a new plane of jubilant expectation. And finally there is the musical dimension: when the hymn is sung well, the choir and congregation are communally uplifted by the soaring expression of hope, culminating in the rising fifth interval on *unknown*, taking us to the tonic chord and also up to the highest note of the tune, in such a way that the music shapes yet also somehow transcends the meaning of the text.

All these elements can contribute to the philosophical understanding of the ideas that are at work here. The underlying theology is influenced by the apophatic tradition, as the musical climax on 'God *unknown*' makes clear: what is effected in the hymn is an act of worship unmistakeably directed to God, yet coupled with an explicit acknowledgement that this is a *hidden* God, whose qualities cannot be humanly encompassed. Is this a coherent idea? Again, the hymn seems to supply the answer: for the underlying reality that is 'unknown' is *nevertheless manifest in terms of a personal address that is individually directed*. 'God unknown, he alone calls my heart to be his own'. The unknown God becomes known in the moral call felt by the worshipper.

Yet this 'knowledge' does not imply that God has to be neatly categorized in terms of the standard theological properties such as omnipotence. Indeed, the words 'he through *change and chance* me guideth' seem to acknowledge a radical contingency in life, and to accept that God cannot be considered as a kind of micro-manager who is supposed to sort out all difficulties for the convenience of his worshippers. It is significant that some users of the hymn were apparently unable to stomach this reference to 'chance', and had this line of the hymn bowdlerized, substituting the far less challenging version found in some hymnals: 'he my guide through changing order'. But the layers of meaning that surround the transmission history of the hymn give the lie to this comfortable and cosy reading of the way that divine 'guidance' operates; for it turns out that the title Howells gave to the tune was the name of his son Michael, who had just tragically died of spinal meningitis. The composer was far too well aware of the shattering 'changes and chances of this mortal life'[58] – the direst need (*Not*) of which the original German version speaks[59] – to subscribe to a banal conception of a world in which all is miraculously 'ordered' to have a happy ending.

We shall return to the theme of suffering and its place in religious understanding in a later chapter; but the main point to be made for present purposes is that the God in whom hope is joyfully placed in this hymn is not principally disclosed through philosophical analysis or theological theorizing, but revealed instead in a call to moral transformation made to each individual from the source of all goodness (the one who is 'only good and only true'). It is not solely or even primarily an intellectual call to consider arguments or evidence, but a personal call to allegiance, and one, moreover, that is addressed not to the analytic mind, but to the heart – to the emotions and the will. All this of course raises further important questions about the nature of the awareness of God that is presupposed here and its wider implications for the philosophy of religion; these are the subject of our next chapter.

---

58 From the *Book of Common Prayer* [1549/1662].
59 For the German text, see note 57, preceding.

3

MEANING AND MODES
OF ACCESS

Was ist Gott? unbekannt, dennoch...
('What is God? Unknown, and yet...')
Hölderlin[1]

1. SPEAKING OF GOD

In our discussion of the various issues in the philosophy of religion that have been addressed in the two previous chapters, a certain picture of the subject should gradually have begun to take shape – a picture that diverges in important respects from the way the subject has often been tackled by philosophers and theologians. The emerging picture rejects the construal of the subject that assimilates it to the kind of inquiry appropriate to the sciences – the evaluation of evidence from a distanced and neutral standpoint. It mistrusts the way of understanding religious claims that interprets them as explanatory hypotheses about the nature or workings of the cosmos rather than as hermeneutic frameworks for understanding the human moral and spiritual predicament. It casts doubt on ways of philosophizing about religion that confine themselves exclusively to the resources of the analytic intellect, and shy away from literary, poetic, and imaginative forms of discourse as if these are always liable to contaminate our reasoning and distort our apprehension of the truth. It acknowledges that religion is a phenomenon that arises from deep longings of the human heart, often against the background of dire need and distress; and while not supposing that such conditions

---

1 Friedrich Hölderlin, 'Was Is Gott?', from *Hymnische Entwürfe* (Sketches for Hymns), 1800–1805, in *Selected Poems* (London: Penguin, 1998), p. 270.

in themselves validate or support the resulting beliefs, it nevertheless attempts to pay attention to the context within which religion operates rather than always trying to abstract isolated propositions for detached scrutiny and analysis.

Notwithstanding all these points, if the theistic world picture is to be tenable, or even a candidate for consideration, it must be a coherent one, whose features can be at least partly articulated in a way that makes communicable sense. Yet as was pointed out in Chapter 2, the standard view of God as transcending the phenomenal world generates problems about how we could have knowledge of the divine or ascribe properties to it. Two worries present themselves here. There is an obvious epistemic issue (to be considered later on in section three) about how we can have knowledge of or access to the divine; but first there is a prior and more fundamental question about expressibility and meaning. How could language whose significance and usage are necessarily based on our human activities and interactions move wholly outside the contexts where it is at home, and somehow be employed to characterize a transcendent being – a being who is 'Wholly Other', as the eminent Swiss theologian Karl Barth put it in his early writings.[2] Of course, as Barth himself later came to underline, in Christian doctrine the 'Otherness' of God is mitigated, or overcome, by the idea that God becomes man and is thus manifest in our human world and in human terms. And historically speaking, as Charles Taliaferro has observed, 'Christianity has long held in creative tension the thesis that God is utterly different from the creature and yet encounters us in images and words we can understand'.[3]

Even granting this, however, the problem of language and meaning is not entirely removed. For an encounter between God and the human world – even if it is manifest in human terms we can grasp, or 'sifted to suit our sight', as the poet Gerard Manley Hopkins put it[4] – is still taken by the theist to be an encounter with a transcendent divine reality, which is conceived of as more than just a mysterious blank. So it seems

2 See Karl Barth, *Epistle to the Romans* [*Romerbrief*, 1919], trans. E. C. Hoskins (Oxford: Oxford University Press, 1968).

3 Charles Taliaferro, 'Religious Rites', in C. Taliaferro and C. Meister, *Christian Philosophical Theology* (Cambridge: Cambridge University Press, 2010), p. 191.

4 Gerard Manley Hopkins, 'The Blessed Virgin Compared to the Air We Breathe', from *Poems (1876–1889)*, ed. H. H. Gardner (Harmondsworth: Penguin, 1953).

that there must be at least some attributes that mainstream theism will need to apply to God qua God; and then the difficulty will be that any language we try to use for this purpose will have to be wrenched out of the original human context that gave it meaning. Anthony Kenny, for example, makes just this allegation with regard to the ascription of mental properties such as thought and knowledge to God: 'The language that we use to describe the contents of human minds operates within a web of links with bodily behaviour and social institutions. When we try to apply this language to an entity outside the natural world, whose scope of operation is the entire universe, this web comes to pieces, and we no longer know what we are saying'.[5]

This might at first sight seem an overly harsh conclusion, since one could point to several other cases where words are employed in unusual or transferred contexts, and yet we still have a workable grasp of what we are saying. One example arises in modern science, where metaphors such as 'wave', or 'particle', drawn from the ordinary world around us, are used to describe the behaviour of the unimaginably small micro-phenomena of quantum physics. In the scientific case, however, it seems that such metaphors are simply a convenient shorthand: physicists do not have to rely exclusively on the metaphors, but are able to talk authoritatively about the phenomena under investigation because they have at their disposal precise mathematical models and equations that enable them to describe what is going on. Such mathematical resources are clearly not available to the theologian – nor would one want them to be, on pain of moving away from the central moral ideas, such as divine goodness and love, that are the lifeblood of theism; to characterize God in mathematical or scientific terms would risk reducing the divine role to that found in the view sometimes labelled 'deism', that is to say, thinking of God as some remote and abstract 'force' that is indifferent to humans and has no clear relevance to the human predicament.

At the other extreme, we find in Scripture many ways of talking about God that are very much drawn from human experience. The Psalms, for example, affirm that 'the LORD is my rock, and my fortress, and my deliverer; my God, my strength, in whom I will trust; my buckler, and the horn of my salvation, and my high tower'(18:2, King James

---

5 Anthony Kenny, *What I Believe* (London: Continuum, 2006), p. 11.

Version). Opinions differ amongst philosophers about how much is achieved by characterizing God via such frankly metaphorical language. What may be called the 'hard-line' view is that metaphorical descriptions of God can have at best a heuristic role in stimulating further reflection or inquiry, but there must remain an irreducible core of literal truth for theism to have a genuine propositional content.[6] Against this, others have argued that metaphors can stimulate the imagination in such a way as genuinely to enhance our understanding of reality, and that relying on metaphors when we talk of God is not just unavoidable but entirely legitimate.[7] This is not an easy dispute to adjudicate. Defending the validity of metaphorical language in theistic contexts is certainly in line with our argument in the previous chapter about the illuminating power of imaginative, symbolic, and poetic forms of discourse; but on the other hand it seems that if one wishes to retain the core content of traditional theism, one cannot dispense with at least some key properties – for instance, creativity, reason, justice, and love – that are taken to be strictly and literally true of God. It is striking, for example, that all four of these latter properties figure in the Bible as an ineliminable part of the Judaeo-Christian conception of God.[8]

Yet for all that, it is hard to deny that our understanding of these terms stems from their use in the ordinary human world. When we talk of a creative action, for instance, what comes to mind is probably something like artistic creation, such as that of a sculptor making a statue; yet since this is done by chiselling and shaping pre-existing materials, such as a block of marble, it will be creation in a very different sense from the mysterious creation ex nihilo, out of nothing, that is traditionally ascribed to God. A similar sort of disparity between human context and divine ascription will also evidently apply in the case of the other key predicates directly attributed to God. So, to come back to Anthony

6 For this view, see W. P. Alston, *Divine Nature and Human Language* (Ithaca, NY: Cornell University Press, 1989), pp. 26–30; Peter van Inwagen, 'Metaphysics', in Adrian Hastings et al. (eds.), *The Oxford Companion to Christian Thought* (Oxford: Oxford University Press, 2000), p. 427.

7 Andrew Louth, *Discerning the Mystery* (Oxford: Clarendon Press, 1983), p. 19; compare Janet Martin Soskice, 'Theological Realism', in W. Abraham and S. Holtzer (eds.), *The Rationality of Religious Belief* (Oxford: Clarendon, 1987).

8 For creativity, see, for example, Genesis 1:1 and John 1:3; for rationality (*logos*), John 1:1; for justice, 2 Thessalonians 1:6; love (in Hebrew *hesed*), Psalm 26:3, or (in the Greek New Testament *agape*), 1 John 4:7–8.

Kenny's challenge, can we really 'know what we are saying' when we ascribe central notions such as rationality and love to God?

2. THOMISTIC ANALOGY AND ANSELMIAN PERFECTION

A possible answer to the question just posed of how we are to understand the properties attributed to God is provided by the Thomist doctrine of *analogical predication*. A term is used 'analogically' of different things, says Aquinas, when 'there is some order or relation to some central thing'.[9] As noted in the previous chapter,[10] Aquinas denies that anything can be predicated of God in the just same sense that it is predicated of any of his creatures. But certain predicates, like goodness and wisdom, can nevertheless be applied to God quite literally and correctly, according to Aquinas; indeed, he thinks that in a way they are *most* appropriately and *most* truly applied to God, because God is the source of all wisdom and goodness. Giving an example from Scripture, Aquinas cites a passage from Paul's letter to the *Ephesians* (3:14) – 'I bow my knees to the Father of our Lord Jesus Christ from whom all fatherhood in heaven and on earth is named'; and he observes that 'the same seems to apply to other words used both of God and of creatures, namely, that these words are used *primarily* of God'.[11]

'Primarily' cannot here refer to how we first came to learn these terms, since Aquinas is quite well aware that language is learned in ordinary human contexts: 'we know creatures before we know God, and hence our words apply to creatures before they apply to God'.[12] Rather, the thought seems to be that God is in one respect somewhat like a Platonic 'Form' – the eternal, central, paradigmatic instance from whom all lesser mundane instances are somehow derived:

when we say God is good or wise, we do not simply mean that he causes wisdom or goodness, but that he possesses these perfections transcendently. We conclude, therefore that from the point of view of what the word means

---

9 Aquinas, *Summa theologiae*, Ia, 13, 6.
10 Chapter 2, section 4, this volume.
11 Aquinas, *Summa theologiae*, Ia, 13, 6, emphasis supplied.
12 Aquinas, *Summa theologiae*, Ia, 13, 6.

it is used primarily of God and derivatively of creatures; for what the word means – the perfection it signifies – flows from God to the creature.[13]

Though further complex issues are raised by this account,[14] it does indicate one way in which the theist might set about ascribing concepts like reason and love to God. An important part of the background here is that God, in Aquinas's conception, is perfectly simple; and this implies that he is not to be thought of as having a list of separate and potentially detachable properties, like the ordinary objects we are familiar with, but rather should be conceived of as an utterly unified being whose perfections are somehow welded together into a perfectly simple and indivisible whole. This in turn means that God is *identical with each of his attributes*: he is not to be thought of as really separable from any of his attributes, but neither are the attributes really separable from each other. It follows from this that, for example, God is identical with his goodness, or as one commentator has put it, 'the divine nature is itself preeminent goodness'.[15] So just as for Plato there is a 'Form of the Good', an eternal perfection from which all lesser goods take their goodness by imitation or participation, so God is inseparable from his essential goodness, which flows out to his creatures, so that, in the words of the letter of James (1:17), he can be thought of as the author of 'every good and every perfect gift'. Aquinas's conception of the divine thus turns out to be a complex synthesis of elements drawn from Plato, and also from Aristotle (from whom he took the concept of analogical predication).[16] Of course the fact that Aquinas's ideas about the nature of God are carefully worked out from elements drawn from Plato and Aristotle does not in itself show that the resulting picture of God is philosophically unproblematic (we shall come back to the crucial idea of God as both the essence and the source of goodness in a later chapter);[17] but it does perhaps go some way to showing how the

---

13 Aquinas, *Summa theologiae*, Ia, 13, 6.
14 For an acute discussion of some of these, see Roger M. White, *Talking about God: The Concept of Analogy and the Problem of Religious Language* (Farnham: Ashgate, 2010), ch. 4.
15 Eleonore Stump, 'Dante's Hell, Aquinas's Moral Theory, and the Love of God', *Canadian Journal of Philosophy* 16 (1986), 181–198, at p. 186.
16 For the many relevant Aristotelian texts, see White, *Talking about God*, chs. 2 and 3.
17 See Chapter 4, this volume.

analogical use of language might provide the theist with a possible way of talking about a transcendent reality.

The Thomistic line just canvassed turns out to harmonize surprisingly well with the Anselmian notion of God, already referred to in Chapter 1 and discussed at greater length in Chapter 2[18] – namely, the idea of God as *that than which nothing greater can be thought*. Leaving aside the vexed question of whether this notion can be used to establish the real existence of God (something which Aquinas himself doubted),[19] Anselm's conception of the divine in terms of unsurpassable perfection nonetheless seems well suited to accommodate the idea of the transcendence of God, since it places God beyond the horizon of full human cognition, as something we can reach towards in our thought but never fully attain. Yet this acknowledgement of transcendence does not leave us with an unknowable blank, but on the contrary accommodates and entails the supreme moral perfection of God, since any limitation to God's goodness would be a violation of the original definition of something than which nothing greater can be conceived. What is more, it carries with it not just the essential goodness of God, but all the other traditional perfections, such as supreme power and knowledge, since again these could not be subtracted without violating the original conception. In addition, the Anselmian conception harmonizes with and supports the Thomistic principle of the simplicity and indivisibility of God, since the idea of supreme, unsurpassable perfection embraces and unites all the divine attributes in a single, unique, and inseparable unity such that it makes no sense to think of it as composed of parts or different elements. Finally, all this seems to square with an analogical understanding of the properties such as goodness, love, justice, power, and knowledge, that are ascribed to God – predicates that are drawn from our human understanding, yet are applied by analogy to the ungraspable creative power that is the supreme pattern and source of whatever measure of those qualities may be found in created things.

The traditional Anselmian and Thomistic ideas just referred to may thus go some way towards vindicating the coherence of the standard theistic idea of a transcendent deity. But although analysing and unpacking those ideas may have a certain philosophical appeal, it is

18 Chapter 1, section 4; Chapter 2, section 2, this volume.
19 Aquinas, *Summa theologiae* [1266–1273], Part I, q. 2, art 1, reply to Obj. 2.

important, in line with the general approach taken in this book, to keep in mind the vital connection between philosophizing about religion and the primary context in which religious belief operates. As pointed out in our opening chapter, religious belief does not seem to be about the kind of knowledge science seeks to achieve, nor is it mainly about the formulation of explanatory hypotheses about how the cosmos came into being; and by the same token, it does not chiefly appear to be concerned with abstract metaphysical theorizing about the divine nature.[20] If we consult the rich historical resources of religious scripture, tradition, and praxis, we cannot but observe that the primary focus of theistic belief has always been on the urgent need for humans to change their lives – on an authoritative call towards moral transformation and redemption. To make sense of this process, not much metaphysical speculation may be required; indeed, all that seems to be presupposed is the idea of a divine author of the moral call – the God who, in the words of the hymn discussed at the end of Chapter 2, is 'only good and only true' and who 'calls my heart to be his own'.[21] In short, it is the 'immeasurable goodness' of God, to use a Cartesian phrase,[22] and our urgent human need to respond to the moral demands such a God places on us, that is the power that drives the engine of traditional theistic religion.

Just as a purely heuristic exercise, it may be worth reflecting on how many of the properties theologians have traditionally ascribed to God could be set aside without destroying this all-important moral core of the religious outlook. If it turned out, for the sake of argument, that God was not all-powerful, would the believer have less reason to love God, and to turn away from the empty preoccupations of the self? If it turned out that, like Plato's 'demiurge', God did not create the world but had to work with recalcitrant pre-existing materials, would this diminish the joy and thankfulness with which the believer contemplates the beauty of the cosmos, or stands in awe before the majesty of the moral law?[23]

---

20 For more on this, see John Cottingham, 'What Difference Does It Make? The Nature and Significance of Theistic Belief', *Ratio* 19:4 (December 2006), 401–420.
21 For the phrases quoted, see the final section of Chapter 2, this volume.
22 '*Immensa Dei bonitas*': René Descartes, *Meditations* [1641], Sixth Meditation, penultimate paragraph.
23 See Immanuel Kant, *Critique of Practical Reason* [*Kritik der Practischen Vernunft*, 1788], trans. T. K. Abbott (London: Longmans, 1873; 6th ed. 1909), antepenultimate paragraph.

If the scope of God's knowledge was somehow restricted, or his supposed omnipresence compromised, would that be reason for the believer to abandon his allegiance to God? If the divine strength was laid aside and 'made perfect in weakness', to use a Pauline phrase,[24] and even if there was absolutely no guarantee of the ultimate triumph of the good, would that be reason for the believer to reject the divine call and revert to a life of self-absorption and the pursuit of power over others? Once these sorts of questions are asked, it should become clear that *nothing* ought to be enough to separate the authentic believer from the love of God, except, *per impossibile*, that the *goodness* of God were somehow compromised. It should be stressed again that these speculations are simply offered as a heuristic exercise, not some presumptuous attempt at theological revisionism (and we have seen earlier in this section that both for Anselm and for Aquinas such putative separating off of any of the divine perfections would be incoherent). But the point of the exercise is to suggest that authentic theistic belief does not necessarily have to be bolstered by a complicated panoply of metaphysical descriptions of the divine, provided it can hold fast to the core idea of the unsurpassable goodness of God that is the prime mover and moral heart of the religious impulse.

3. EXPERIENCE OF THE DIVINE?

Even if the various problems of meaning and language discussed in the previous section can be dealt with in a philosophically satisfactorily way, and even if, as envisaged towards the end, one were to posit a metaphysically pared down theism that focused simply on the moral demand placed on humans by a supremely perfect God, there would evidently still remain important epistemic problems that any philosophical defender of theism would need to confront. If religious belief is to be established as a viable option, the philosopher will not just have to be satisfied of the philosophical coherence of the idea of God but will also have to give some account of our supposed awareness of God – of the putative *modes of access* to the divine, and of their status and cognitive credentials. Of course, if the atheist worldview is correct, and there is

24 2 Corinthians 2:9.

no such thing as the divine, it will follow that the putative modes of access are illusory, and that the belief in any such being is due to one or more suspect causes, such as indoctrination (Dawkins), socioeconomic conditioning (Marx), infantile fears or fantasies (Freud), or other distorting influences.[25] But if it is claimed that the theistic worldview is correct, then the philosophical defender of theism will have to provide some indication of the relevant modes of access to the transcendent reality we call God, and of why they should be taken to be, at least in part, veridical. For example, if, in line with the emphasis suggested at the close of the previous section, we focus especially on the goodness of God, then we will need to inquire into how our human experience could possibly give us the basis for a belief in a transcendent source of goodness.

What kind of experience might be relevant here? The kind of observational data collected by the natural scientist could hardly fit the bill, since natural science is by definition concerned with the phenomenal world around us, not with any putative transcendent domain or source of meaning and value. And in any case, there seems good reason to think that the complex investigative techniques of the scientific researcher could not provide the right model for access to the divine. Given that the call to turn to God as described in scripture and tradition is primarily a moral and spiritual call, then if one accepts the basic picture in Abrahamic monotheism of a universally loving and compassionate God, one would prima facie expect the call to be able to be heard without special training or expertise or intellectual prowess. To put it in the Christian terms famously rehearsed by René Descartes in his *Discourse on the Method*, the kingdom of heaven must be 'no less open to the most ignorant than to the most learned'.[26] So one might conclude that knowledge of God cannot in principle be something complicated for

---

25 See Richard Dawkins, *The God Delusion* (London: Bantam, 2006), ch. 9; Karl Marx, *Critique of Hegel's Philosophy of Right* (*Zur Kritik der Hegelschen Rechtsphilosophie*, 1843]), trans. A. Jolin and J. O'Malley (Cambridge: Cambridge University Press, 1970), Introduction; Sigmund Freud, *Civilization and Its Discontents* [*Das Unbehagen in der Kultur*, 1929], in Penguin Freud Library (London: Penguin, 1991), Vol. 12, p. 195. Deflationary accounts of religious experience are considered in Chapter 4, this volume.
26 'Le chemin [au ciel] n'en est pas moins ouvert au plus ignorants qu'aux plus doctes'. René Descartes, *Discours de la Méthode* [1637], part i.

humans to attain: rather, it seems one ought to expect that, like the divine mercy of which Portia spoke, it would drop 'as the gentle rain from heaven upon the place beneath'.[27]

Yet although not requiring complex inferential processes or other learned investigations, such knowledge need not be supposed to be quite as universal and freely available as the drops of rain which fall on all alike whether they like it or not. The Pascalian thought that God provides 'enough light for those who desire to see, and enough darkness for those of a contrary disposition'[28] suggests that instead of an unavoidable rain shower, a rather more apt simile for how awareness of God comes about might be the fleeting appearance of morning dew – certainly not something that needs complicated techniques to experience, but something that requires you to be interested enough to get up early in the morning and go out into the fields. A somewhat similar point has recently been put by Stephen Evans, who has argued that we ought to expect knowledge of God to be (i) *widely accessible* (given the deity's benign purposes), but also (ii) *easily resistible* (as it ought to be if human freedom is to be respected):

One thing we might expect, given God's intentions for humans, is that the knowledge of God would be widely available, not difficult to gain. If we assume God cares about all humans, and that all of them are intended by God to enjoy a relationship with God, then it seems reasonable to believe that God would make it possible at least for very many humans to come to know his existence.... [But on the other hand we should expect that] knowledge of God is not forced on humans. Those who would not wish to love and serve God if they were aware of God's reality [should] find it relatively easy to reject the idea that there is a God. To allow such people this option, it is necessary for God to make the evidence he provides for himself to be less than fully compelling. It might, for instance, be the kind of evidence that requires interpretation, and include enough ambiguity that it can be interpreted in more than one way.[29]

---

27 'The quality of mercy is not strained./It droppeth, as the gentle rain from heaven/upon the place beneath'. William Shakespeare, *The Merchant of Venice* [c. 1597] Act IV, scene 1.

28 Pascal, *Pensées*, ed. Lafuma, no. 149, final paragraph; see Chapter 1, section 4 and Chapter 2, section 4, this volume.

29 C. Stephen Evans, *Natural Signs and Knowledge of God* (Oxford: Oxford University Press, 2010), pp. 13 and 15.

What kind of knowledge might fit these conditions? There is a long-standing distinction in Western philosophical theology between on the one hand the 'natural light' of human reason, and on the other super-natural revelation (for example, the revelations reported in Scripture, or handed down via apostolic authority), which must be believed on faith. But the stark dichotomy between these 'two sources of illumination', as René Descartes put it – the *lumen naturale*, the natural light of reason, and the *lumen supernaturale*, the supernatural light of faith[30] – suffers from the following problem: it suggests that *either* evidence has to be such as to be accessible by purely natural human secular reason, *or else* it has to be revelatory, and/or perceptible only to the eyes of faith. Aquinas's idea of faith 'making up' for the deficiencies of the ordinary natural senses[31] reflects in part the same idea. However, it seems worth-while to investigate the possibility of a third alternative. Let us consider, for example, those who are not convinced by the various philosophical arguments for God's existence, or are for some other reason dissatis-fied with the weapons of standard natural theology. Or let us consider the vastly larger number of human beings who are ill-equipped or disin-clined to devote themselves to investigating the philosophical arguments or supposed evidence for God, or simply have no time or resources to do so. Does it follow that to come to knowledge of God they are now dependent on the 'supernatural light', or that they have to rely solely on faith and revelation?

To make the latter supposition would seem to be a clear violation of Evans's 'wide accessibility' condition. For if revelation is taken to refer to miraculous incursions of the divine into the natural order, even the most enthusiastic believer in revelation or miracles must surely

---

30 'The clarity or transparency which can induce our will to give its assent is *of two kinds* (*duplex*): the first comes from the natural light (*lumen naturale*), while the second comes from divine grace. . . . Those who read my books will not be able to suppose that I did not recognize this supernatural light (*lumen supernaturale*), since I expressly stated in the Fourth Meditation that it produces in our inmost thought a deposition to will, without lessening our freedom'. René Descartes, *Meditations* [1641], Second Replies (AT VIII 148: CSM II 105–106).

31 In the hymn *Pange lingua* [1260]. Aquinas's position on the relation between faith and reason is not what is sometimes called a 'fideist' one, that faith *substitutes* for reason; the two, rather, are complementary. Thomas elsewhere describes an 'ascent' via natural reason, coupled with a 'descent' from God via revealed truth: *Summa contra Gentiles* [1259–1265], trans. A. C. Pegis (Notre Dame, IN: Notre Dame University Press, 1975), Bk IV, ch. 1, and see Introduction to Vol. I, p. 39.

acknowledge that there are countless numbers of people in the past, and perhaps even more in our busy and overpopulated contemporary world, who go through their lives without ever being confronted with visions of angels (as were Joseph and Mary in the Nativity story),[32] or voices from heaven (as was Saul of Tarsus in the story of his conversion),[33] or any other such dramatic manifestations of the divine. Yet there may nevertheless be certain aspects of universal or near universal human experience that function, if you will, as a kind of *bridge* between what we can establish by detached rational investigation, through the 'natural light' alone, and what seems to depend on the gracious bestowal of something more extraordinary and special.

4. INTIMATIONS OF THE TRANSCENDENT

To explore the idea just broached in more detail, consider the 'transcendent' moments that very many people will from time to time have experienced, the times when the drab, mundane pattern of our ordinary routines gives way to something vivid and radiant, and we seem to glimpse something of the beauty and significance of the world we inhabit. William Wordsworth described these moments as 'spots of time', when our mind is 'nourished and invisibly repaired' by our encounters with the natural world;[34] elsewhere he speaks of how the mind can be impressed by the 'quietness and beauty' of nature, that we are lifted up by 'a cheerful faith that all that we behold is full of blessing'.[35] The poet Sylvia Plath, even in the midst of the depression to which she was prone, could write in similar terms: 'I felt my lungs inflate with the onrush of scenery – air, mountains, trees, people. I thought, "This is what it is to be happy."'[36] And the same lesson is reiterated in a very simple and poignant manner in the famous diary of Anne Frank:

---

32 Luke 1:26–38; Matthew 1:18–21.
33 Acts 9:1–8.
34 William Wordsworth, *The Prelude*, Book 11, line 265 [1805 version], in S. Gill (ed.), *William Wordsworth: A Critical Edition of the Major Works* (Oxford: Oxford University Press, 1984).
35 Wordsworth, *Lines Written a Few Miles above Tintern Abbey* [1798], lines 135–136, in S. Gill (ed.).
36 Sylvia Plath, *The Bell Jar* [1963] (London: Faber, 1966), ch. 8.

The best remedy for those who are afraid, lonely or unhappy is to go outside, somewhere they can be alone, alone with the sky, nature and God. For then and only then can you feel that all is as it should be and that God wants people to be happy, amidst nature's beauty and simplicity. As long as this exists, and that should be for ever, I know that then there will always be solace for every sorrow, whatever the circumstances may be. And I firmly believe that nature can bring comfort for all who suffer.[37]

The peculiar sense of joy and healing experienced amid the beauties of nature is testified to by many other writers. It does not require special training, complex argument, scientific investigation or philosophical theorizing, but merely a simple act of accepting the gift that is offered. What 'lifts us up', in Wordsworth's phrase,[38] is the sense that our lives are not just a disorganized concatenation of contingent episodes, but that they are capable of fitting into a pattern of meaning, where responses of joy and thankfulness and compassion and love for our fellow creatures are intertwined; and where they make sense because they reflect a splendour and a richness that is not of our own making.

Notice that what is involved here is not thought of as a 'religious experience', if that latter term is understood in the rather narrow way that has become common in our culture, when philosophers speak, for example, of the 'argument from religious experience'. What is often meant under this latter heading is some kind of revelation which is taken to be evidence for, or to validate, the supposed truths of some particular creed or cult – a paranormal vision, for example, or the sense (reported by one of William James's correspondents) of 'the close presence of a sort of mighty person'.[39] This kind of notion is I think uppermost in many people's minds when they insist that they have never had a 'religious experience'. By contrast, the kinds of 'transcendent' experience described by Wordsworth and many other writers involve not so much a revelation of supernatural entities as a heightening, an intensification, that transforms the way in which we experience the world. Terms like 'transfiguration' or 'epiphany' come to mind here,

37 Anne Frank, *Diary* [*Dagboekbrieven 14 juni 1942 – 1 augustus 1944*], trans. S. Massotty (London: Puffin, 2007), entry for 23 February 1944.
38 Wordsworth, *The Prelude*, Book 12, line 218 [1805 version], in S. Gill (ed.).
39 William James, *Varieties of Religious Experience* [1902] (London: Fontana, 1960), ch. 3, p. 75.

but not in the sense that there is necessarily an explicit invocation of metaphysical objects that transcend ordinary experience, but rather because the categories of our mundane life undergo a radical shift: there is a sudden irradiation that discloses a beauty and goodness, a meaning, that was before occluded. Other examples could be drawn from our responses to great art, the sense of uplift we get from sublime works of literature, painting, or music. Thus Roger Scruton, describing the experience of a great work of music, speaks of 'sacred' moments, moments 'outside time, in which the deep loneliness and anxiety of the human condition is overcome', and 'the human world is suddenly irradiated from a point beyond it'.[40]

A rather different example of a widespread human pattern of experience that has often been thought of as a mode of access to the divine can be found in the exercise of our human moral faculties. The Danish philosopher Knud Løgstrup speaks of the 'ethical demand' in terms of trust and self-surrender that are a basic part of human life.[41] His particular focus is the openness and responsiveness to another person that is morally required in any human encounter or relationship. But a phenomenologically somewhat similar process seems to take place in our responsiveness to central moral values. What philosophers have come to call 'normativity' is one way of referring to a remarkable feature of moral values like the wrongness of cruelty, for example, or the goodness of compassion: such values exert a demand upon us; they *call forth our allegiance*, irrespective of our inclinations and desires. When we contemplate such properties, with the required combination of attentiveness yet receptivity, we transcend ourselves, as Pascal might have put it (one thinks here of his dictum *l'homme passe l'homme* – humanity transcends itself).[42] We are taken beyond our own inclinations or endogenous attitudes to something higher and more authoritative. No matter what you or I may feel about cruelty – even if there are those who develop a taste for it – it remains wrong, wrong in all possible worlds. And no matter how disinclined you or I may be to show compassion,

---

40 Roger Scruton, 'The Sacred and the Human' [2010], http://www.st-andrews.ac.uk/gifford/2010/the-sacred-and-the-human, accessed 30 March 2010; see also Scruton, *The Face of God* (London: Continuum, 2012).
41 Knud E. Løgstrup, *The Ethical Demand* [*Den Etiske Fordring*, 1956], ed. H. Fink and A. MacIntyre (Notre Dame, IN: University of Notre Dame Press, 1997).
42 Pascal, *Pensées* (ed. Lafuma), no 131.

the goodness of compassion retains its authority over us and demands our admiration and our compliance, whether we like it or not.

Now all the cases just mentioned, our vivid awareness of natural beauty, our responses to the mysterious power of great art and music, and our sense of awe before the authoritative demands of morality – all these may be described by the believer as revelations of the sacred, as intimations of the divine reality that is the source of all truth, beauty, and goodness. But it is also striking that they do not necessarily present as supernatural or miraculous irruptions into the natural world; they are in a way perfectly 'natural'. They are not, to be sure, everyday or routine occurrences, since they characteristically raise us up to something higher than our mundane habits and inclinations; but the relevant experiences depend on faculties and sensibilities that are an integral part of our human heritage. Except in tragic cases where these sensibilities have been irretrievably damaged by trauma or abuse or serious illness, such heightenings, or intensifications, transforming the way in which we experience the world, can come to all of us, from time to time, and if we honestly interrogate ourselves we are hard-pressed to deny it.

Since such experiences are part of our ordinary human birthright, irrespective of our particular religious allegiances or lack of them, they might well be grouped by the theist under the category of *awareness of God by means of the natural light*. In other words, they could be thought of as natural intimations of the transcendent, glimpses of the sacred dimension that forms the ever present horizon of our natural human existence. To speak this way is, to be sure, to widen somewhat the traditional extension of the phrase 'natural light', since that is normally taken to be the natural light of *reason*: the terms 'natural light' and 'light of reason' are virtually interchangeable in many Christian writers.[43] But this standard restricted construal of the 'natural light' of the human mind seems to be an instance of an intellectualist bias that is prevalent amongst many philosophers and theologians. If something can't be turned into an argument or a logical insight, then it is supposed to be not worth its salt. And the only alternative to purely rational inference or insight is taken to be the 'supernatural light', which, as Descartes put

---

43 In Descartes, for example, the *lux rationis* or 'the light of reason', found in the *Regulae* [c. 1628] (AT X 368: CSM I 14), becomes, in the *Meditations*, *lumen naturale*, 'the natural light' (e.g., AT VII 40: CSM II 28).

it, 'whisks us up at a stroke to infallible faith'.[44] So if the latter is proposed as a mode of access to the divine, it is likely to be dismissed by the sceptic as illusory, or else rejected as question-begging. Whether such sceptical dismissals are fair or unfair is an interesting question, but it is outside the scope of the present argument. For the kinds of experience we have been focusing on in this section are on the one hand not taken to involve celestial visions or disembodied voices or other 'special' religious experience. Yet, on the other hand, they do not arise from engaging in intellectual analysis or exercising our rational or inferential faculties. What we are talking about is something much more natural, spontaneous, direct, and intuitive, and much more readily available to all.

The kinds of transformative experience being discussed here are ones where the ordinary world is 'transfigured' and we seem to have glimpses of a deeper and richer reality that calls forth responses of joy, wonder, awe, and respect. Yet what kind of human faculty could enable us to have such experiences? One possible answer is that they might be seen as exercises of the human imaginative faculty – but with the important caveat that this label can be misleading if it is taken to refer to something fictive and fanciful, as in the popular song – 'Imagination is funny/it makes a cloudy day sunny . . . Imagination is crazy, your whole perspective gets hazy . . .'[45] In this pejorative sense of the term, imagination could never be a guide to the truth, since it moves us away from reason and cognition into some murky bog of emotional sludge. But there is another sense of the term, which has a long philosophical history going right back to Plato in the *Symposium*, where the imaginative faculty has the power to lift the mind up to the highest realities. This is Wordsworth's view, when he speaks of the imagination as

> but another name for absolute strength
> And clearest insight, amplitude of mind,
> And Reason in her most exalted mood.
> This faculty hath been the moving soul
> Of our long labour: we have traced the stream
> From darkness . . .

44 René Descartes, *Preface* to the 1647 French translation of the *Principles of Philosophy*, AT IXB 4: CSM II 181.
45 'Imagination', music by Jimmy Van Heusen, lyrics by Johnny Burke [1940].

> ... followed it to light
> And open day; accompanied its course
> Among the ways of Nature, afterwards
> Lost sight of it bewildered and engulfed;
> Then given it greeting as it rose once more
> In strength, reflecting from its solemn breast
> The works of man and face of human life;
> And lastly, from its progress have we drawn
> The feeling of life endless, the one thought
> By which we live, Infinity and God.[46]

The picture is a powerful one, and although expressed in poetic terms, it arguably presents a more realistic account of our human cognitive capacities than one that focuses on the purely intellectual powers of logical and probabilistic inference as if these were the only routes to the truth. But it is now time to look more closely at its philosophical credentials.

5. ASSESSMENT AND CRITIQUE

If imagination has the power to sweep us up to a higher plane, it is also important for the philosopher to make sure that it does not carry us away so far that we lose our powers of critical judgement. Many philosophers may acknowledge that honesty compels them to admit the power and widespread nature of the kinds of experience so far discussed; but they may still, quite reasonably, wish to question whether any kind of transcendent interpretation is required. Ought we not to be sceptical about the move from 'transcendent' experiences to a transcendent *object* of those experiences? May there not be other ways of explaining those experiences, *immanentist* ways, as it were – ways that do not have to involve reference to anything other than the natural world we inhabit?

Part of the answer to this seems to hinge on the *phenomenology* of the experiences involved. A religious interpretation of these experiences will point to their uplifting character, the fact that they seem to take us 'out of ourselves', so that whatever our previous state of

---

46 William Wordsworth, *The Prelude*, Book 13 [1805 version], lines 168–184, in S. Gill (ed.).

gloom, depression, or sense of futility, the renovating power of nature can transform us into a deeper, richer, more joyful state of exaltation and thankfulness. Yet to put the matter this way is at once to see that this is not an automatic process: there is no guarantee that anyone who is confronted with the relevant data will respond in the way described. Because of this, when one interprets these transformative experiences as 'modes of access' to the divine there can be no question of being able to offer a coercive argument, or indeed even a probabilistic one, if probabilistic is interpreted in the normal way, in terms of impartially and impersonally accessible evidence. What is involved instead is more like a challenge, or appeal, to the integrity of the listener; and integrity is itself a moral category, and that indicates something important about the kind of 'evidence' we are speaking of. Just as the Cartesian 'encounter' of the finite mind with the infinite requires a certain kind of submission to the light,[47] so the power exerted by the values of beauty and goodness may require a moral change in the subject if it is to be fully apprehended. Moral and aesthetic realities, like religious ones, may be amongst the set of truths that are subject to what I have elsewhere called 'accessibility conditions': they do not manifest themselves 'cold', as it were, but require a focused and sincere receptivity on the part of the subject.[48]

It is significant here that what is experienced in the cases we have been looking at is described by many of the writers concerned in terms of a *gift* or *blessing*. And the giving of a gift (though this is perhaps not always immediately obvious) is necessarily a two-way process: it requires not just the bestowal or presentation of something good, but a willing acceptance on the part of the receiver. A good example of what happens when the latter does not occur is provided in some of the work of the poet A. E. Housman, who in many ways has just as keen a sense of the beauties of nature as Wordsworth, but ends up with a very different reaction. In his fine poem 'Tell me not here, it needs not saying/what tune the enchantress plays', he paints the changing cycle of the seasons, the cuckoo call and 'blanching mays' of Spring, the 'aftermaths of soft September' in Autumn, the stripping of the beech woods for Winter; and he concludes:

---

47 For Descartes, see Chapter 1, section 4, this volume.
48 See further John Cottingham, *Why Believe?*, ch. 5, section 2.

Possess, as I possessed a season,
  The countries I resign,
Where over elmy plains the highway
  Would mount the hills and shine,
And full of shade the pillared forest
  Would murmur and be mine.

For nature, heartless, witless nature,
  Will neither care nor know
What stranger's feet may find the meadow
  And trespass there and go,
Nor ask amid the dews of morning
  If they are mine or no.[49]

The poem gives a vivid sense of the wonder at nature that we found in the other writers quoted earlier, but there is a sour note of nihilism that has gradually emerged in earlier verses: the pools in the pine forest are not calm and still, but 'idle'; 'the cuckoo, harbinger of spring, is reduced to futility – he 'shouts all day at nothing'. The spell cast by the 'enchantress' Nature turns out to be a trick. And here in the final verses, the poem ends in disillusionment – the poet is leaving, 'resigning' the woods and fields, and nature is now not even an 'enchantress' but an utterly blank, silent, impersonal power that will 'neither care nor know' whether he returns. None of this is to deny the evocative craftsmanship of the lines – and the present discussion is not at all about apportioning literary merit or its lack (we are not engaged in the absurd exercise of trying to say that all poetry should be positive and cheerful, or that it ought to have an orientation compatible with a religious outlook). What is relevant for our present purposes is that there is a moral malaise at the heart of the poem: the writer complains at the loss of the forest that he wanted to *possess* ('murmur and be *mine*'), and it is significant that the verb 'possess' occurs twice in the first line of this verse, and the emphatically stressed word 'mine' recurs in the poem's final line. The gift, though perhaps partly glimpsed, has been rejected; and this is somehow connected with the protagonist's orientation towards self. He cannot simply let nature *be*, as an object of wonder and praise: he wants to *have it*; and the final complaint that his desire is not reciprocated is

49 A. E. Housman, *Last Poems* [1922], XL, repr. in *Collected Poems* (Harmondsworth: Penguin, 1956), pp. 152–153.

inevitable; for possessive love is by its nature defective and can never be returned in the way that the subject desires.

All this reinforces the point that the 'modes of access to the divine' that are under discussion in this chapter cannot be construed as objective evidence, or the basis for a coercive argument. What they make reference to instead is a phenomenon that is indeed part of our universal human birthright, but which, if the theist is right, is a gift that requires a certain response in order for its significance to be grasped. The glimpses of the transcendent, the believer will want to say, are there to be had by everyone; but nothing in logic makes it incumbent on us to so interpret them; and nothing enables us to see them in the appropriate light in the absence of the right kind of receptivity. The speaker in Housman's poem takes an ultimately bleak view of the 'heartless, witless' character of nature. So far from feeling, with Wordsworth, that 'all that we behold is full of blessing', he is left with a self-oriented and melancholic resentment that his 'possession' of the countryside is temporary, and that no one will care that he is leaving. He has made no mistake in logic or his assessment of the data; his aesthetic and perceptual capacities are not defective; and yet he has missed something. What he has missed – and this very fact perhaps shows how ultimately inadequate it is to divide up our sensibilities into separate capacities labelled 'aesthetic', 'moral', 'imaginative', 'intellectual' – is something that can only be grasped by someone for whom these various powers fuse together into an act of joyful receptivity.

But even if they are not themselves arguments or intuitions of the intellect, can these glimpses of the transcendent at least be the *basis* for intellectual inference to God? Well, in a sense perhaps they can, in the following way: since it is a rational requirement, a requirement of intellectual integrity, to take proper account of all aspects of our experience, any worldview that wantonly ignores, or fails properly to accommodate, these aspects of our experience is to that extent intellectually weakened in comparison with its competitors. Yet in another sense it is clear that construing such experiences as grist for an inferential mill would be a distortion. For if we take on board the lessons of 'Pascalian' epistemology, or what we earlier called the 'epistemology of involvement',[50] we should see that there is not here a body of evidence

---

50 See Chapter 1, section 6, this volume.

from which there is a logical or probabilistic conclusion to be drawn by anyone who responsibly attends to the data. In the first place, no one can be compelled to have, or to acknowledge, such experiences: they require a certain kind of focused attention, a certain motivational stance that might best be described as a listening or attunement.[51] And in the second place, such experiences are not 'data' presented for our speculative assessment and inference. Rather, we ourselves are part of the evidence, as we open ourselves to something that is resistible, something that does not compel our assent, but which if we are responsive has the power to transform us – not in such a way as to enhance our store of knowledge, or to allow us to make better inferences, but so as to irradiate our lives with meaning and value that we cannot create for ourselves.

There are of course several possible objections that the sceptic or the atheist can make here. One would be to argue that these so-called modes of access to the divine are no such thing, since there is nothing objective to be accessed, merely a subjective projection on the part of the beholder. Another would be to accept that there is indeed something objective that is accessed, or detected, in these experiences, but to argue that it is nothing more than a set of properties of the kind a purely secular or naturalist worldview can accommodate. We shall consider both these kinds of response in looking further at the special case of moral responsiveness in the following chapter. Yet a third objection would be that the benign interpretation of reality supposedly suggested by the experiences in question is belied, or at least seriously threatened, by the amount of disorder and distress to be found in the world; this will be discussed in Chapter 5. But whether or not these difficulties can be countered, the results of the foregoing discussion perhaps go some way towards making sense of the notion of 'modes of access' to the divine – not as an abstruse metaphysical doctrine, or an appeal to mystical experience or special revelation, but as something that can be understood by appealing to human capacities and sensibilities that are widely shared and readily acknowledged by all. In a sense we are

---

51 For the term 'attunement', compare Heidegger's term *Stimmung* (cf. *Being and Time* [*Sein und Zeit*, 1927], trans. J. Macquarrie and E. Robinson (New York: Harper and Row, 1962), H 137), as interpreted in George Steiner, *Heidegger*, 2nd ed, (London: Fontana Press, 1992), p. 55.

thus brought back full circle to the claim in Paul's letter to the Romans highlighted in Chapter 2, namely, that God's power and divine nature are indeed manifest in creation.[52] For the believer, such manifestation is plain to see, in the beauty and wonder of nature, in the glory of the works of music and art that celebrate that natural and human world, and in the majesty of the moral law that inspires the human race with awe and longing. But nothing in logic or ordinary observation compels us to see things in such a transfigured light, so it will hardly be surprising that such manifestations often for various reasons pass people by, or are rejected, or are interpreted in a sceptical or deflationary way.

And the context, in any case, is quite unlike that of ordinary human reasoning, scientific investigation, or speculative inquiry. In the very special character of our distinctive human responses to the transcendent there is always, for the theist, an implied call, a call to change and to bring our weak and wasteful lives into closer harmony with the enduring source of being and value. The standard Christian view is that we cannot do that unaided, and that our salvation requires faith, and a voluntary act of openness to divine grace. But the special theology of faith and grace, if the argument we have been developing is accepted, builds on the ordinary natural responses that are already at work in our experience of the natural and human world. So, to come back to the point made in the previous section, there may be good reason to reject too rigid and exclusive a dichotomy between distinct sources of illumination, the 'natural' and the 'supernatural' light: in theological terms, there may be a bridge between the workings of nature and of grace, which together have the power to guide us home to our ultimate source and end. Or perhaps we may allow the last word to William Wordsworth, this time not from *The Prelude*, or *Tintern Abbey*, but from his celebrated Ode, 'Intimations of Immortality':

> Hence in a season of calm weather
> Though inland far we be,
> Our Souls have sight of that immortal sea
> Which brought us hither.[53]

---

52 Romans 1:21; see Chapter 2, section 2, this volume.
53 William Wordsworth, 'Ode: Intimations of Immortality, from Recollections of Early Childhood' [1807; title added 1815], lines 165–168, in S. Gill (ed.).

The 'sight' that Wordsworth refers to is intimately bound up with the glories and beauties of nature and its transforming power, a sight for which humans have an innate capacity, and which once enjoyed is never entirely lost. It does not deliver objective evidence, but neither is it 'insider knowledge', restricted to the club of believers or the 'saved'. It arises out of a pattern of response that is part of our natural human heritage: we only need to find the time to attune ourselves to it and allow ourselves to glimpse its true meaning.

4

MORALITY

Ki-attah adonay tov v'salach; ve'rab-hesed le-kol qoreykha.
('For you Lord are good and ready to forgive; abounding
in love to all who call to you.')
Psalms[1]

1. THE SOURCE OF GOODNESS

A theme that has surfaced at many points in the foregoing chapters is the idea of what may be called the *primacy of the moral in religion.* Religious belief is not chiefly to do with abstract metaphysical theories or the formulation of explanatory hypotheses about the origins and workings of the world, but takes as its central focus the deep structural problems of human life and our pressing need for moral transformation. A pivotal point of difference between a theistic and a nontheistic outlook, and arguably the most important area where the philosophical battles need to be fought, will thus concern the domain of value and morality: what is it that grounds our judgements of value, and what determines how we should act and live our lives?

For the believer, as suggested in the preceding chapter, perhaps the most crucial element in the way God is conceived is his *goodness.* The God who is the object of worship in the Judaeo-Christian and Islamic traditions is conceived of as the pattern and source of beauty and goodness. In the words of the seventeenth-century Cambridge

---

1 Psalms 86 [85]:5. A useful online resource for biblical texts in many different versions and translations (including a transliteration of the Hebrew) may be found at http://biblos .com.

72

Platonist philosopher Peter Sterry, the 'stream of the divine love' is the source of 'all truths, goodness, joys, beauties and blessedness'.[2] For the worshipper, involved in the praxis of daily or weekly liturgy, this idea is pretty much central, the basis of the sense of joy and exaltation experienced as one turns to God in praise and thanksgiving.

What exactly does it mean, however, to say that God is the source of goodness? To begin with, it evidently implies a firm denial of relativism. If goodness derives from an objective being that exists independently of us, then this rules out pragmatic and relativistic conceptions according to which the good is simply what works for us, or what is currently approved in our culture circle; nor can the good be something we can create or invent by our own choices or acts of will, in the way Friedrich Nietzsche envisaged.[3] To see goodness and beauty as stemming from God, as Sterry does in the quotation, means they cannot simply be 'in the eye of the beholder' – just a function of the subjective tastes of various human beings. But in addition to underwriting *objectivity* and *nonrelativity*, the idea of a divine source of goodness also implies a certain kind of *authority*. This connects with the notion (by no means confined to theists) that beauty and goodness exert some kind of normative pull on us. Beauty is *to be admired*; goodness is *to be pursued*. These values in a certain sense constrain us, whether we like it or not. We can of course deviate from them, or turn away from pursuing them, and we often do, but that does not seem to alter their validity. They are, to use an apt metaphor employed by Gottlob Frege in a rather different context, rather like 'boundary stones which our thought can overflow, but not dislodge'.[4]

The Oxford philosopher John Mackie famously put the point, or something close to it, by observing that there is something 'queer' about properties like goodness. They have a magnetic quality, a kind of inbuilt 'to-be-pursuedness'; and it is hard, Mackie pointed out, to see how such normativity could be just a function of mere empirically observable

---

2 Peter Sterry, *A Discourse of the Freedom of the Will* [1675]; repr. in C. Taliaferro and A. J. Teply (eds.), *Cambridge Platonist Spirituality* (Mahwah, NJ: Paulist Press, 2004), p. 179.
3 Friedrich Nietzsche, *Beyond Good and Evil* [*Jenseits von Gut und Böse*, 1886], §203.
4 G. Frege, *The Basic Laws of Arithmetic* [*Die Grundgesetze der Arithmetik*, Vol. I, 1893], trans. M. Furth (Berkeley: University of California Press, 1964), p. 13.

features of things. For there is, Mackie noted, an unexplained connection involved in the transition from 'this action wilfully inflicts distress' to 'this action is bad and to be avoided'; or from 'this action helps someone in distress' to 'this action is good and to be pursued'; and establishing this 'synthetic connection' as he put it, was the kind of thing that might be done by God. Mackie himself was a convinced atheist, and was also a subjectivist about value (he followed the Humean line that goodness is simply a projection of our own inclinations and desires). But in his book *Ethics: Inventing Right and Wrong* he concedes that if there *were* such a thing as objective goodness, then it might provide a good argument for theism. For if objectivism were true, argues Mackie, then there would have to be some objective relationship (a 'supervenience' relation) between a natural empirical property of an action (e.g., its tendency to alleviate suffering) and the property of its being good: 'If we adopted moral objectivism, then we should have to regard the relations of supervenience which connect values and obligations with their natural grounds as synthetic: they would then be in principle something that god may conceivably create; and since they would otherwise be a *very odd sort of thing*, the admitting of them would be an inductive ground for admitting also a god to create them.'[5]

An obvious challenge for the theist, however, is to explain exactly *how* God is supposed to create these connections. Before we come on to specifically moral cases (to do with right and wrong action) let us continue for a moment thinking about goodness in general. The Genesis account of the creation says that God looked at the world he had made and 'saw that it was good'. This is an interesting phrase, since it seems to suggest (pace Mackie's thought) that God did not have to *institute a connection* between the various observable features of things and their goodness, but rather that the goodness was already there plain to see, as it were, in virtue of the observable natural features themselves. What was good about the world was the majestic brilliance of the sun and stars, the freshness and lushness of the plants, the symmetry and vigour of the animals, and so on. In the words of the poet John

---

5 J. Mackie, *The Miracle of Theism* (Oxford: Clarendon, 1982), p. 118; emphasis supplied. See further J. Cottingham, *The Spiritual Dimension* (Cambridge: Cambridge University Press, 2005), ch. 3.

Milton, which he puts into the mouth of Eve, as she contemplates the creation:

> All seasons and their change, all please alike.
> Sweet is the breath of morn, her rising sweet,
> With charm of earliest Birds; pleasant the Sun
> When first on this delightful land he spreads
> His orient Beams, on herb, tree, fruit and flower,
> Glistring with dew; fragrant the fertile earth
> After soft showers; and sweet the coming on
> Of grateful evening milde, then silent Night
> With this her solemn Bird and this fair Moon
> And these the Gemms of Heav'n, her starrie train.[6]

The inference is that all that God has to do to bring goodness into the world is to create the various items possessing their own various good-making properties; apart from the act of creation itself, no further 'addition' of goodness is required of God. Yet this in turn highlights a serious worry for theistic theories of value: to put it crudely, God seems to risk dropping out of the picture when it comes to goodness and becoming redundant from an explanatory point of view. For if the goodness of nature arises out of the good-making properties of things – the glittering freshness of the dew, the fragrance and fertility of the earth, and so on, then we seem to be on the way to understanding goodness without invoking God at all. So it seems that any 'creation', even one produced in a purely naturalistic way, as in the atheist's universe, would be good, or at least contain good elements, provided it had these relevant natural good-making features.

But what of the strange 'magnetic' aspect of goodness highlighted by Mackie? On the face of it, this seems to require something beyond a merely natural, empirically observable, property. But the 'something more' could turn out to be quite ordinary and innocuous. Adam and Eve, as described in Milton's eloquent reworking of the Genesis story, do not just *observe* the lushness of the plants, and the warmth of the

---

6 From Eve's description of the creation in John Milton, *Paradise Lost* [1667], Bk IV, lines 640ff. Spelling based (with a few adaptations) on the text edited by H. Darbishire (London: Oxford University Press, 1958), which aims to follow the editions printed under Milton's own supervision.

sun, but they have reason to admire and value these things. What reason? The answer seems obvious: because they are part of a natural environment that is clearly beneficial to their comfort, delight, and welfare. So a 'deflationary' account of goodness looms – one that simply analyses goodness as the 'second-order' property of providing us with reasons to choose or value something in virtue of the ordinary natural first-order properties it has.[7] So I call a bunch of grapes good, for example, because it has the natural properties – sweetness, nutritional value, ability to quench hunger and thirst – that give me reason to seek it out and value it.

The threat of explanatory redundancy is the most serious objection that theistic accounts of value have to face; indeed, many philosophical critics of theism take it to be unanswerable. To explore this in more detail, let us now turn to the more specific case of moral goodness, and the question of how far (if at all) a theistic outlook contributes to our understanding of such things as moral obligation and the rightness and wrongness of action.

2. DIVINE COMMANDS AND THE EUTHYPHRO DILEMMA

The spectre of explanatory redundancy just referred to makes itself felt with particular force in the moral arena through the argument that has come to be known as the 'Euthyphro dilemma' (named after an argument originally developed by Plato in his dialogue *Euthyphro*).[8] Many theists see God as the source not just of goodness but also of moral obligation, an idea seemingly supported by scriptural narratives such as that of Moses and the Ten Commandments, where God is thought of as issuing rules or commands to his people, which thereby become injunctions they are morally obliged to obey. The Euthyphro dilemma is often regarded as fatal to such accounts. In a nutshell, the problem is that if merely being *ordered* to do something by God is enough to make it good or right, this seems to make morality arbitrary and potentially irrational ('Do this because I say so!'); but if on the other hand the God-given demands of morality are based on moral

---

7 Compare the 'buck-passing' account of goodness offered by Tim Scanlon in *What We Owe to Each Other* (Cambridge, MA: Belknap Press, 1998), pp. 95ff. See also P. J. Stratton-Lake, *Ethical Intuitionism* (Oxford: Clarendon Press, 2002), p. 15f.

8 Plato, *Euthyphro* [c. 390 BC], 6–10.

reasons ('Do this because it is just/kind/virtuous'), then the appeal to God seems to become redundant – why not simply base morality on the relevant reasons of justice or kindness or virtue? And similarly, *mutatis mutandis*, for acts that are forbidden: why not base the obligation to refrain simply on the features of the acts in question, such as injustice, cruelty, or viciousness?

Of the two horns of the Euthyphro dilemma, arbitrariness or redundancy, the first charge is now standardly countered by theists via a line of argument developed by Robert Adams: the God of traditional theism is taken to be supremely good, loving, and just in all his works; and therefore his commands, so far from being arbitrary edicts, are ones we have every reason to obey.[9] But then the other horn of the dilemma threatens: does the fact that God commands something really add any additional normative force to the reasons (based on beneficence, love, and justice) that already obtain in favour of the commanded course of action?

An answer recently offered by C. Stephen Evans leans on the distinction between a theory of the good and a theory of obligation.[10] Evans argues that we cannot explain moral obligations merely in terms of what is reasonable to do to achieve the good. Obligations have a special, overriding force, which make it incumbent on us to abide by them – and this is precisely what is provided for by the commands of a supremely perfect God: 'If God commands us to love our neighbors as ourselves, and tells us that all human persons must be considered our neighbors, then we have powerful and overriding reasons to consider the good of others when acting.'[11]

But more needs to be said about where exactly this additional normative power is supposed to come from. It seems correct that merely having a goodness-based reason to do X does not in itself create an obligation to X – otherwise I would be obliged to go to look at a fine painting in the National Gallery merely because it would be good to do so. This last example involves aesthetic goodness rather than moral

---

9 Robert M. Adams, *Finite and Infinite Goods* (Oxford: Oxford University Press, 1999), esp. chs. 10 and 11.

10 'Divine command theory' is 'a theory of the nature of obligation only, not of moral properties in general.... [It] presupposes a theory of the good.' Adams, *Finite and Infinite Goods*, p. 251.

11 C. Stephen Evans, *God and Moral Obligation* (Oxford: Oxford University Press, 2013), p. 73.

goodness, but the same seems to apply to the latter as well: it would be morally good, an act of kindness, if you called me to wish me well on my birthday, but you are not obliged to do so. So what converts a reason based on goodness to an obligating or overriding reason? The issuing of an order does not seem anywhere near enough to do the trick. There is admittedly a kind of weak institutional normativity that an order may have: if the Sergeant says 'Left Turn!' and I am a private soldier, then I ought to turn left. But this 'ought' comes from something beyond the mere ordering. It arises because I have enlisted and committed myself to obey my NCO, or else prudentially, because I want to avoid being put on a charge or shouted at. But the mere issuing of the order doesn't *in itself* seem to do any normative work, absent this kind of institutional background. And in any case, the kind of institutional normativity involved here is still reasons-based: we need an army, let us assume, for legitimate reasons (like self-defence); if there is to be an army there has to be a hierarchically structured chain of command; therefore duly issued orders have to be obeyed. But the fact that I ought now to turn left hinges on these prior reasons; if they fail to obtain (as in the case of an army that finds itself controlled by a racist or tyrannical regime), there is no moral obligation to obey (indeed there may be a moral obligation to disobey). Moreover, even when the institution is legitimate and serving a valid moral purpose, the obligation to obey an order is still *weak*: if I know that turning left would trigger a bomb, I ought to disobey. So we are still not anywhere near the idea of a command, even from a good source, having overriding normativity.

But suppose (to come closer to the line of argument developed by Robert Adams) that the issuer of the order has some very special status. Suppose it's not the Sergeant but the Colonel himself – someone the whole Regiment is in awe of. Suppose further that I know this particular commanding officer cares deeply about every member of the regiment, and also that he would never address a private soldier directly unless there were some very important reason in favour of a given action. Well, maybe the order would then have a special overriding force for me. But it still seems that the normative force would derive, once again, from the goodness of the reasons the good Colonel is presumed to have in this case, not from the order as such.

There are two features Adams identifies that purport to show what is doing the normative work when we think of obligations as divine commands. He points out firstly the 'reasons for compliance that arise from a social bond or *relationship* with God'; and secondly he notes that 'it contributes importantly to our reasons for complying with demands if the personal *characteristics* of the demander are excellent or admirable'.[12] These features, relationship and character, at first sight appear to move beyond the reasons based on the goodness of the action itself, towards something extra related to the mere fact of its being commanded. But this may be an illusion. If we take *relationship* first, then one might accept that a personal dependency or other such bond could create a prima facie presumption that I should comply with an order, but it certainly does not generate anything like an overriding obligation. If an abusive therapist with whom a patient has a special relationship tells the patient to do something improper, there is no resulting obligation whatever. This is not to ignore Adams's valid premise that a surpassingly good God would never issue abusive commands; the point of the example is that the normativity in relationships of trust flows from the good towards which those relationships are supposed to be oriented, not from the command itself. As for Adams's second reason for compliance, 'the personal characteristics of the demander are admirable', a similar argument applies. To revert to the military case, if my commanding officer is a truly admirable soldier for whom I have the utmost respect, that may certainly predispose me (motivationally) to do what he says; but in reaching the strong normative conclusion that I have an overriding obligation to do it, once more it must be the presumed goodness of the command that is doing the work, not the fact of the command or the character of the commander. So on further reflection it seems that a command, qua command, has no normative moral force whatsoever.

Adams himself appears to be sensitive to these points, judging by the following passage:

Reasoning will play an important part in our cognitive access to divine commands.... It is crucial to the prospects for a divine command theory as part of a coherent... ethics that human claims about what God has commanded are subject to rational assessment and criticism. If a divine command theory is embedded in a theory of the good, and presupposes it... we must expect this assessment to involve judgements about the compatibility of purported

---

12 Adams, *Finite and Infinite Goods*, pp. 252–253.

commands with the goodness of God – that is, with the character of a deity who is to serve as the supreme standard of goodness. We may inquire both about the goodness of what is commanded and about the appropriateness of sanctions or adverse reactions against what is forbidden. These considerations will constrain our judgements of obligation.[13]

Admittedly, this passage is not directly about the ontological question of what constitutes moral obligation but only about the epistemic question of 'cognitive access' – about how we *know* whether something is commanded by God. But it seems nevertheless to have clear implications about how reasons-based considerations must necessarily call the shots when it comes to normativity. If we take seriously the idea of divine commands being *embedded* (in Adams's phrase) in a theory of the good, then the normative weight exerted by the embedding (as indeed is quite appropriate) means that there is no real normative force left over to be exerted by the command. As Adams allows as a possible objection but never seems fully to deflect: 'it may be suspected that all the [normative] work is being done by the supposed goodness of God and [the goodness of] God's commands'.[14]

At this stage in the dialectic we seem to have reached an *aporia*. On the one hand, the reasons I'm obliged to do something appear to stem ultimately from reasons involving the good. But on the other hand, we have seen that mere reasons of goodness don't in themselves seem enough to create an obligation: it seems there must be something to bridge the gap between 'it would be good to do x' and 'one morally must do X'; and it is still unclear how invoking divine commands can do any useful work here.

3. THEISM AND THE FORCE OF OBLIGATION

To explore further the gap between 'it would be good to x' and 'one ought to X', and the question of what theism might contribute to bridging the gap, let us briefly consider the so-called *Mandatum* – the command reported in the Fourth Gospel to have been given by Jesus to his disciples in the course of a long discourse the night before his crucifixion: 'A new commandment I give to you, that you love one another: as I have

13 Adams, *Finite and Infinite Goods*, p. 264.
14 Adams, *Finite and Infinite Goods*, p. 255.

loved you, that you also love one another' (John 13:34).[15] The Greek word used here is ἐντολή (*entolē*), the term normally used in the Septuagint Greek version of the Hebrew Bible to translate מצוה (*mitzvah*), plural מצוות (*mitzvot*), the commandments given by God to the Israelites via Moses. So not only the solemn context (the night of his betrayal and arrest leading to his death), but also the specific terminology of command used by Christ make this saying pregnant with authoritative force. The disciples are solemnly enjoined to love one another.

If commands flowing from God generate moral obligations, then the inference from this (for those who accept the doctrine of the divinity of Christ) will be that the disciples of Christ were placed under a moral obligation to love one another. Indeed, assuming that this saying of Christ was meant to apply not just to those actually present at the time but to disciples of Christ generally, it will follow that all Christians are under an obligation to love one another. And a further short step, if we combine this with other teachings of Christ such as the parable of the Good Samaritan, will take us to the conclusion that all followers of Christ are under an obligation to show love to any fellow human being in need.

If divine commands generate obligations, the striking result follows that something that in many other ethical systems (for example, Aristotelian or Confucian ethics) is not thought of as required at all becomes, according to Christian ethics, obligatory. This would be consistent with the general view of Richard Swinburne, for example, that 'God's command to us to do some action makes it obligatory for us to do that action when it would not otherwise be obligatory'.[16] The obligation to help any human in need will arguably also obtain in Jewish ethics, since despite the description of Christ's injunction as a 'new commandment', it has clear antecedents in the so-called Old Testament, as Nicolas Wolterstorff shows in his fascinating book *Justice: Rights and Wrongs*, where he links Christ's teaching with the frequent injunctions in the Hebrew Bible to show concern not just for fellow-Israelites but for strangers and aliens and the vulnerable generally.[17] The upshot is that

---

15 *Entolēn kainēn didōmi humin, hina agapate allēlous, kathōs ēgapēsa humas hina kai humeis agapate allēlous* (John 13:34).
16 Richard Swinburne, *Was Jesus God?* (Oxford: Oxford University Press, 2008), p. 11.
17 Nicolas Wolterstorff, *Justice: Rights and Wrongs* (Princeton, NJ: Princeton University Press, 2008), ch. 3.

Judaeo-Christian ethics makes obligatory what in many other ethical systems is not seen as required – loving one's fellow human being. And to come finally to the key point at issue for present purposes, what creates the obligation here might seem to be *just the command* – the command of the Lord God in the Hebrew Bible, or of Christ speaking with direct divine authority in the Fourth Gospel.

However attractive such a position might appear to be, it turns out to be problematic, as we shall shortly see. One philosophical attraction the view might have if it were correct is that this kind of overriding obligation, created by command, might be a way of resolving the problem of the 'dualism of practical reason' which so exercised the philosopher Henry Sidgwick and has preoccupied many others since. If our reasons for action flow merely from what is good, then if we are rational and unbiased we may recognize an obvious good in some action that serves the interests of others; but we can also recognize a clear and equally valid good in an alternative action that serves our own personal interests. And it's simply not clear from rational analysis alone why the former (the altruistic reason) should have any overriding force. The tension or 'dualism' between 'disinterested benevolence' and 'rational self-love'[18] was one that Sidgwick was unable to resolve, since, as he ruefully put it, 'I cannot persuade myself... that Christian self-sacrifice is really a happier life than classical insouciance.'[19] Merely considered in terms of rational action aimed at the good, there seems no reason to give up one's own good for the sake of others.

If a command from a certain source can generate special normativity, then Sidgwick's tension might be defused. But now comes the crucial question: in a standoff between selfish and altruistic reasons, is it really the divine command that is the normative tiebreaker as it were? Adams speaks of 'the motivational or reason-generating power of the belief that something actually is demanded of me by an unsurpassably wonderful being who created me and loves me'.[20] But the hybrid phrase

18 Henry Sidgwick, *Methods of Ethics* [1874], 7th ed. (London: Macmillan, 1907), Bk III, ch. 14.
19 E. M. Sidgwick and A. Sidgwick (eds.), *Henry Sidgwick, A Memoir* (London: Macmillan, 1906), p. 90; cited in Barton Schultz, 'Henry Sidgwick', *The Stanford Encyclopedia of Philosophy* (Fall 2012 Edition), Edward N. Zalta (ed.), http://plato.stanford.edu/archives/fall2012/entries/sidgwick/.
20 Adams, *Finite and Infinite Goods*, p. 256.

'motivational *or* reason-generating' appears to elide two quite different things: the fact that I might be psychologically *swayed* by such a
thought, and the fact that the demand might *in itself have normative
force*. And it is not easy to see how the latter could be possible.

In fact, if we look at the Johannine narrative more closely, there are
clear indications of more than a mere command at work here. Having
commanded his disciples to love one another, Christ immediately adds
a kind of gloss: '*as I have loved you*, that you also love one another'.
And when, much later in the discourse in chapter 15, he recapitulates
the command, we once again find not just a bald instruction but the
same closely associated reciprocal clause: 'this I my commandment, that
you love one another *just as I have loved you*'.[21] One could read this as
merely an adverbial comparison – 'love one another in the same way,
or with the same degree of concern'; but it seems much more plausible
to read it as a reason that *grounds* the command, or comes very close to
doing so. It is significant that earlier in the same discourse we have the
episode of Christ's washing the disciples' feet (an act of humble service
with which the Mandatum is still closely associated in the Church's
liturgy for Holy Thursday), and here again we have exactly the same
reciprocal link: 'If I your master and teacher have washed your feet, so
too you ought to wash one another's feet.'[22]

Why should we love others? The teaching of Christ here suggests a
possible reason – namely, that whether we like it or not we are bound in
relations of reciprocity. And indeed this seems to be an essential aspect
of what it is to be human. I am not an isolated autonomous independent
figure who can dole out benefits either to myself or to others as I see fit,
on the basis of my lordly assessments of the requirements of 'practical
reason'; on the contrary, I need the love and concern of others every day
of my life, from birth to death. And once I recognize my dependency,
and the fulfilling and healing power of the loving action of another
towards me, I cannot but recognize the strength of the reason that calls
me to reach out in a similar way to others who need my care. This is
surely the force of Christ's demonstrating his love for the disciples in the

---

21 This is my commandment: that you love one another *just as I have loved you*. (*Autē
estin hē entolē hē emē hina agapate allēlous hathōs ēgapēsa humas*) (John 15:12).
22 *Ei oun egō enipsa humōn tous podas ho kyrios kai ho diaskalos, kai humeis opheilete
allēlōn niptein tous podous* (John 13:14).

foot-washing, and of his subsequently *directly associating his own love for them* with his appeal to the disciples to love each other. Although it's phrased as a commandment, it is in fact a piece of *teaching*, a guiding towards the rational enlightenment that discloses the reasons-based imperative of love, grounded in the objective facts of human dependency and mutuality. The point is not to add an obligation-generating command to what would otherwise be a normatively defective array of reasons but rather to highlight the strength and appeal of the reasons that already obtain.

This takes us a considerable way towards the idea of an overriding obligation, but it does not yet go the whole way. For it is clearly possible to acknowledge the facts of human mutuality and dependency just outlined and yet to set one's face against them, as it were. One might admit that humans indeed need each other and crave the love and care of others, but say with Nietzsche that the individual of true strength and creativity should rise above all this, harden his heart against 'weak' feelings of compassion and concern, and exercise the 'will to power' so as to achieve true greatness.[23] This is, for most of us, a repulsive ethic; but its mere existence indicates that the obligation to love and care for others is not something that logic compels everyone to recognize. So the problem of the 'gap' between the relevant good-making reasons and the idea of an obligation still remains. To see how this might be bridged, a further step in the argument is needed: we need to see how the love-teaching of Christ fits into a normative framework where the relevant reasons operate so as to generate an overriding call upon us. If we ask what that framework might be, the answer is not hard to seek, given the fundamental premise of Christian theism about the essential nature and purpose of humanity. If we are created by a source that is itself pure love, if we are made in that image, then our deepest fulfilment will lie in realizing that love in our lives. However imperfectly we may be able to pursue it, love must be the key to meaningfulness in the lives of each of us. Self-interested goods (such as Nietzschean creativity) may perhaps be, as far as they go, authentic goods; but in the absence of love, as St Paul's famous analysis in the first letter to the Corinthians tells us, they lose their significance and their pursuer becomes merely

---

23 Friedrich Nietzsche, *Beyond Good and Evil* [*Jenseits von Gut und Böse*, 1886], §37,

a 'sounding gong', or a 'tinkling cymbal'.[24] This fundamental teleological framework, affirmed by a long line of writers from St John
to Dante and beyond, has *nothing to do with the normative force of
commands*. It has to do with the way our human lives are inescapably
oriented towards a final supreme end, the good whose principal nature is
love.

This theistic teleological structure, with its associated vision of the
ultimate good of human life, is as it were the normative *fulcrum* which,
on the argument here proposed, generates the force of obligation. Without that structure, as for example in the typical naturalist-atheist worldview, our human nature is simply the product of a series of contingent
processes, which has delivered whatever mix of drives and desires happened in the past to be conducive to the survival of our species. So the
situation on the secularist view is that although no doubt humans get
some satisfactions and benefits from exercising compassion and love
towards their fellow-humans, we also get considerable benefits from
more restrictive altruism (reserved for kin, clan, or allies), or even from
outright egoism. And there is nothing, in this mix of desires and benefits, to generate overriding obligations – nothing which, as it were,
pins a 'gold star'[25] on any one drive or impulse amongst the plurality
competing for attention. There is nothing, to come back to Sidgwick,
with the power to resolve the 'dualism of practical reason' in a philosophically satisfying manner. By contrast, a theistic worldview, on the
view advanced here, is in a good position to do just that. But the
suggested resolution does not come from the invoking of an edict or
instruction, even one promulgated by a being of unimaginably exalted
status. Rather, it comes from the reasons based on goodness that are
fully sufficient to explain obligation's overriding force – but *only* once
it is accepted that, as the poet Tennyson put it, 'God [is] love indeed/
and love Creation's final law.'[26] And 'law' here, in line with what we

---

24 I Corinthians 13:1. See further John Cottingham, 'Meaningful Life', in Paul K. Moser
and Michael T. McFall (eds.), *The Wisdom of the Christian Faith* (Cambridge: Cambridge University Press, 2012), pp. 175–196.

25 See this chapter, section 3.

26 Alfred Tennyson, *In Memoriam* [1849], Canto 8. Immediately after the lines quoted,
the poem goes on to agonize over evidence (of 'nature red in tooth and claw') that seems
to count against the benign view of the cosmos; we take up this problem in Chapter 5,
this volume.

have been at pains to argue, should not be construed as 'commandment' or 'edict', but instead teleologically, as the ultimate principle and final goal of the cosmos – what Dante famously called 'the love that moves the sun and the other stars'.[27] To spell it out more explicitly, if the pattern after which we are shaped, whether we like it or not, is one that allows us true fulfilment only if the love that is deep in our nature wells up and overflows towards our fellow-creatures, only then have we the highest and most compelling reasons to live in accordance with that love.

4. LOVE, JUSTICE, AND MERE PREFERENCE

The argument developed in the previous section draws specifically on Christian texts and ideas, with the primacy they accord to love as both the essence of the divine nature and the wellspring of our human nature, and the overriding force of the resulting reason for us to love our fellow human beings – even our enemies (Matthew 5:44). Before moving on, it is worth just adding that although the injunction to love one's enemies is sometimes taken to be unique to Christianity, it has clear antecedents in the Hebrew Bible: 'If you meet your enemy's ox or his donkey going astray, you shall bring it back to him' (Exodus 23:45); 'If your enemy is hungry, give him bread to eat; and if he is thirsty, give him water to drink' (Proverbs 25:21); and there are also passages in the Quran that point in a similar direction (41:34; 42:43). But however that may be, the requirements of love and charity clearly do not exhaust the field of morality as generally understood; and hence it is natural to go on to ask whether a theistically based outlook such as we find in the three great Abrahamic faiths can be used to generate the basic obligations of justice, which are regarded as of central importance in many moral outlooks, both religious and secular. These include paying one's debts, or keeping one's promises, not to mention fundamental 'negative' obligations such as the obligation not to murder or rape.

Standard theism conceives of the goodness of God in terms of justice as well as loving-kindness. Psalm 33 for example is amongst many

---

27 'l'amor che move il sole e l'altre stelle', Dante Alighieri, *The Divine Comedy: Paradise* [*La Divina Comedia: Paradiso, c.* 1320], final stanza, ed. G. Bickersteth (Oxford: Blackwell, 1981).

passages in the Hebrew Bible that refer in the same breath to God's justice (*mispat*) and loving-kindness (*hesed*): 'the LORD loves righteousness
and justice; the earth is full of his loving kindness' (verse 5). Moreover,
the Thomistic view of the simplicity of God that we looked at earlier[28]
implies that God's justice is inseparable from his love – the latter being
something Aquinas explicitly underlines.[29] So everything said in the previous section about love as the essence of the divine nature would also
apply to justice; and the moral teleology sketched out earlier, according
to which the final destiny and goal of God's creatures is to find their
deepest fulfilment in perfect love, would equally apply to justice. It will
follow that human nature, on the theistic worldview, is such that we
have the strongest and most compelling reasons to be just, just as we do
to be loving. The theistic picture, if our analysis is correct, thus provides
a unified account of the way in which moral obligations are, as it were,
cosmically grounded.

Yet since most secular ethicists also acknowledge the obligations of
justice, one may reasonably ask whether such 'cosmic' theistic grounding for moral obligation is really necessary. Those who combine a secular worldview with maintaining that there are genuine moral obligations
will obviously give a negative answer. And interestingly, one of the most
eminent of contemporary theistic philosophers, Richard Swinburne,
seems to agree, at least in the case of some moral obligations: although
he regards God as *a* source of moral obligation (since on his view
'[God's] command to us to do some action makes it obligatory to do that
action when it would not otherwise be obligatory'), he considers that
God is not *the* (sole) source of obligation, since 'many truths of morality
hold whether or not there is a God'. Swinburne cites the case of keeping promises, which is clearly obligatory; this, he claims, is one of the
moral truths that hold 'independently of God'.[30] Now clearly there are
many atheists who have a strong sense of their moral obligations and
scrupulously abide by them. But it is not so clear that Swinburne is
correct in supposing that the *moral truths themselves*, the fact or reality
of such obligations, can be said to apply irrespective of whether there
is a God.

28 See Chapter 3, section 2, this volume.
29 Thomas Aquinas, *Summa theologiae* [1266–1273], Part I, art. 21, Q4.
30 Swinburne, *Was Jesus God?*, p. 11.

For what is the precise status of moral obligations in a naturalistic or atheistic universe? A good many philosophers have supposed that the most plausible answer here is a reductionist or deflationary one. The so-called positivist theory of obligation, for example, is that things are obligatory only insofar as there exist laws backed by sanctions to enforce certain types of conduct.[31] So when we say that we have an obligation not to kill, on this view this will simply be shorthand for saying that in a given jurisdiction there is law against it, and any further talk of an additional 'real' moral obligation, irrespective of the positive law of the land, will be rejected as a sham. Or again, various emotivist or projectivist accounts of moral obligation have been developed according to which such talk is simply a way of expressing our emotional horror at killing, or a way of projecting our own strong preferences or desires onto reality.[32] According to these views, it is simply an error to think there could be obligations that objectively constrain us independently of our feelings and passions.

One serious problem faced by views of this kind is that they run strongly against most people's intuitions: since we all *talk* of obligations, and nearly everyone has a strong *sense* of obligations as constraints on conduct which we have overriding reasons not to violate, proponents of the deflationary accounts under discussion have to maintain that our moral language and moral intuitions are radically erroneous: we talk *as if* there are real facts about morality and obligation (hence the term 'quasi-realism' often favoured by projectivists),[33] but in reality there are only truths about society and its laws, or about human beings and their emotions and preferences. Such deflationary accounts of moral demands do not seem to be inconsistent – indeed, they may be the most consistent approach for the defender of an atheist worldview to take – but the price they pay, of having to argue that whole swathes of our human discourse rest on false presuppositions, is one that many have found unacceptable. So we find a variety of influential contemporary accounts which aim to do justice to the reality of moral demands, while still adhering to a broadly naturalist worldview.

---

31 See John Austin, *The Province of Jurisprudence Determined* [1832].
32 See A. J. Ayer, *Language, Truth and Logic* [1939], 2nd ed. (London: Gollancz, 1946), ch. 6; Simon Blackburn, *Ruling Passions* (Oxford: Clarendon Press, 1998), ch. 1.
33 Blackburn, *Ruling Passions*, pp. 311–320.

5. SECULAR ACCOUNTS OF MORAL OBJECTIVITY

One of the most committed defenders of moral objectivism in recent times has been the British moral philosopher Derek Parfit. In his mammoth study *On What Matters*, Parfit argues that the leading philosophical theories of right action such as consequentialism and Kantianism, despite their different starting points, all turn out when properly understood to arrive at the same recommendations on how we should act. Parfit's conclusions give strong support to ethical objectivism. For if morality was a matter of our personal tastes or preferences, or if it depended just on a given society's choices or conventions, then we might expect lots of different standards; but if the most plausible interpretations of the most prominent ethical theories turn out to converge, then it seems very unlikely that morality could be an illusion, or a mere projection of subjective tastes. It seems much more likely that there are genuine moral truths, objective truths, which, if we think clearly and conscientiously enough, we can hope to reach, just as we can hope to reach the truth in science, or in other matters of fact.

Parfit is adamant that there are indeed such objective truths in morality. As the title of his book suggests, he thinks that some things really *matter* – they really matter in themselves. How we treat people really matters; whether we look after our planet so that humanity survives really matters. These are genuine moral truths. As Parfit puts it, 'In believing that some things matter, I am believing that there are some irreducibly normative truths.'[34] In other words, there are some moral truths that have objective authority over us, that give us decisive reasons to act in certain ways. But what grounds this objectivity? What makes the truths true?

In science, what grounds objectivity is the way the world is – the actual existence and configuration of stars and planets and atoms and molecules and all the rest. The better our scientific theories map on to or reflect these realities, the truer they are. But what is the basis of the truths in the moral as opposed to the physical domain? Like most contemporary philosophers, Parfit rejects the theistic answer: he cannot accept God as the reality underlying the objective moral order.

---

34 Derek Parfit, *On What Matters* (Oxford: Oxford University Press, 2011), Part II, p. 464.

Yet he continues to insist that there are objective moral truths. So what reality grounds them? The perhaps amazing answer that Parfit gives is: *none*. So although he insists they are true, 'in the strongest sense true', he maintains there is no underlying reality that makes them true. 'Like numbers and logical truths, these normative properties and truths have *no* ontological status.' Or again, 'For such claims to be true, the reason-involving properties need not exist either as natural properties in the spatio-temporal world, or in some non-spatio temporal part of reality.'[35]

To say the least, this seems puzzling. Nor is one's puzzlement much assuaged by the analogy Parfit draws with numbers and other logical properties, where we all believe there are genuine truths. For the standard models of what makes logic and mathematics true do not seem favourable to Parfit's case. Some philosophers of mathematics are *conventionalists* – they think that the truths of logic and mathematics are just true in virtue of human conventions about how we use symbols. This type of answer would obviously be unacceptable to Parfit in the moral sphere: he very much does *not* want to say that morality is reducible merely to our human customs and conventions: on the contrary he wants to say it really, objectively matters. Other philosophers of mathematics are *realists*: they maintain there is a kind of Platonic realm of mathematical objects, existing independently of us, which it is the job of the mathematician to investigate. But Parfit doesn't approve of this solution either: he can't accept a Platonic realm in which values just 'waft by' or float around in some nonphysical sense. On his view, which has become the overwhelmingly dominant one in contemporary anglophone philosophy, only the natural world exists; as he puts it, there is no case for positing 'strange entities as parts of reality'.[36] So we are left with Parfit's assertion that there are ultimate moral truths that have authority over how we should live, but which are simply *true*, true without there being any truth-makers, yet '*as true as any truth could be*'.[37] Maybe all explanation must stop somewhere, but this seems to reach a blank wall rather too soon for comfort. It also raises problems about how, if there is nothing beyond the natural world, we humans

35 Parfit, *On What Matters*, Part II, pp. 486, 487.
36 Parfit, *On What Matters*, Part II, p. 487.
37 Parfit, *On What Matters*, Part II, p. 487; emphasis supplied.

could have evolved in such a way as to be able to grasp these supposed objective ethical truths.[38] How, in a purely naturalistic cosmos, could our minds turn out to be, in a phrase of Thomas Nagel, 'instruments of transcendence'[39] – capable of grasping these irreducibly normative truths which according to Parfit have no truth-makers? It is far beyond the scope of the present volume to delve in more detail into Parfit's intricate and complex account of the moral landscape; but at least it may be said in the light of the foregoing that his attempt to preserve the objectivity and normativity of morality within an ontologically minimalist framework leaves many questions unanswered.

An alternative approach that tries to ground the idea of obligation within an entirely naturalistic worldview is the so-called enriched naturalism of John McDowell.[40] According to McDowell, our moral sensibilities are ultimately products of human culture. These are perfectly 'natural', in the sense that they were developed out of our ordinary contingent activities as biological and social creatures of a certain kind, and hence they do not require us to posit any transcendent properties or entities. But he argues that there are nonetheless genuine ethical realities and requirements, to which we gain access by being inducted as children into a certain ethical culture; and in virtue of the access thereby gained, we do indeed become subject to moral requirements and demands. As McDowell puts it,

the rational demands of ethics are not alien to the contingencies of our life as human beings. . . . Ordinary upbringing can shape the actions and thoughts of human beings in a way that brings these demands into view.[41]

This is a subtle and carefully worked out position, but the problem it faces is that the 'reality' of the moral demands to which we are subject turns out in the end to be simply a function of a given human culture with a given biological and social history. There is no further, no more ultimate, moral reality to constrain it or measure it against. Yet that

---

38 Parfit discusses these at length in *On What Matters*, Part II, ch. 32.
39 Thomas Nagel, *Mind and Cosmos* (Oxford: Oxford University Press, 2012), p. 85.
40 For a highly perceptive discussion of 'enriched' or 'expansive' naturalism, which develops the notion in a way that has fascinating implications for the philosophy of religion, see Fiona Ellis, *God, Value, and Nature* (Oxford: Oxford University Press, forthcoming).
41 John McDowell, *Mind and World* (Cambridge, MA: Harvard University Press, 1994), p. 83.

comes straight up against the problem first highlighted by Friedrich Nietzsche in the *Genealogy of Morals* (1887). As Nietzsche put it, once we start to think about the conditions under which man invented the value judgements good and evil, we can start to ask *what value these value judgements themselves possess.*[42] Once we accept that ethics has a contingent genealogy, once we can see that our moral principles might easily have been otherwise, this frees us from acknowledging their ultimate authority.

The celebrated British philosopher Bernard Williams in his later work was seriously occupied with this problem of the 'radical contingency of the ethical', as he called it:

A truthful historical account is likely to reveal a radical contingency in our current ethical conceptions. Not only might they have been different from what they are, but also the historical changes that brought them about are not obviously related to them in a way that vindicates them against possible rivals.[43]

The thought is a troubling and disorienting one. Nietzsche's sinister conclusion, at any rate, was that we can, if we are strong enough, decide to *invert* eternal moral values. In a godless universe, where God is 'dead', we are not subject to any higher moral principle, and so questions of value become merely a function of the projects we autonomously decide to pursue. So as Nietzsche frighteningly suggested, there might be conclusive reasons to steel ourselves *against* impulses of love and mercy, to harden our hearts against compassion and forgiveness, since such sentiments might get in the way of our will to power, or our passion for self-realization as a new and stronger kind of being.[44] The disturbing implication is that sooner or later we are bound to lose our sense of obligations as something authentic that provide conclusive reasons for us to act in certain ways, or to refrain from certain absolutely wrong courses of action. Morality loses its authoritative status and becomes,

---

42 Friedrich Nietzsche, *On the Genealogy of Morals* [*Zur Genealogie der Moral*, 1887], Preface, §3.
43 Bernard Williams, *Truth and Truthfulness* (Princeton, NJ: Princeton University Press, 2002), ch. 2, p. 20.
44 Nietzsche, *Beyond Good and Evil*, §37, and (for 'inverting' eternal values) §203. See also J. Cottingham, 'The Good Life and the "Radical Contingency of the Ethical"', in D. Callcut (ed.), *Reading Bernard Williams* (London: Routledge, 2008), ch. 2, pp. 25–43.

in Williams's significant phrase, a 'peculiar institution' – that is, merely one amongst many potentially valid ways for us to conduct our lives.[45]

Defenders of McDowell's enriched naturalistic model for ethics might respond by saying that the historical contingency of our ethical structures need not be as worrying as these criticisms imply; for although our species and our history might no doubt have been otherwise, it remains true that humans have developed in such a way that certain values are deeply embedded in their sensibilities and their culture, and this is all the ultimate grounding for morality that is needed. The worry with this, however, is twofold: first history suggests that the 'embedding' of the morality system is by no means deep enough to provide the required stable grounding (one only has to think of the horrific values eagerly adopted and extolled by the totalitarian regimes of the twentieth century); and second, even on a more optimistic reading of where our contingent origins have brought us, we are plainly, on any showing, a conflicted species beset by competing inclinations and impulses. As Hume put it, 'a particle of the dove is kneaded into our frame along with elements of the wolf and serpent'.[46] And why should one of these natural impulses have superior normative power?

Yet another highly influential approach to obligatoriness, which aims to take us beyond the flux of our contingent inclinations, is the 'constructivism' of Christine Korsgaard; this attempts to achieve objectivity by reference to the rational procedures whereby we arrive at moral conclusions rather than by reference to any supposed independent domain of moral reality. But what gives the moral values and maxims so arrived at their authority over us, or their normativity? Korsgaard's answer, in the end, turns out to be that if we were to violate them we would lose our sense of integrity and self-worth, perhaps partly echoing an earlier suggestion of Bernard Williams that the normative force of obligations derives ultimately from 'the *ethos*, the projects, the individual nature of the agent'.[47] Yet this seems to get things backwards. The reason I couldn't with integrity live with myself if I betrayed a comrade is not that

---

45 Bernard Williams, *Ethics and the Limits of Philosophy* (London: Collins, 1985), ch. 10.
46 David Hume, *An Enquiry concerning the Principles of Morals* [1751], ed. T. L. Beauchamp (Oxford: Oxford University Press, 1998), section 9, Part 1.
47 Christine Korsgaard, *The Sources of Normativity* (Cambridge: Cambridge University Press, 1996), p. 102. Compare Bernard Williams, *Shame and Necessity* (Berkeley: University of California Press, 1993), ch. 5, p. 103.

I have a certain conception of myself I can't give up; rather it is because I recognize something objectively morally repugnant about betrayal.[48] Or if this is denied, and my own self-conception or 'self-constitution'[49] is supposed to be the bedrock on which normativity rests, the question arises as to why some values should take precedence over others in determining how I conceive of or constitute myself. So we are back with the general worry that seems likely to beset all purely naturalistic frameworks for ethics: without some kind of teleological framework for understanding the nature and ultimate destiny of humanity, there seems no basis for regarding any one of the many competing impulses and goals that provide us with reasons to act as having overriding normative force.

6. THE LIMITS OF ARGUMENT

In most contemporary moral philosophy, theistic theories of ethics are scarcely mentioned, yet the discussion in this chapter apparently points us towards the conclusion that a theistic approach is a serious contender when it comes to understanding the nature of moral obligation, especially in the light of the flaws that seem to beset some of the leading alternative approaches. The term 'theory', however, is a very over-used one in philosophy, especially amongst those who construe philosophy as a quasi-scientific enterprise; and it is time to add a note of caution to any suggestion that the theistic outlook provides the 'best theory' of morality. We have already noted the possible option of denying the reality of moral obligation; and those who take this line will of course reject the very idea that there is something 'real' that needs to be accounted for or grounded (as opposed to explained away as an illusion). And as for those who accept the idea of genuine normativity but offer to explain it within a purely secular or naturalist framework, constraints of space have allowed us only to look briefly at a limited number of alternative approaches in a large and complex field; and even if an exhaustive case by case examination were feasible, it would be a mistake to

---

48 As Angus Ritchie aptly points out (following Thomas Nagel), in Ritchie, *From Morality to Metaphysics* (Oxford: Oxford University Press, 2012), pp. 96–97 and 101–102.

49 See Christine Korsgaard, *Self-Constitution* (Oxford: Oxford University Press, 2009), chs. 1 and 2.

suppose that this is an area where decisive refutation is feasible by the use of coercive philosophical argument.[50]

Argument and analysis are important, but their role in determining us to adopt or relinquish a given philosophical position is probably much less significant than we often like to think. In the all-important area of morality, how we interpret it will depend in large part on how far we are gripped by a certain picture of reality, or how far we can with sincerity live with that picture. Can we embrace the vision of the projectivists and accept that there is no final court of appeal beyond our desires and preferences, and that talk of objective moral constraints is ultimately a sham? Or if on the other hand we hold on to the idea of genuine objective moral values, are we happy to understand these entirely within the framework of a world that developed without purpose or goal, and delivered us along with our ethical beliefs and sensibilities out of an eddying stream of circumstances that simply happened to occur that way? Secularist philosophers who give an affirmative answer to this last question may still wish to preserve the idea of some kind of strong authority or normativity as attaching to moral principles, but the question will remain as to what grounds such authority. And from the alternatives presented, the stark choice will be between a picture where truths that matter to us more than anything are left in limbo with no ultimate grounding, and one where, in our search for a grounding, we are in the end brought back face to face with nothing more than ourselves, our own self-conception, or our own contingently evolved capacities and sensibilities.

For the theist, there is an objective grounding. So far from the 'radical contingency of the ethical', there will be its complete opposite: ethics will be grounded in the eternal necessity of an unsurpassably perfect being. But to revert to the term 'theory', the believer would be ill-advised to boast about having devised a brilliant explanatory account of morality; for to explain puzzling phenomena like objective goodness and justice by positing a transcendent being who is himself good and just will seem to the naturalist critic to be little short of circular. Nevertheless, to come back full circle to the discussion of God as the source of goodness with which this chapter opened, the theistic picture continues to resonate

---

50 For the limitations of 'coercive argument', see Robert Nozick, *Philosophical Explanations* (Oxford: Oxford University Press, 1981), Introduction.

with many people because it presents us with a world in which the natural, observable, good-making features of things are not just randomly occurring features that happen to suit whatever desires or needs we happen to have evolved to have, but are aspects of a creation shot through with rationality and love. And indeed the cosmos as revealed by modern science does turn out to be an astonishingly beautiful and unified whole, seemingly able to generate, over billions of years, the intricately ordered processes of life and, eventually, the amazing human capacities for rationality and reflective thought and responsiveness to beauty and goodness. Of course the beauty and goodness we discern are not (to say the least) all-pervasive features of the cosmos; there is much that is amiss – and the problem of evil and suffering, which is clearly the main objection to a benign theistic teleology, will be the chief subject of our next chapter. But the wonder and joy that humans naturally experience in contemplating the glory and variety of creation and the power of the moral order, nevertheless remain; and this is something that integrity requires us to acknowledge.

The glory and variety of creation, and the unique beauty and goodness of each created thing, is something to which the poet Gerard Manley Hopkins gave consummate expression in the first eight lines of a famous sonnet:

> As kingfishers catch fire, dragonflies draw flame;
> As tumbled over rim in roundy wells
> Stones ring; like each tucked string tells, each hung bell's
> Bow swung finds tongue to fling out broad its name;
> Each mortal thing does one thing and the same:
> Deals out that being indoors each one dwells;
> Selves – goes itself; *myself* it speaks and spells,
> Crying: *What I do is me: for that I came.*[51]

Scholars have debated the philosophical influence of Duns Scotus in this celebration of the 'thisness' of things; but there is a simpler and more basic underlying idea in these verses that is found in many other theistic writers – that all things, each in their own way, bear the signature of the divine. They all cry 'for this I came'; that is, they are not random

---

51 'As Kingfishers Catch Fire' [c. 1877]. From *Poems (1876–1889)*, in W. H. Gardner (ed.), *The Poems and Prose of Gerard Manley Hopkins* (Harmondsworth: Penguin, 1953), no. 34.

processes in a senseless cosmos but are pregnant with purpose and meaning. Or as Hopkins put it in one of his notebooks, in language that strongly recalls both this and several other poems he wrote: 'All things therefore are charged with love, are charged with God, and if we know how to touch them give off sparks and take fire, yield drops and flow, ring and tell of him.'[52]

As we move to the start of the 'sestet' (the six lines that form the second part of the sonnet) this idea reaches its climax:

> I say more: the just man justices
> Keeps grace; that keeps all his goings graces...

As each natural thing glorifies God by expressing its unique self, so the human being finds fullest self-expression in doing what is morally required – in 'justicing'. So the poet is telling us that even as the bell joyfully rings out, expressing the purpose for which it 'came', so humanity finds its fullest expression and ultimate purpose in works of justice. And to complete the picture, this achievement is not a self-determined invention, preference, or 'project', as many secular theories of morality would have it,[53] but is a manifestation of 'grace' – something that flows, like all being and goodness, from a source that is pure love, but which has to be freely accepted and 'kept'. No philosophical argument could convince every sceptic that such a picture of reality is correct; but it is a picture that resonates with many of our deepest human sensibilities, and one that arguably tells us more about the normativity of love and justice than could be delivered by any other means.

52 G. M. Hopkins, *Note-books and Papers*, ed. H. House (Oxford: Oxford University Press, 1937), p. 342; cited in *Poems and Prose*, ed. Gardner, p. 231.
53 See, for example, Bernard Williams, cited earlier at note 47.

5

MISFORTUNE AND MISERY

Misère de l'homme sans Dieu... Félicité de l'homme avec Dieu.
('Wretchedness of humanity without God; happiness of
humanity with God.')
Pascal.[1]

I. THE DEMISE OF TELEOLOGY?

The philosophy of religion, as was pointed out in our opening chapter, cannot function properly as an isolated specialism but sooner or later must inevitably concern itself with the grand synoptic question of what kind of 'worldview' or overall picture of reality we are to adopt. The arguments of Chapter 4 have underlined that the theistic worldview is of a cosmos that is fundamentally benign: a cosmos where the natural world reflects a goodness and beauty stemming from the divine source of all reality, where our human moral impulses orient us towards an eternal and objective moral order, and where the deepest fulfilment of our human nature lies in responding to the imperatives of love and justice.

This is more than a 'theory'; it is a kind of joyful affirmatory vision, which is a source of inspiration and hope for the believer. It is not something to be accepted or rejected as one might accept or reject the theory of plate tectonics, or a theory of the causes of the Napoleonic wars, but something that has an impact on every aspect of one's life. If it is a true vision, it confers a deep sense of meaning and purpose in life; if it is false, it is the most pitiable delusion. Any philosophical

---

1 Blaise Pascal, *Pensées* [1670], ed. L. Lafuma (Paris: Seuil, 1962), no. 6.

examination of religious belief must take account of these facts: it is no use pretending that the issues involved are not ones in which we have the deepest personal and emotional stake.

As argued earlier, it would be a mistake to suppose that valid philosophical inquiry must always strive to bracket off or filter out the emotions as if they had no role to play in human understanding.[2] Nevertheless, it must also be an essential part of philosophical inquiry to strive for accuracy and clarity of vision and to take account of all the relevant aspects of our experience when assessing a given position. So it will not do simply to set out the theistic vision and extol its uplifting character; we have to look carefully at those aspects of the world, and of our own human situation, that might count against it. And the most striking of these, and the most worrying for the theist, are those aspects of reality that have come into prominence in the light of modern Darwinian understandings of who we are and how we got here. Richard Dawkins, drawing precisely on these Darwinian understandings, has put the point by declaring that 'the universe we observe has precisely the properties we should expect if there is, at bottom, no design, no purpose, no evil and no good, nothing but blind, pitiless indifference'.[3]

A philosophically more sophisticated expression of the same idea has been developed by Bernard Williams, in a way that is highly relevant to the argument developed in the previous chapter concerning a 'theistic teleology' as the basis for the objectivity and normativity of the moral order.[4] Williams takes the Aristotelian teleological worldview as his target, but his comments implicitly bring into their sights the Christian worldview (whose philosophical articulation, most prominently by Thomas Aquinas, was of course significantly influenced by Aristotle).[5] Williams writes:

[The] most plausible stories now available about [human] evolution, including its very recent date and also certain considerations about the physical characteristics of the species, suggest that human beings are *to some degree a mess*, and that the rapid and immense development of symbolic and cultural

---

2 See Chapter 1, section 4, this volume.
3 Richard Dawkins, *Rivers Out of Eden* (New York: Basic Books, 1995), p. 133.
4 Chapter 4, section 3, this volume.
5 For more on Aquinas's debt to Aristotle, see, for example, Joseph Owens, 'Aristotle and Aquinas', in N. Kretzmann and E. Stump (eds.), *The Cambridge Companion to Aquinas* (Cambridge: Cambridge University Press, 1993), ch. 2.

capacities has left humans as beings for which no form of life is likely to prove entirely satisfactory, either individually or socially.... [This contrasts with the Aristotelian view, a] deeply teleological outlook... according to which there is inherent in each natural kind of thing an appropriate way for things of that kind to behave. On that view it must be the deepest desire... of human beings to live in the way that is in the objective sense appropriate to them.... The first and hardest lesson of Darwinism, that there is *no such teleology at all*, and that there is *no orchestral score provided from anywhere* according to which human beings have a *special part to play*, still has to find its way fully into ethical thought.[6]

The point that human beings are 'to some degree a mess' can be set aside for present purposes since it does not present an obvious contrast between the theistic and the secular worldviews. Some atheistic creeds (one thinks here of certain forms of communism) have taken a decidedly upbeat, not to say crassly optimistic, view of human nature and its supposed aptitude for harmonious living given only the right economic conditions. And conversely it is a commonplace of much Western religious thought that humans are conflicted beings, whose impulses often pull them in contrary directions with disastrous results. The 'wretchedness' of which Pascal speaks in our opening epigraph, and the resulting need for salvation, is a theme that finds powerful symbolic expression in the story of the Fall; and many other texts in the Judaeo-Christian scriptures strongly emphasise the conflictedness of our nature.[7] So pace Williams, we did not need the results of evolutionary theory to arrive at the idea that human nature is problematic. But in any case, to come to the crucial point, there is no automatic conflict here with the vision of a benign creation. For a theistic teleological framework certainly does not imply that things have arrived at perfection – on the contrary, it typically points to an end-state that is not yet fully realized. Thus, for example, in Paul's vision in his letter to the Romans, the whole creation is 'groaning in travail', straining towards its future redemption.[8]

6 Bernard Williams, *Making Sense of Humanity* (Cambridge: Cambridge University Press, 1995), pp. 109–110; emphasis supplied. The importance of this passage is well brought out in David McPherson, 'Cosmic Outlooks and Neo-Aristotelian Virtue Ethics', *International Philosophical Quarterly*, forthcoming June 2015.

7 See, for example, Romans 7:19.

8 Romans 8:22.

There remain, however, at least two important issues for the theist that are implicitly raised by Williams's comments about the supplanting of teleology by the modern Darwinistic outlook, but they need to be carefully distinguished. The first is the question of the correctness or otherwise of 'Darwinism' (we may take this term to be a convenient label for Darwin's theory of evolution by natural selection as supplemented by modern genetics); the second is whether the 'lesson' that Williams draws from Darwinism does in fact follow.

On the first question, few can fail to recognize the formidable explanatory power of natural selection and genetic mutation for understanding the way in which biological systems have developed on earth. That is not to say that no questions remain. The philosopher Thomas Nagel, for one, has expressed doubts about 'the likelihood that [in the available geological time] as a result of physical accident, a sequence of viable genetic mutations should have occurred that was sufficient to permit natural selection to produce the organisms that actually exist'.[9] Working out the exact probabilities is of course a highly complex matter. But we need to beware of the use of words like 'accident', which are so often used in discussions of evolution. For if we suppose that the biological process is accidental in the sense of not consciously guided, it doesn't follow that it must therefore be inherently random and chaotic. On the contrary, most biologists (and we may include Darwin himself)[10] would maintain that once the relevant combination of circumstances happens to arise, then, given the natural properties of the relevant structures, the resulting evolutionary processes can be expected to occur in an in principle perfectly predictable and lawlike fashion. The British astronomer Martin Rees suggested some time ago that the universe may be 'biophilic' – intrinsically apt to produce life (and we might add 'noöphilic' – apt for the eventual emergence of intelligence).[11] More recently, the physicist Brian Cox has put the point as follows: 'far from being some chance event . . . the emergence of life might have been an inevitable consequence of the laws of physics [so that] a living cosmos might be the only way our cosmos can be'.[12] Although Nagel is

---

9 Thomas Nagel, *Mind and Cosmos* (Oxford: Oxford University Press, 2012), p. 6.
10 See Charles Darwin, *On the Origin of Species by Means of Natural Selection* [1859], final paragraph.
11 Martin Rees, *Our Cosmic Habitat* (London: Weidenfeld & Nicolson, 2002).
12 Brian Cox, *The Wonders of Life*, BBC television series, first broadcast January 2013.

perfectly entitled to express his doubts about this supposed 'inevitability', the issue appears to be one for scientists to investigate, not for philosophers to try to decide in advance.

The waters have been muddied here by the so-called theory of Intelligent Design, some of whose supporters would like to promote a designer God as a scientific alternative to Darwinian evolution.[13] But as a general strategy that seems radically misguided. Science necessarily operates within the natural world, investigating the structure of things and attempting to discover the hidden mechanisms of nature that account for how things behave. It searches, in one of Daniel Dennett's more helpful pieces of terminology, for 'cranes' – solid workmanlike mechanisms that perform the laborious task of explanatory lifting. And although the Darwinian 'cranes' so far proposed may turn out to need further refinement or even (as Nagel suggests) replacement with or subsumption under a new scientific paradigm, it doesn't help in the meantime to invoke divine 'skyhooks' – attempts to short-circuit all the hard work of empirical scientific research by appealing to a miraculous solution from on high.[14]

As for the 'lesson' that Williams draws from the success of Darwinism – namely, that there is 'no teleology at all', and that Darwinism has decisively refuted the picture according to which there is an objective good for each natural kind – this seems far more questionable. For even should the evolutionary account turn out to be quite sufficient to explain the complex unfolding of the physical and biological universe, there seems no good reason to suppose that accepting such an account is inconsistent with belief in a theistic teleology. In other words, a 'compatibilist' position vis-à-vis religion and science seems quite feasible. On this view, we look purely to science for a valid explanatory account of the mechanisms and processes by which the universe developed from its original state, and by which, over vast swathes of time, life and intelligence arose. But the religious outlook, so far from being construed as providing a *rival* account to this scientific one, is understood instead as *interpreting* the entire natural world and all its beautiful and intricate physical processes as a manifestation of divine creativity.

13 See, for example, Stephen C. Meyer, *Signature in the Cell* (New York: HarperCollins, 2009).
14 Daniel Dennett, *Intuition Pumps* (London: Allen Lane, 2013), ch. 6, §38.

This does not necessarily imply that human beings have a 'special part to play', in Williams's phrase. The somewhat scathing expression is presumably supposed to suggest an outmoded anthropocentrism; but many theistic writers, past as well as present, have allowed the possibility of innumerable other worlds in which God's creative purposes may be unfolded.[15] But a religious perspective does nevertheless imply that humans do indeed have *a* part to play in the wider cosmic scheme of things. And central to understanding this, for the theist, will be an acknowledgement of the significance of those distinctive intellectual and moral capacities of which we find ourselves possessed: an acknowledgement that what has happened on this planet (and for all we know elsewhere in the universe) is, in Thomas Nagel's significant phrase, 'the development of consciousness into an instrument of transcendence that can grasp objective reality and objective value'.[16] All this is strikingly compatible with a theistic teleological interpretation of reality. For it will mean, on the theistic view, that amongst what Williams elsewhere calls our 'rather ill-sorted *bricolage* of powers and instincts',[17] there is a fundamental awareness of the good, a responsiveness to something objective that is not merely a projection of our various contingently evolved inclinations and preferences, and that the ultimate destiny and fulfilment of human beings must lie in our orienting ourselves towards that good.

2. EVIL AND THEODICY

Even if, as just argued, Darwinian understandings of our history need not be intrinsically subversive of the concept of a benign, divinely established teleology, nevertheless the worry remains for the theist that the actual mechanisms of the evolutionary process seem such as to severely threaten belief in a surpassingly good God. The bitter struggle for survival, the endless extinction of whole life forms, the pain and suffering

15 For example, René Descartes, *Conversation with Burman* [1648], AT V 168: CSMK 349; G. W. Leibniz, *Theodicy* [*Essais de théodicée*, 1710], trans. E. M. Huggard (London: Routledge, 1951), Part I, §19.
16 Nagel, *Mind and Cosmos*, p. 85.
17 Bernard Williams, 'Replies,' in J. Altham and R. Harrison (eds.), *World, Mind, and Ethics* (Cambridge: Cambridge University Press, 1995), p. 199; cited in McPherson, 'Cosmic Outlooks.'

endured by countless individual sentient beings in the process – can this really be compatible with an interpretation of reality according to which 'God is love indeed/ and Love creation's final law'?[18] This question is of course part of the complicated issue known as 'the problem of evil', with its associated vast array of philosophical literature stretching back to Augustine.

The best-known aspect of Augustine's approach to 'theodicy' (the attempt to vindicate God's justice in the face of all the evil and suffering found in the world) is the so-called free will defence, which focuses on *moral* evil – the widespread suffering caused by the deliberate choices of human beings. In a world where people are not automata but free agents, with the genuine two-way power to act or not to act in certain ways, it will always be possible for them to turn away from the good, and, for example, to pursue cruel or selfish policies that will cause pain to their victims. Even if this line of argument is successful however, it plainly does not cover the many kinds of *natural* evil – deformity, disease, all the fear and pain repeatedly caused in the struggle for survival (for example, by lions, wolves, and other predators behaving simply in accordance with their nature), not to mention the distress and agony humans and other sentient creatures undergo as the result inanimate natural causes (earthquakes, floods, forest fires, and so on). The catalogue of the resulting innocent suffering, over the millennia, is enormous and appears to be an integral part of the ordinary natural process arising out of the geological and biological development of the planet over time.

The explanations of such natural evil that have been offered by some theistic philosophers can seem almost embarrassingly inadequate. In the *Theodicy* of Gottfried Leibniz in the early eighteenth century, for example, we find the following:

A little acid, sharpness or bitterness is often more pleasing than sugar; shadows enhance colours; and even a dissonance in the right place gives relief to harmony. We wish to be terrified by rope-dancers on the point of falling and we wish that tragedies shall well-nigh cause us to weep. Do men relish health enough, or thank God enough for it, without having ever been sick? And is

18 In Tennyson's phrase; see citation at note 26 in Chapter 4, this volume.

it not most often necessary that a little evil render the good more discernible, that is to say, greater?[19]

While it is true that we would not want a bland universe without contrasts or challenges (indeed, for humans, moral development may be enhanced by struggle and stress, as many have pointed out),[20] the *amount* and *degree* of suffering found in the world is clearly too great for this kind of 'argument from contrasts' to carry enough explanatory weight. But Leibniz's 'optimistic' view of creation is part and parcel of a more general metaphysical outlook based on a priori reflections on the nature of God:

Supreme wisdom, united to a goodness that is no less infinite, cannot but have chosen the best; . . . there would be something to correct in the action of God if it were possible to do better; . . . so it may be said that if there were not the best (*optimum*) among all possible worlds, God would not have created any.[21]

This is linked to Leibniz's 'Principle of Sufficient Reason' – that 'no proposition can be true unless there is a sufficient reason why it should be thus and not otherwise, even though in most cases these reasons cannot be known to us'.[22] And from this, and the concept of the infinite goodness of God, Leibniz concluded that 'any perfection which God could put into things, without derogating from the other perfections in them, has been put there'.[23] The 'without derogating' clause is important, since Leibniz holds that only certain combinations of properties and things are 'compossible' (can exist together).[24] So a delicate and fast-running herbivore, perfect of its kind, cannot also be equipped with massive tusks to resist a carnivorous predator; nor can a tiger, perfect of its kind, be the creature it is and yet have the ability to flourish without hunting and killing its prey.

19 Leibniz, *Theodicy*, Part I, §12.
20 See, for example, Richard Swinburne, *The Existence of God* (Oxford: Clarendon, 1979), p. 219; 2nd ed., p. 264.
21 Leibniz, *Theodicy*, Part I, §8.
22 G. W. Leibniz, *Monadology* [1714], §32, trans. in Leibniz, *Philosophical Writings*, ed. G. H. R. Parkinson (London: Dent, 1973), p. 184.
23 Leibniz, *Correspondence with Clarke* [1715–16], Fourth Paper, in *Philosophical Writings*, p. 220.
24 Leibniz, *Resumé of Metaphysics* [c. 1697], §8, in *Philosophical Writings*, p. 145.

These considerations take us some way forward insofar as they suggest that abolishing suffering, even for an omnipotent being, is not simply a matter of waving a magic wand and eliminating any feature of nature that may be unwelcome to any given species. Nature is an intimately interrelated whole, 'all of one piece like the ocean', as Leibniz put it,[25] and any supposed 'improvement' in one part may turn out to carry costs for other parts of the system – something that modern ecological awareness is increasingly underlining. But what of the more general claim that there must be a 'sufficient reason', albeit often unknown to us, which explains the presence of any given, or indeed all, the natural evil and suffering in the cosmos? The claim does not appear to cut much ice in the context of the present debate. For an atheist cosmology may simply doubt that the universe *is* ultimately rational in this way; or alternatively, it may accept that there are always in principle sufficient explanations for what occurs, but deny that these have to reflect any ultimate goodness (suffering may be the result of a lawlike but 'blind and pitiless' processes, as Dawkins maintains). Nevertheless, the Leibnizian thought that sufficient justifying reasons for evil do not have to be ones that we are aware of does turn out to be relevant to the debate over evil and suffering, at least in one respect. As several contemporary philosophers have pointed out, the existence of massive suffering could never be a logically conclusive refutation of the existence of God, since even when we cannot conceive what the reason for such suffering might be, there is no possibility of establishing that there *could* not be such a reason.[26] So even if one were to evaluate and reject all the suggested reasons that Leibniz and the many other philosophical defenders of theism have actually come up with here, it would still be logically possible for the theist to stand his ground.

Nevertheless, the extent of the suffering found in the world, though not a logically watertight refutation of God's existence, has seemed to many to tip the balance of probabilities against the theistic view. Amid all the intricacy and harmony that so impressed eighteenth-century

---

25 Leibniz, *Theodicy*, Part I, §9; cf. Part II, § 119.
26 For a careful survey of this and other arguments relating to God and evil, see Trent Dougherty and Jerry L. Wells, 'Arguments from Evil', in C. Taliaferro, V. Harrison, and S. Goetz (eds.), *The Routledge Companion to Theism* (London: Routledge, 2013), pp. 370ff.

writers like Archdeacon Paley,[27] the detailed work of biologists in the following two centuries or so has increasingly disclosed so much that seems wasteful, so much that appears makeshift and awkward,[28] so much that condemns species and individuals to lives of grinding struggle and ever present danger and distress. In short, what our increasing understanding of the mechanisms of nature seems to have done, in the light of the Darwinian revolution, is to produce, in many people's minds, a deep loss of confidence in the idea of a cosmos that is at bottom benign. Further ingenious explanations by theistic philosophers following the pattern set by Leibniz and others could of course conceivably tip the balance the other way. But it seems more likely (to revert to a theme that has already surfaced in earlier chapters) that this is one of those areas where further argument and analysis, or further empirical evidence, cannot really settle the matter. The facts are pretty well established by now; the question is whether it is possible, with integrity, to maintain a theistic interpretation of those facts, and hold on to the idea of an underlying goodness in the cosmos against the background of widespread suffering. The latter question is clearly not a scientific question but a hermeneutic or interpretative one. So it may be that the most fruitful way forward here is to shift the focus and look at how the suffering that is an inescapable part of the human condition is actually portrayed in religious tradition and scripture.

3. SUFFERING AND THE RELIGIOUS PERSPECTIVE

If we move away from abstract intellectualizing about suffering and start to look at how it is presented in the canonical writings of the great religions, we find something remarkable: so far from being glossed over as an embarrassment for the believer, suffering is something that religious writers characteristically both acknowledge and indeed emphasize again and again. At the very start of the human story, in Genesis, the human lot is spoken of as one of sweat and toil, pain and sorrow, and inevitable death; and the subsequent narrative in the Hebrew Bible is a

27 See William Paley, *Natural Theology* [1802].
28 See, for example, Richard Dawkins, *The Blind Watchmaker* (London: Penguin, 1986), pp. 93–94.

long catalogue of bitterness and tragic loss – war, slavery, exile, disease, fear, and famine.

In condemning Adam and Eve, in Genesis, chapter 3, to a hard and painful life, God is described as pronouncing a punishment for their sin of disobedience; and this may prompt a familiar picture of the religious interpretation of suffering, namely, that it is something deserved by humans through their wrongdoing. Let us for convenience call this the 'penal story'. There is no doubt that this represents one significant strand in the Judaeo-Christian tradition. But the penal story is problematic for many reasons. In the first place, there is evidently a great deal of suffering that is by no stretch of the imagination deserved by wrongdoing (one may think again here of the results of 'natural evils', like earthquake damage, or all the suffering undergone by infants and children as a result of genetic disorder or infectious disease). If one responds to this by taking the Genesis condemnation narrative in a strict and literal sense and insisting that the sin of Adam and Eve incurs a blanket penalty for all their descendants, this not only fails to show that the resulting suffering is deserved, in any normal sense of the term, but it also carries the incoherence of representing an unsurpassably good God as inherently unjust.

The penal story is also inconsistent with many other moral insights that emerge elsewhere in the Bible. The story of Job, perhaps the most striking reflection on the problem of suffering anywhere in literature, makes it clear that the horrible torments Job undergoes are completely undeserved. And the teachings of Jesus, in line with this, resolutely reject the idea that a natural evil like congenital blindness can be attributed to the sin either of the individual sufferer or his ancestors (John 9:2). Or again, the large number of people who were crushed when the Tower of Siloam collapsed were in Jesus' eyes, certainly *not* being singled out for punishment (Luke 13:4). None of this of course implies that moral wrongdoing does not carry any bad consequences for the wrongdoer; but it does reject the simplistic conception of God as a micro-manager who constantly manipulates natural events so as to protect the righteous and bring harm upon transgressors. Curiously perhaps, the complaint that this is not so, or that the universe is not made that way, is something that is frequently voiced by atheists, who would appear to have no reason to expect any such thing. David Hume, for example, seems to have been strongly piqued by the fact that, in the world as we find it, such is the disorder and confusion in human affairs, that no perfect or regular distribution of happiness and misery is ever, in this life, to be expected. Not only are the goods of fortune, and the endowments of the body ... unequally divided between the virtuous and the vicious, but even the mind itself partakes, in some degree, of this disorder.... In a word, human life is more governed by fortune than by reason.[29]

And taking up Hume's theme, the contemporary philosopher John Kekes has observed: 'Good people deserve good things, bad people deserve bad things, but contingencies [prevent] this from happening... this offends our sense of what the world ought to be like.'[30] The implicit train of thought in the minds of those who take this line appears to be somewhat as follows: '(1) the daily flow of natural events *ought* to be such that virtue is always rewarded and vice punished; (2) religious people must believe that it *is* this way; (3) but [melancholy fact] it just *isn't* that way; therefore (4) so much the worse for the religious view.' But the trouble with this is that it depends on a caricature of what a religious worldview amounts to. In reality, as we have just seen in the examples from Job and from the Gospels, there are key religious texts that declare that suffering is very often *not* deserved.

The possibility of a more nuanced religious approach to suffering, which does not rely on penal or other simplistic interpretations, is often ignored by critics of religion. Thus Galen Strawson speaks of the 'unsurpassably disgusting' practice of theodicy, which in its attempt to justify suffering 'shows contempt for the reality of human suffering, or indeed any intense suffering'.[31] This is a familiar accusation whose roots can be traced to Voltaire,[32] and which does little justice to the complexities of the treatments of suffering in scripture and subsequent theodicy writings. What does admittedly seem true is that some otherwise highly acute and sensitive philosophical writers on this topic have been tempted by the ambition to show how not just some but *all* suffering must be deserved, or else justified in some other way via some larger divine plan. Examples of this include attempts to justify cases like the genocidal

---

29 David Hume, 'The Sceptic,' in *Essays Moral and Political*, Vol. 2 [1742], last four paragraphs; repr. in Hume, *Selected Essays*, ed. S. Copley and A. Edgar (Oxford: Oxford University Press, 1993), pp. 111–112.

30 John Kekes, *The Human Condition* (Oxford: Oxford University Press, 2010), p. 14.

31 Galen Strawson, 'Religion Is a Sin', *London Review of Books* 33:11 (June 2011), 26–28.

32 See Voltaire, *Candide* [1759].

command to the Israelites (ascribed to God in the book of Deuteronomy) to slaughter all the Canaanites, men, women, and children, which include the thought that God might offer salvation to the Canaanites 'posthumously', and the idea that the deaths of the Canaanites 'were partially instrumental in making possible the coming of Jesus'.[33] But in reality, such horrendous suffering, whether the result of natural or of moral evil, seems beyond all morally acceptable justification. So many might be inclined to agree with Mark Johnston, that 'nothing that *subsequently* happens can diminish the tragedy or the horror.... [T]he attempt to put an otherworldly frame around such things, so they seem not to be the tragedies or the horrors that they manifestly are, borders on... the obscene'.[34]

But if one decisively rejects the idea that all suffering is deserved or justified by some wider plan, what recourse *is* left to the theist? We have identified some false steps in theodicy, but could there be an authentic theodicy? Or will any suggestion of trying to put an 'otherworldly frame' around such sufferings be as abominable as Johnston suggests? One 'otherworldly frame' that might come to mind here is the idea of the afterlife (to which we shall return in the next chapter); but whatever one's view of that notion, it plainly cannot do *all* the work. For the implicit worry (irrespective of whether we are considering natural or moral evil) is why a supposedly omnipotent and unsurpassingly good God does not do something *at the time* to alleviate or reduce suffering of the innocent victims.

If we now come back to the way in which suffering is portrayed in Scripture, we find in the Christian narrative of the Crucifixion a paradigm case of apparent divine inaction in the face of the most hideous suffering. For theologians, of course, there are many competing theological interpretations of this event, involving complex theories about the precise status of Christ, conceptions of sacrifice, the doctrine of the atonement, of the Resurrection, and so on; and it may be very hard, if not impossible, to consider the event in a way that prescinds from all the theological theory. But for the purposes of the present discussion, we

---

33 D. Baggett and J. L. Walls, *Good God: The Theistic Foundations of Morality* (Oxford: Oxford University Press, 2010), p. 140. It should be added that the quoted suggestion is but one part of an otherwise highly nuanced and well-argued discussion.

34 Mark Johnston, *Saving God: Religion after Idolatry* (Princeton: Princeton University Press, 2009), p. 15, emphasis supplied.

are simply asking what is disclosed here about the bare phenomenon of extreme innocent suffering and what an appropriate religious response to it might be.

Considered in purely human terms, the figure of Christ may in one respect be considered as an archetype who stands for all humankind, insofar as we know of countless cases (and there must be uncountably many more we do not know of) where innocent people have cried to be delivered from agony, and no deliverance has been forthcoming – no end, until death, to the torment. Whatever else the religious believer knows about God, then, one thing is already known – that in these cases there is no divine micro-managerial intervention to put a stop to horrendous evils while they are occurring. This does not entail that miracles never happen or that prayer is wholly pointless – these are quite different questions that raise a host of complex further questions in their own right. But it does mean that the religious outlook must, like any outlook that claims to be coherent, take account of the world as we find it: we live in a world where utterly terrible things often happen, *and this, moreover, is something that is not denied but is fully acknowledged in many religious writings.*

What then does a theistic outlook of the Judaeo-Christian kind do with such happenings? Johnston's answer is that it tries, obscenely, to put an 'otherworldy frame' around them that tries to deny the horror and the tragedy. But the actual accounts found in the relevant texts are hardly such as to make the gory details recede from view. The misery of Job as he sits in the ashes and scrapes his sores with a piece of broken pottery; Christ's scourging, his agonizing thirst on the cross, the brutality of the solders, and all the rest: these are details more consonant with the horrific details in the paintings of, for example, the German Renaissance painter Matthias Grünewald[35] than the calm ethereal gold of a Byzantine icon. Any portrayal, of course, must in part be an interpretation; and the various biblical narratives, like the various perspectives offered by different schools of painting, each have their own distinctive value, and give varying emphasis to the 'transcendent' and the 'down-to-earth' aspects of the events they describe. But the common factor we nevertheless find, in the portrayals of these momentous events whether in Scripture or art, is not so much the attempt to put an 'otherworldly

---

35 See, for example, the Grünewald *Crucifixion* from the Isenheim Altar (1512–1515).

frame' round the terrible facts, as to put a framework of *moral significance* around them. We have referred in early chapters to the 'primacy of the moral' in religion: that is to say, the idea that religious belief is not chiefly to do with abstract theological theories or the formulation of explanatory hypotheses about the origins of the world, but instead takes as its central focus the deep structural problems of human life and our pressing need for moral transformation.[36] The reason the crucifixion story has resonated so powerfully down the ages, touching so many ordinary people and inspiring so many great artists and musicians, hinges on something much deeper and more universal than the intellectual theorizing of theologians – the sense that this event somehow reflects a profound moral truth about the true meaning of human suffering.

4. THE DYNAMICS OF TRANSFORMATION

The moral and hermeneutic dimensions just alluded to are hard if not impossible to explore fruitfully if we take science as our best model for how philosophical inquiry should be conducted. This perhaps explains why religious thinking is often disregarded or despised by those contemporary academic philosophers who would like to see philosophy move in an increasingly 'scientific' direction, and who tend, like the early Wittgenstein, to mistrust any departure from what can be stated in plain descriptive language. But it is worth remembering here that even in his early philosophy, when he was concerned to argue for an austerely restrictive conception of the limits of philosophical inquiry, Wittgenstein had the insight to allow that there is that which is unsayable (*es gibt Unaussprechliches*) but which can somehow *make itself manifest*, or 'show itself' (*zeigt sich*).[37] Moral insights, like aesthetic and religious ones, he later suggested, cannot be forced into a scientific template 'as a teacup will only hold a teacup full of water [even] if I were to pour out a gallon over it'.[38]

---

36 Chapter 1, section 4, Chapter 4, section 1, both this volume.
37 Wittgenstein, *Tractatus Logico-Philosophicus* [1919], §6.552.
38 Wittgenstein, 'A Lecture on Ethics' [1929], in *Philosophical Occasions*, ed. J. Klagge and A. Nordmann (Indianapolis: Hackett, 1993), p. 40.

The first and hardest step, if we are to tease out what is 'made manifest' in scriptural accounts of suffering, may be to free ourselves from a common but ultimately unsatisfying construal of the way suffering must be understood from a religious perspective. We have already put on one side the 'penal account' – not in order to claim it has no truth but because it plainly cannot cope with all that needs to be explained. And by the same token, we may now need to put on one side a number of other familiar accounts that try as it were to 'tidy up' suffering – that try to show that a religious perspective incorporates it into a justifying schema that *leaves no remainder*. An example of what I mean here would be if someone were to say: 'Job's sufferings were permitted because his righteousness was being tested; and once he had been through the test, his goods were restored to him, so it was all made all right.' The very 'tidiness' may give this some appeal for those who like their answers to be simple (and there may even be elements of truth in what has been offered); but the cost is very considerable, namely, that the story is turned into a banal fairy tale where everyone lives 'happily ever after'. Too much will have been lost of what makes the story challenging and pregnant with moral significance. In a similar way (though the component elements are far more complex), the following familiar kind of construal of the Crucifixion would be ultimately unsatisfying, or at least incomplete. Someone, for example, might say: 'the suffering of Christ was a penalty due for the sins of others, and that explains why it had to happen, namely, in order that sinners who believe in him can go to heaven'; or 'the suffering of Christ was the necessary preliminary to his triumph and Resurrection'. To be wary of such accounts is not (to repeat) necessarily to maintain they contain no truth. The problem, rather, is that they are too 'thin'; they gloss too quickly over what gives the event its *depth* and moral significance. And it is no accident, in this connection, that over-schematic explanations of this kind form an ideal target for contemporary critics who prefer to dismiss the theistic perspective from a safe and superior distance.

A telling feature of the kinds of account just alluded to is their implicit emphasis on the 'happy ending'. The underlying conception of religious thought is that it deals with the problems of human life by offering a quick way out. God is construed as a kind of deus ex machina, who ensures a favourable outcome, at least for the favoured group of believers. This way of thinking is one that can easily slide into what Mark Johnston has dubbed 'servile idolatry and spiritual materialism'.[39] Spiritual materialism involves retaining our ordinary selfish desires (for security, comfort, success, etc.) and trying to get them satisfied by manipulating supposed supernatural forces; idolatry is similar, placating the gods to get what we want. Authentic spirituality, by contrast, must address the 'large-scale structural defects in human life' – arbitrary suffering, ageing, the vulnerability of ourselves and our loved ones to time and chance and, ultimately, death. The religious or redeemed life, Johnston argues, is one where we are *reconciled* to these large-scale defects.[40]

This in turn makes a vital difference to ethics. In addressing the central question of how we should live our lives, the ordinary secular virtues (self-confidence, fairness, good judgement, etc.) 'take life on its own unredeemed terms and make the most of it'[41] By contrast, the theological virtues (faith, hope, love) are 'not merely intensifications of ordinary virtue but conditions of a transformed or redeemed life'. Johnston is thus deeply sympathetic to the resonant insights of Scripture – for example, the story of the Fall, which shows how we are by our nature caught in an oscillation between self-will and the 'false righteousness' which conforms to the good out of fear or self-interest. So his conclusion is that the salvation Christ proclaimed (and something similar might be said about the message of many of the prophets of the Hebrew Bible) was not about placating a supernatural God, or about 'making it all better', but rather was about 'the grace of finding a way to live that keeps faith with the importance of goodness and love even in the face of everything that can happen to you'.[42]

Taking a favourable view of these insights need not imply agreement with all of Johnston's position (for example, his controversial and idiosyncratic conception of the prospects for personal survival after death).[43] But what does emerge from his comments on the narratives of the Fall and the Crucifixion is the importance of interpreting

39 Mark Johnston, *Saving God* (Princeton, NJ: Princeton University Press, 2009), p. 51.
40 Johnston, *Saving God*, pp. 14–17.
41 Johnston, *Saving God*, p. 16.
42 Johnston, *Saving God*, p. 180.
43 See further Mark Johnston, *Surviving Death* (Princeton, NJ: Princeton University Press, 2010).

religious thought in a way that preserves the crucial connection between authentic religious allegiance and accepting the call for moral transformation. If one preserves this connection, then the scriptural examples we have been considering will be seen as anticipating what has come to be thought of as a Kantian insight: that true moral worth attaches only to an attitude that turns towards what is right for its own sake, out of pure 'good will', as Kant put it, and not from any ulterior motive.[44] Thus the Judaeo-Christian moral framework requires the kind of moral rebirth that leads to wholehearted and totally committed love of God and of one's neighbour. As we saw in the last chapter, there is a kind of cosmic teleological framework supporting this: humans are thereby called towards their ultimate destiny and deepest fulfilment. But there is no conflict here with the Kantian idea of 'deontology' – that the moral agent acts rightly simply because it is right and not for any beneficial result. For the teachings of Christ make it plain that following what is right can demand great self-sacrifice; so that for anyone who is still in the grip of 'spiritual materialism', following the path for utilitarian or self-interested reasons will not be acting rightly. The way of the Cross is the starkest possible reminder of what a morally transformed life may require.

So where does this leave the problem of suffering? If, as just suggested, an authentic religious perspective must in a certain sense embrace it, are we not left simply with a bleak world in which doing what is right often carries terrible costs? Adding the teleological framework which, as it were, draws us on to that goal in the name of the good and the right does not seem quite enough. For one feels that a theistic outlook must do more. Granted, it should not, as we have seen, offer base rewards or bribes for right action; but it must surely have more to say about the way in which enduring suffering for the sake of the good might be redemptive.

A possible way forward here is suggested by Eleonore Stump, who explores the problem of suffering by considering four biblical narratives: the stories of Job, Samson, Abraham, and Mary of Bethany (the sister of Martha and Lazarus). Each of them, as portrayed in the stories, undergoes appalling suffering: Job, physically and emotionally

---

44 Immanuel Kant, *Groundwork of the Metaphysic of Morals* [*Grundlegung zur Metaphysik der Sitten*, 1785], ch. 1.

tormented and stripped of all that has given his life meaning; Samson, 'eyeless in Gaza at the mill with slaves',[45] fallen from his former glory as champion and become an object of scorn; Abraham, confronted with the horrifying command to sacrifice his beloved son; and Mary, prostrate in the desperate grief of bereavement, her earlier pleas for help having been apparently ignored by the one she most trusted. Eschewing the easy answer of invoking post-mortem rewards, Stump develops a distinctive interpretation of the moral significance of the suffering undergone in each of these cases, which invokes the idea of the 'glorifying' power of suffering.

Drawing on the account of love given by Thomas Aquinas, Stump argues that people can be 'ultimately and deeply united with each other only if they are united in goodness'.[46] A corollary of this is that internal integration is a vital requirement for two parties truly to love each other. If you desire union with someone, you desire to be intimately close and personally present to them; but such closeness is undermined if one of the parties suffers from internal conflict or psychic dissonance.[47] Now in the four biblical cases discussed, the biblical protagonists start out in a state of something like double-mindedness: they are unable to enter into a fully loving relationship with God either because they lack a wholehearted commitment to the good, or because they lack a wholehearted trust in God's goodness. Thus Abraham (as indicated by his earlier behaviour towards his other son Ishmael) longed to be the father of a nation, but tried 'to bring about the fulfilment of the divine promises by devices of his own'.[48] Only *in extremis*, in the anguish of being ready to sacrifice Isaac, is he finally willing to trust God to keep Isaac safe, and this 'makes Abraham into something glorious. It moves him from being a prosperous nomad with powerful religious experiences to being the father of faith, and so it brings Abraham to the flowering of his life'.[49] In the case of all the protagonists Stump discusses, what happens as a result of their terrible suffering is that they are somehow brought to a 'gloriousness' that could not have been achieved had their goals, as they originally envisioned them, been brought about. So Mary

45 John Milton, *Samson Agonistes* [*c.* 1660].
46 Eleonore Stump, *Wandering in Darkness* (Oxford: Clarendon Press, 2010), p. 95.
47 Compare Stump, *Wandering in Darkness*, p. 130.
48 Stump, *Wandering in Darkness*, p. 281.
49 Stump, *Wandering in Darkness*, p. 306.

of Bethany loses, she thinks irretrievably, what she thought she wanted more than anything. But

> as it turns out, what seemed to be irretrievable loss was not; and however much it seemed to Mary that Jesus betrayed her trust, in fact in the story he did not. She was not wrong to be heartbroken.... Nonetheless she was mistaken about what she thought she knew.... When Lazarus is restored to her... what Mary is given is more what she really desires than she would have known how to want.[50]

By a close examination of these particular scriptural narratives then, it seems one may be able to glimpse the *meaning* of such suffering on an authentic religious outlook. In the cases described, the suffering, terrible as it is, ends up playing a role in the person's ultimate flourishing by bringing them, in the end, closer to God. Is this a theodicy – that is to say, an indication of the morally sufficient reasons for God's allowing such suffering? In the cases described, one can begin to see how the desires of those involved are be reconfigured or 'refolded', in Stump's striking expression, so that they become 'interwoven with a deepest desire for God', or for the good. This is a moving and powerful conclusion. But plainly this kind of model cannot be extended to all suffering – nor is it intended to be, since Stump has the integrity to admit cases where 'the suffering a person endures breaks that person beyond healing'.[51] To come back to the issue of 'natural' evil, there are clearly countless instances where accident, disease, and natural disaster does not just crush a life, but does so in a way that is utterly unrelated to even the possibility of moral transformation. The upshot is that lamentable and horrific suffering can sometimes, despite all appearances, be a catalyst for redemptive changes in the agent. This in itself is a highly significant fact about the human condition. But it is a fact of limited scope, which still leaves much apparently unredeemed.

5. THE FEARFUL RESIDUE

The lesson to be drawn from the foregoing discussion is in many ways a positive one. In a centuries old debate that has often seemed either

---

50 Stump, *Wandering in Darkness*, p. 367.
51 Stump, *Wandering in Darkness*, p. 480.

sterile or disrespectful of the terrible reality of suffering, we can see how the problem can be tackled in a way that takes us away from the barren arena of adversarial sparring. A hermeneutic approach, exploring specific examples in all their rich detail and striving to discern how the meaning of what happens is unfolded, can significantly help us to see how a religious perspective operates in such cases. And along the way, by encouraging empathetic reflection on the cases discussed, it can itself contribute to the growth of our moral sensibilities. On the negative side, however, what emerges is that even the most sensitive illuminations of the moral dimension of suffering cannot exclude a large residue of cases where such a dimension is simply absent – where the darkness remains unbroken by any glimmer of light that might hold out hope of redemption.

Here we are brought back to the world as we find it. For despite our desire for security and comfort, we know we inhabit a wild, untameable universe of change and decay, where suns explode with cataclysmic force, producing heavier elements that after countless further collisions and explosions sometimes end up as temporary lodgings for those immensely delicate and fragile parts of the cosmos that are living beings. And we are amongst them, part of that ceaseless process of change and decay. 'All things which are bounded with time', the seventeenth-century philosopher Anne Conway aptly observed, 'are subject to death and corruption, or are changed in to another species of things, as we see water changed into stone, stones into earth, earth into trees, and trees into animals or living creatures'.[52] Can all this be more than an impersonal flux, magnificent perhaps, but void of ultimate moral significance, like the 'fountain' of which the theologian and philosopher Don Cupitt spoke – someone who was once in his younger days a theist but who later abandoned any hope of a transcendent ground of meaning and value, and whose only consolation was to strive to be content with a world that is 'passing rapidly', and where we will soon be 'forgotten along with everything else'.[53]

Argument cannot finally settle this. This does not mean that theism, or its denial, are irrational positions held in despite of the evidence. As

52 Anne Conway, The Principles of the Most Ancient and Modern Philosophy [1690], ch. 5, §6; repr. in Taliaferro and Teply (eds.), Cambridge Platonist Spirituality, p. 191.
53 Don Cupitt, The Fountain: A Secular Theology (London: SCM Press, 2010), p. 29.

we have seen, there is plenty of evidence on both sides; it is simply that there is no neutral detached court of appeal from which the status of the evidence can be assessed and the final verdict can be dispassionately determined. There could, in the end, be nothing but the 'fountain', a continuous flux and reflux of atoms until the universe finally expires; and in any such world it seems that a residue of brute unredeemed suffering is bound to occur. But as we have seen, for humans, caught up in the process, true moral action and moral growth is nevertheless possible, though the way is fearfully hard, and for many it may be tragically barred through accident, disease, or any of the 'thousand natural shocks that flesh is heir to'.[54] The terrible residue of such suffering is not something a theist has any business trying to deny. But the authentic theistic response to this is not to be in denial, but to endure the 'forsakenness' of which the Psalms and the Gospels speak,[55] out of which trust can somehow spring. And for the theist, there is hope that the struggle will not be in vain. This, at any rate, was how the religious poet R. S. Thomas saw things, a writer who lived on the remote Welsh coast, and often in his writings saw the wild moving expanse of the sea as a metaphor for the ambiguous, wonderful yet fearful, creation of which we are a part:

> Let despair be known
> as my ebb-tide; but let prayer
> have its springs, too, brimming,
> disarming him; discovering somewhere
> among his fissures deposits of mercy
> where trust may take root and grow.[56]

54 William Shakespeare, *Hamlet* [*c.* 1601], Act III, scene 1.
55 Matthew 27:46; Mark 15:34; Psalms 22:1.
56 R. S. Thomas, 'Tidal,' in *Mass for Hard Times* (Newcastle: Bloodaxe Books, 1992), p. 43. For a more extensive exploration of the oceanic metaphor, see Thomas's poem 'Alive,' in *Laboratories of the Spirit* (London: Macmillan, 1975), p. 51.

6

MORTALITY AND
MEANINGFULNESS

Herr, es ist zeit. Der Sommer war sehr groß.
Leg deinen Schatten auf die Sonnenuhren,
Und auf den Fluren laß die Winde los.
('Lord, it is time. The summer lasted long.
Upon the sundial draw your lengthening shade
And on the meadows let the winds blow strong'.)
Rilke[1]

1. THE THEISTIC OUTLOOK AND THE HUMAN CONDITION

The characteristic theistic voice of hope in the face of suffering, with which the previous chapter ended, marks a transition to the rather more practical aspects of the religious outlook, which will be our main concern in the remaining chapters. These aspects do not always receive much prominence in philosophy of religion as commonly studied, but no philosophical inquiry into religion can afford to ignore them. For subscribing to a particular worldview is never simply a matter of assenting to certain doctrines or propositions; it characteristically makes a crucial difference to how we live – both to our overall sense of the meaning and purpose of life, and to how we come to terms with the constant stresses and changes that mark human existence, and with the bodily deterioration and eventual demise that sooner or later awaits us all.

Thinking about the human condition inevitably raises questions about what is the essential nature of a human being; philosophers have differed widely on this, and even on the question of whether there

---

1 Rainer Maria Rilke, *Herbsttag* [Autumn Day, 1902], trans. J. C.

is such an essential nature at all.[2] Socrates, in the *Phaedo*, famously characterizes human life as a 'preparation for dying': the goal of our existence is to purify the soul from its damaging attachment to the body and ready it for the pure rational activity that is its ultimate destiny.[3] On this dualistic view, which has of course profoundly influenced much subsequent religious thinking, it seems to follow that illness, old age, and even death are not to be regretted, since they bring us nearer to our próper destination, the life of an immortal soul freed from the body. Our liability to physical infirmity and decay would seem, on this dualistic view, to be a help, not a hindrance, in the necessary Socratic process of learning to despise the bodily pleasures and attachments that hinder the functioning of the immortal part of us.

For all its apparent purity, the Platonic position (vividly reinforced in the *Phaedo* by the dramatic and moving account of the noble death of Socrates) is by no means free of problems, and despite the influence it has had, it is far from clear that it offers the right model for a theistic account of the human condition. Even on Plato's own terms, the account he presents faces difficulties. If our ultimate destiny is separation of the 'immortal part' of us from the body, then the typical trajectory of a human life can hardly be construed as a fitting preparation for this, as Socrates claims it to be in the *Phaedo*; for the crucial activities attributed by Plato to the soul (such as philosophical reasoning and theoretical contemplation) are self-evidently *not* facilitated or enhanced by the increasing decrepitude of the body. On the contrary, ordinary observation, supported by a wealth of medical and scientific evidence, clearly indicates that intellectual activity starts declining from its peak quite early in adult life and is diminished further in varying degrees by the gradual infirmities of ageing, and, in the case of some specific conditions (such as Alzheimer's and other forms of dementia), may be curtailed or even eliminated altogether.

The determined dualist could of course argue that the activity of the soul is not actually being damaged or eradicated in such cases but simply subjected to swamping or interference from distracting bodily

2 This is implied by Jean-Paul Sartre's slogan 'existence precedes essence', which suggests that human beings have no predetermined nature but are free to shape their existence as they choose; *Existentialism Is a Humanism* (*L'existentialisme est un humanisme*, 1946].
3 Plato, *Phaedo* [c. 380 BC], 67e.

signals (rather as the operation of a radio receiver might be temporarily swamped by an external source such as an electrical storm, without the radio losing its pristine power to do its job perfectly once the storm has subsided).[4] But our unavoidable biological liability to a long and gradual weakening of our powers and capacities nevertheless emerges as a kind of meaningless deterioration, without any intelligible role to play in what is taken to be our true destiny on the Platonic view, and on the religious views that take this as their model. The senescence of the body, admittedly, does not emerge from the Platonic account as something intrinsically terrible, since it turns out to be irrelevant to our ultimate destiny as immortal souls. Nevertheless, the actual typical conditions of ageing emerge as likely to interfere with the functioning of the most important part of us; so the normal processes of growing older are seen as taking us ever deeper into a 'limbo', where the soul has to put up with a greater or lesser interference with its powers, until it can escape from the body entirely. It is hard to see how all this provides much scope for a persuasive religious picture of the meaning and value of the normal human biological cycle of birth, ageing and death.

In contrast to this, Aristotle's position on human nature, in the light of his famous definition of man as a 'rational *animal*', seems considerably more 'body-friendly' than Plato's: our biological or corporeal nature, on the Aristotelian account, is an essential part of what we are.[5] Many aspects of Aristotle's view made their way through into the Christian vision of the human condition developed by Thomas Aquinas; and although subsequent theological debate has oscillated somewhat between 'Platonic' or dualistic and Aristotelian or embodied conceptions, it is probably fair to say, especially in the light of much recent 'incarnational theology',[6] that few religious thinkers today would see an authentic religious perspective as requiring the downgrading or despising of our bodily nature. On the Judaeo-Christian view, human

---

4 Compare Richard Swinburne's defence of traditional substance-dualism in *The Evolution of the Soul* [1986] (Oxford: Clarendon, 2005).

5 Soul and body are related in Aristotle not as two separate things or substances but as form is related to matter; hence in any biological creature the bodily structures have a certain form that enables them to function as they do. See Aristotle, *De Anima* [c. 320 BC], Bk. II, ch. 1.

6 See, for example, Peter Jonkers and Marcel Sarot (eds.), *Embodied Religion. Ars Disputandi: The Online Journal for Philosophy of Religion*, Supplement, series 6, ed. M. Sarot (2013).

beings – that is to say, living, breathing, biological creatures of flesh and blood – are formed in the image and likeness of God (Genesis 1:26; 2:7); and one should beware of 'spiritualizing' this, since the creation language of Genesis is robustly corporeal. So simply in virtue of our human status we participate in some way in that infinite worth that is God. Building on this foundation, the Christian vision takes the extraordinary further step of declaring that our corporeal human nature is actually 'divinised' – raised up to the fullest dignity by Christ's humbling himself to take our bodily nature upon him. As the poet and priest Gerard Manley Hopkins so vividly puts it:

> In a flash, at a trumpet crash,
> I am all at once what Christ is, since he was what I am, and
> This Jack, joke, poor potsherd, patch, matchwood, immortal diamond,
> Is immortal diamond.[7]

Nothing, on the face of it, could be more undignified than this 'Jack' – a common, ordinary fellow, of undistinguished worth; this 'patch', a mere fool or ninny; this potsherd, a broken fragment, like that with which the wretched Job, reduced to the utmost indignity, scraped his sores (Job 2:8); weak and feeble, as perishable as matchwood. Yet all at once, by Christ's sharing in our bodily nature, this paltry individual becomes 'immortal diamond' – of infinite worth and dignity.

This Christianized vision takes us into a distinctive conception of the human condition, which diverges radically from that found in Aristotle and from most secular accounts. On these latter conceptions of human flourishing, what matters is the maximally vigorous flowering of our various human capacities, intellectual, aesthetic, physical, emotional and moral; and the extent to which this happens will of course widely vary from person to person. The scope for developing one's abilities will depend on accidents of birth, education and environment, and hence the 'excellence' that is the goal of Aristotelian-type accounts of human well-being will inevitably be something that is achieved by comparatively few; moreover, the degree to which someone achieves success or 'excellence' of this kind will inevitably be reduced by the ordinary infirmities of the ageing process, which are inseparable from human life

---

7 G. M. Hopkins, 'That Nature Is a Heraclitean Fire'; *Poems (1876–1889)*, no. 49, final stanza.

as it moves inexorably towards its normal biological term. A theistic account of the human condition, by contrast, while denying none of the facts just mentioned, sets them against a background where God is the loving father of all humankind. In this picture, God does not show favouritism;[8] and the 'kingdom of heaven' is open to everyone, rich and poor, young and old, learned and ignorant, irrespective of talent or ability.[9]

Set against this background, the misfortunes of life and the eventual ills and infirmities of ageing appear in a rather different light. For the question becomes not 'How well is this individual exercising those characteristic activities that make for human excellence?' but 'Is this individual a child of a loving God who desires the salvation of all?' And salvation, again in accordance with the fundamental moral insights of the Judaeo-Christian tradition, depends not on achievement but on the right moral orientation – turning to God and to fellow-man in love and humility. This is perhaps the meaning of St Paul's remarks, written in conditions of great stress and affliction: 'For which cause we faint not; but though our outward man perish, yet the inward man is renewed day by day'.[10] In short, a religious view of the human condition (of the kind now being considered) presents it in a light that seems to offer a measure of hope for all alike, as compared with the typical secular view. More needs to be said, however, about the precise basis for this hope, since it is widely regarded, both by believers and their critics, as hinging on what is supposed to happen in some future world, after the biological term of life is complete.

2. THE NEXT WORLD

There is a long line of Christian 'consolation' literature that offers what purports to be the Christian 'answer' to the grim facts of human suffering and death by invoking the next world. There are of course differing conceptions of the 'life of the world to come' (as it is put in the concluding phrase of the Nicene Creed, written in the fourth century); but in the

---

8 Acts 10: 34–5; cf. Romans 2:11.
9 Descartes aptly sums up this standard Christian teaching in the *Discourse on the Method* [*Discours de la méthode*, 1637], part i, where he remarks that 'the kingdom of heaven is no less open to the most ignorant than to the most learned.'
10 II Corinthians 4: 16 (the letter dates from around AD 57).

light of the problematic nature of the Platonic-dualistic conception of the human condition,[11] it is worth pointing out what mainstream and long-established Christian doctrine actually asserts. It speaks not of the survival of an immaterial soul or disembodied consciousness (what we now think of as a 'Cartesian' purely mental substance), but rather of the 'resurrection of the body', to quote the penultimate phrase of the Apostles Creed, a summary of Christian doctrine whose origins also go back to the very early centuries of Christianity.

In our popular culture, the possibility of a person's adopting a religious worldview often seems inextricably linked with whether he or she can accept the idea of a post-mortem existence; thus one often hears people come out with phrases like 'I could never be religious – I think that when you die, that's the end'. It may be that what is doing a lot of the work here in making many reject the doctrine of the afterlife is the march of modern science, which has increasingly disclosed such intimate links between consciousness and brain activity that it seems to many people that the permanent cessation of brain function at death must mean the final end. And as for the reactivation or 'waking up' of this particular body that is mine, in the way envisaged in medieval paintings of the dead rising from their graves at the Last Day, this seems beyond all feasibility, given what we now know of the ceaseless processes of biological decomposition and the recycling of organic materials throughout the biosphere during the millions of years of the life of our species.

It is, however, by no means clear that believers in the afterlife have to understand it in terms of either of the unpalatable alternatives mentioned – the survival of a disembodied Platonic (or Cartesian) incorporeal soul, or the reactivation of a particular biological organism (the particular configuration of flesh and blood that now constitutes John Doe or any other living human being). Paul speaks of the Resurrection in a famous passage in one of his letters not in terms of the survival of this biological body, but in terms of its transformation from a biological body (*soma psychikon*) into a 'spiritual body' (*soma pneumatikon*) (1 Corinthians 15: 44). This idea has been understood in different ways, but two points seem worth making. Firstly, that which survives, on Paul's account, is not an immaterial spirit, but, on the contrary, a *body*

11 As discussed in section 1 of this chapter.

(in Greek, *soma*), albeit one of a wholly different kind from that with which we are familiar. Secondly, moving to a present-day perspective, given what modern medical science is now able to do with replacement organs (where the functioning of one biological part is taken over by an artificial prosthesis made of nonbiological materials), it would seem a piece of unwarranted dogmatism for any philosopher to declare that the replacement of a biological organism with a life form constructed from a different type of body is an intrinsically incoherent notion.

At this point in the philosophical debate, the emphasis shifts away from questions about the viability and coherence of the idea of body replacement (or radical transformation) to the metaphysical question of whether the resulting individual could be said to be the same individual as the one whose biological body has died. There is a vast philosophical literature on what makes an individual self-conscious being (or 'person') the same across time and across changes in physical constitution, and it seems fair to say that no consensus has been reached or is likely to be in the foreseeable future. That does not of course mean that the literature is not absorbing, or that studying it cannot be a legitimate part of the philosophical study of religion.[12] But for present purposes we will content ourselves with noting that despite the widespread scepticism in many quarters of the philosophical academy about the possibility of the afterlife, most people if pressed would have to admit in honesty that this is not a matter that can be finally decided on philosophical grounds alone. A belief in the afterlife, though many philosophers see it as out of tune with the dominant contemporary naturalist outlook, cannot be shown to be philosophically or scientifically out of the question.

Given this impasse, it may be more profitable to turn instead to the more practical question of the *role* of this doctrine in the outlook of the religious believer. If one reflects on this, it appears that something of vital moral and religious importance is left out of the picture if one attempts to understand the Christian approach to senescence and death *merely* (or perhaps even *mainly*) in terms of the supposed consolations of the afterlife. Such attempts seem to suffer from analogous kinds of

---

12 The locus classicus is Derek Parfit's *Reasons and Persons* (Oxford: Oxford University Press, 1984). For a fascinating discussion of some of the problems connected with post-mortem survival, see Mark Johnston, *Surviving Death* (Princeton, NJ: Princeton University Press, 2010). For my own views, see J. Cottingham, *Why Believe?* (London: Continuum, 2009), ch. 6, §4.

weakness to the attempts explored in the previous chapter to solve the problem of evil at a stroke by invoking the next world.[13] It is as if, faced with the Gordian knot (the apparently pointless and degrading discomforts of senescence and the final pains of death), we simply get out the knife, cut the knot, and say 'No problem: it will all be made right in the next world'. The worry here is not one about whether the idea of the afterlife is true or coherent (that question has been left mute for the purposes of the present discussion); the danger, rather, is that if the emphasis is moved wholly to the next world in this way we risk ending up with a distorted understanding of the religious perspective on human life. For the viability of a theistic worldview depends in part on its ability to find meaning and value, and the possibility of redemption, in *the world as we have it*, as opposed to retreating into a future world in which the problematic features are no longer present.

It is instructive in this connection to look at what is actually said by the authors of religious consolation literature, one example being a sermon of the nineteenth-century Unitarian pastor Samuel Lothrop, entitled *The Consolations of Old Age*. Lothrop focuses on the 'infirmity and deprivation' that attends the end of our biological life, and refers to the terminal phase of human existence as the 'last and greatest trial of our humanity'.[14] But he does not simply wheel in the afterlife as a panacea. The 'consolations' that are unfolded in the sermon, though they do include the hope of immortality (especially in a grand final peroration), lay great emphasis on the moral growth of the individual over a complete lifetime, and the tranquillity attendant on a life well spent. But none of this allows the author to gloss over the actual physical suffering and infirmity that typically attend the closing stages of life; on the contrary, it is resolutely confronted. It is rather as if the author is interpreting the Christian message as saying that the Resurrection should only be brought in at the *end* of the story: it cannot be anticipated, or invoked, to provide a 'consolation' to the victim still on the cross. Some might find it tempting to rewrite the Gospel stories as a grand triumphalist narrative where the glorification of Christ and the confounding of his foes is all celestially guaranteed in advance, so that the suffering turns out to be nugatory against the backdrop of eternal

---

13 See Chapter 5, section 4, this volume.
14 S. K. Lothrop, *The Consolations of Old Age* (Boston: Eastburn's Press, 1846), pp. 7–8.

triumphant bliss that awaits him. But the actual gospel narrative is more profound and the 'glorification' achieved in the passion of Christ far more complex than that;[15] and the fact that not one element of the horror is omitted from the story is a sign of its moral depth.

'If I am lifted up from the earth', says Christ before his Passion, 'I will draw all people to myself' (John 12:32). The disciples (who in the Gospel narratives are all too human and like most of us never seem to understand anything until it is too late) will evidently assume that this refers to some kind of traditional kingly exaltation, perhaps as the triumphant ruler of a restored independent kingdom of Israel, freed from Roman domination. But the eventual reality of being 'lifted up' turns out to be a glorification of a wholly different kind.

In one of the stories of the post-Resurrection appearances of Christ, some of the disciples ask him; 'Lord, will you now restore the kingdom of Israel?' (Acts, 1:6). With telling insight the narrator seems to be acknowledging here that even after the cataclysmic events of the Passion and its aftermath, some of the closest witnesses to those events *still* did not 'get it': they still had in mind a 'happy ending' that would transform the suffering of Christ into a distant memory, overwritten by a grand regal success in which they could all share. One standard theological interpretation of such passages construes the disciples' mistake as simply that of hoping for a *this-worldly* happy outcome instead of realizing they should look for it in the 'world to come': in other words, they were right to anticipate a spectacular triumph but wrong to think of it in political terms. But one reason such triumphalist[16] readings seem inadequate is that they incur the suspicion of being motivated by 'spiritual materialism' (to use the phrase of Mark Johnston discussed in the previous chapter).[17] This is the desire to have our cake and eat it, to subscribe to the redemptive value of pure love and self-sacrifice yet retain our allegiance to our ordinary mundane bestowers of meaning – security, comfort, esteem, success – by wheeling in the magical

---

15 Compare (though she does not discuss the Crucifixion) Eleonore Stump's account of the term 'gloriousness', in *Wandering in Darkness* (Oxford: Oxford University Press, 2010), pp. 254ff. For more on this, see Chapter 5, section 4, this volume.

16 For a survey and critique of such 'triumphalism' (combined with a theologically rich discussion of the multiple layers of meaning in the Resurrection), see N. T. Wright, *The Resurrection of the Son of God* (London: SPCK, 2003), ch. 19.

17 See Chapter 5, section 4, this volume.

intervention of supernatural forces to guarantee them, albeit in a future existence.[18] This, if you like, is a way of reducing the costs of unconditional love for the good, or God, by conveniently reconciling it with our ordinary desires for success and personal triumph.

Whatever the Resurrection can mean, it cannot, on any satisfying interpretation of the Christian message, mean that. If one were to try to understand the meaning of Christ's self-sacrificial life and death from the fact of his post-mortem victory per se, this would be an all too convenient resolution, an altogether too tidy construal of the mystery of redemptive love and suffering. Rather, the core of meaning in Christ's death and passion must lie somewhere in the fact that human beings are made for love, which is our greatest good; that love requires self-sacrifice; and that here lies the ultimate purpose of our lives. One way of putting this interpretation would be to say that on the Christian worldview the Cross and the Resurrection are wholly inseparable. And indeed the authentic Christian picture has never been that the Resurrection is a kind of external or logically detachable compensation for the Crucifixion. The Church's annual celebration of the mystery of the Triduum gives expression to the fact that the meaning of Easter Sunday is inextricably bound up with that of Good Friday, and vice versa.[19] The glorification of Christ by the Father, in other words, is not that which *confers* meaning on his life ex post facto, but rather that which honours the meaning that is *already there*, in the perfect life he led and the loving death he endured.[20]

This very brief excursus into the interpretation of the central Christian narrative of the Crucifixion may already be enough to offend those who think that philosophy of religion should operate at an entirely abstract level, uncontaminated by the hermeneutic issues that are important to actual believers. But a proper philosophical understanding of a

---

18 See Mark Johnston, *Saving God* (Princeton, NJ: Princeton University Press, 2009), pp. 123–124.

19 In the ancient Latin wording of the Third Preface for Easter, Christ is described as *agnus qui vivit semper occisus* (literally, 'the lamb who lives forever slain'). Timothy Radcliffe aptly comments: 'If the risen Lord did not still bear his wounds, then he would not have much to do with us now.' *What Is the Point of Being a Christian?* (London: Continuum, 2005), p. 75.

20 This paragraph draws on material from J. Cottingham, 'Spirituality', in C. Taliaferro, V. S. Harrison, and S. Goetz (eds.), *The Routledge Companion to Theism* (New York: Routledge, 2013), pp. 654–665.

religious outlook cannot be achieved if we remain at a safe distance from what religious adherents actually think and feel about the scriptural and other narratives in terms of which their worldview is structured. Highly relevant here is the fact that the attacks of many contemporary atheist critics tend to rest on crude and oversimplified accounts of what believers think and feel regarding doctrines such as the Resurrection and the afterlife. And hence, if we want to reach a sensible understanding of these matters, it is a legitimate *philosophical* task to try to enter more closely into the meaning of these concepts, and the true place they have in the life of the believer. The results of our discussion in this section have in no way tried to gloss over the importance of these notions for the believer, but they have begun to suggest that their meaning is not properly captured by simplistic ideas of post-mortem reward, vindication, or compensation, which critics of the religious outlook often take to be the whole story.

3. GOD, THE AFTERLIFE, AND MEANINGFULNESS

With the results of the previous section in mind, let us now turn to the issue of how religious belief in the 'next world' impinges on the question of meaningfulness in human life.[21] In our contemporary secularized culture, many philosophers are inclined to think that belief in the existence of God or in a future life is entirely irrelevant to the question. If we take the existence of God first, an increasingly popular view is that any meaning that life may have must be found entirely from our *own* chosen activities and projects: meaning is something we have to create for ourselves. For what (so runs the view under discussion) could *God* have to do with it? How could his purposes and plans for us (even assuming he exists) generate meaning *for us*? Suppose we found that our origins derived from an alien intelligence, who injected some early version of DNA into some molecules in the primordial terrestrial soup, in order that, over time, humans would emerge on this planet and their struggles and setbacks and temporary triumphs would serve as entertainment when viewed on celestial television by the denizens of

---

21 The discussion in this and the next section draws on Cottingham, 'Meaningful Life', in Paul K. Moser and Michael T. McFall (eds.), *The Wisdom of the Christian Faith* (Cambridge: Cambridge University Press, 2012), pp. 175–196.

a distant galaxy. Would we, if we discovered these facts, be the slightest bit inclined to say our lives were more meaningful as a result? If anything, surely, we might be inclined to conclude the reverse. We might be inclined to think that discovering we were the puppets of these aliens – or, if not that, then at the very least fodder for their entertainment industry – had the effect of making our lives even more absurd, even more futile, than they were in danger of being already.

The word 'aliens', of course, has a rather nasty ring to it, suggesting salivating jaws and metallic mandibles. But even if we uncovered evidence that the beings in question were a rather benign race, who genuinely wanted us to succeed in our little projects and endeavours, who rejoiced at our successes and grieved at our frequent tendency to mess up our own and other people's lives, we might still be inclined to think that their role in the origin of our species detracted from, rather than added to, our ability to see our lives as meaningful. For might it not seem rather humiliating, rather demeaning, to realize that we are not the grand, autonomous beings we like to think we are, but are the creatures of a superior race who were on the stage long before we were, and who planned our very existence as something that would play a role in *their* purposes?[22]

Notice moreover that not much difference is apparently made to this disquieting line of thought by bringing in the idea of an afterlife. For suppose these aliens had a mysterious technology, far beyond our ken, which enabled them to make a complete informational scan of the unique set of total contents of each human being's mind and to preserve it after the death of the body, only to reactivate it on some distant world, either in a new body, or in a body recreated from a rescued single cell from the old body, but purified or reengineered in such a way that it would no longer be subject to decay or mortality. Would that suddenly make sense of things and render human life after all meaningful? It seems by no means clear that it would. For, to begin with, there would still seem to be something disturbingly manipulative about the imagined scenario. Suppose these aliens greet us, on our

---

22 This is perhaps one way to interpret the rationale for Thomas Nagel's at first sight bizarre observation that he hopes there isn't a God because, as he puts it, 'I wouldn't want the universe to be like that'. His thought may be that being a *creature* (a created being) is just too demeaning for his liking. T. Nagel, *The Last Word* (Oxford: Oxford University Press, 1997), p. 130.

post-mortem arrival at the delightful decay-free planet they have prepared for us, and smilingly say: 'You see now! All that pain, all those
diseases, those terrible earthquakes and tsunamis, those terrifying crop
failures, those centuries upon centuries of grinding relentless toil and
premature death – all the time we knew we had *this* place ready for
you: doesn't that make you happy? Doesn't that now make sense of
it all?' In the words of Ivan Karamazov, we might be only too aptly
inclined to answer: 'we respectfully return the ticket'.[23] And even if we
suppose this post-mortem world to have a more traditionally 'moral'
character, and imagine that the aliens have planned to dish out punish-
ments to those who have behaved badly on earth, reserving the rewards
of a blissful new existence for those who have behaved well, would this
really improve matters? The additional feature of the story might gratify
those of us who have strongly retributive instincts and are piqued that
the present distribution of welfare on earth does not appear to match
desert,[24] but it does not succeed in dispelling the residual feeling that we
have somehow been *used*. Nothing appears more corrosive of meaning
than supposing that our struggles and endeavours are being watched by
a secret agent who is assessing us from a superior vantage point, smiling
at our successes and frowning at our failures.

The challenge posed by this line of argument, in short, is that the
kind of world picture presupposed in Christian theism not only fails to
support the meaningfulness of human life but actually erodes it. By making our ultimate goals subordinate to another's purposes, it alienates
us, so runs the objection, from our own autonomous human sources
of meaning. Let us, for short, call this the *alienation* objection. How
might a defender of a theistic, or more specifically a Christian, world
picture respond to it?

4. ALIENATION, OBEDIENCE, AND AUTONOMY

The problem of alienation just raised comes into sharp focus if one considers what many religious traditions take to be a fundamental virtue
and perhaps even the key to a good life, namely, obedience to the will of

---

23 Fyodor Dostoevsky, *The Brothers Karamazov* [*Brat'ya Karamazovy*, 1880], Bk 5,
    ch. 4.
24 As David Hume apparently was: see Chapter 5, section 3, this volume.

God. A paradigm case here is the self-sacrificial life of Christ, as characterized in the Gospels, which at first sight seems to offer hostages to just the kind of 'alienation' worry discussed in the previous section. The most famous prayer left by Christ to his disciples, the Lord's Prayer, designed for daily use and clearly intended to structure the basic framework for the Christian life, contains what appears to be an essentially submissive plea – 'Thy will be done.'[25] And in the supreme crisis of his life, Jesus is reported by all three synoptic gospel writers to have prayed that he would be spared the coming ordeal, but to have added the crucial proviso 'Nevertheless, not as I will, but as thou wilt'.[26]

Deliberately subordinating one's will to that of another seems on the face of it a paradigm of alienation or, in Kantian terms, of heteronomy.[27] So far from our will aspiring to be, in Kant's terminology, *selbstgesetzgebend*, giving the law itself, it appears to be asked to turn in precisely the opposite direction and to submit to the injunctions of another.[28] Hence, insofar as we nowadays identify the meaningful life with the autonomous life, with the life structured around the agent's own freely chosen 'projects',[29] there again seems to be a striking divergence from the Christian conception of meaningfulness. The Kantian insistence on the value of autonomy and the sovereignty of the individual will seems to be reinforced, in our contemporary culture, by a whole barrage of progressivist attitudes that have emerged from these Enlightenment roots. Thus the theologian Daphne Hampson underlines, from a feminist perspective, the damaging effects of the kind of

---

25 Matthew 6:10. The Lucan version (11:2–4) omits this clause.

26 Matthew 26:39; Mark 14:36; Luke 22:42.

27 'Whenever the will seeks the law that is to determine it anywhere else than in the fitness of its maxims for its own giving of universal law, and if therefore it goes outside itself and seeks this law in a property of any of its objects – the result is always heteronomy. In that case the will does not give itself the law; rather, the object gives the law to it, in virtue of its relation to the will.' *Groundwork for the Metaphysic of Morals* [*Grundlegung zur Metaphysik der Sitten*, 1785], ch. 2; Akademie edition (Berlin: Reimer/De Gruyter, 1900–), Vol. IV, pp. 440; trans. T. E. Hill Jr. and A. Zweig (Oxford: Oxford University Press, 2003), p. 241.

28 Autonomy, for Kant, is 'the basis of the dignity of human nature and of every rational nature', according to which our will must be considered as *selbstgesetzgebend* ('giving the law to itself'). *Groundwork*, ch. 2; Akademie edition, Vol. IV, pp. 436, 431; trans. Hill and Zweig, pp. 236, 232.

29 Compare, for example, Bernard Williams, *Shame and Necessity* (Berkeley: University of California Press, 1993).

self-effacement that the Christian ideal apparently enjoins: 'Within the Judaeo-Christian tradition...the relationship to God is at least potentially heteronomous, such that the human must be obedient to what he or she conceives to be God's will, rather than obeying his or her own conscience'.[30] And from a broadly Freudian perspective, we find Jacques Lacan arguing that even within the individual psyche, subordination to the demands of the internalized Other can lead to a radical loss of autonomy: the 'gourmandisme' of the Superego, with its ever more stringent demands for obedience, is never satisfied by anything less than total submission. Like a sinister parasite, the more you feed it, the more it wants.[31]

Someone who is alienated in this way, it is implied, is someone who is adrift in a world without true meaning. Instead of seeing herself as a self-determining being, proceeding along a path that she has chosen, towards goals that are her own, she feels instead a constant pressure to conform, to submit, to bend the will in a direction dictated by another. This is indeed a sinister picture. Yet something has gone seriously wrong with our interpretation of the self-sacrificial life of Christ if we are inclined to interpret the prayer 'Thy will be done' along these lines. To enable us to glimpse an alternative and more compelling interpretation, we need to look at another saying of Christ, this time not from synoptic gospels, but from John: 'I and the Father are one'.[32]

Jesus' declared self-identification with God the Father, according to the fourth evangelist, provoked at the time an immediate and violent reaction ('they picked up stones to stone him'); and on any interpretation it raises a host of complex theological questions that take us beyond the scope of the present discussion. But if we focus simply on the implications of Jesus' extraordinary claim for the issue of autonomy and heteronomy that is in question at this stage of our argument, some interesting results emerge. In the same passage where he claims union with the Father, Jesus also claims to be loved by the Father: elsewhere, he announces his own reciprocal love for the Father, and does so,

---

30 Daphne Hampson, *After Christianity* (London: SCM Press 1996; 2nd ed. 2002), p. 137.
31 Cf. Rajchman, *Truth and Eros* (New York: Routledge, 1991), p. 58.
32 *ego kai ho pater hen esmen*, John 10:30.

moreover, in a way that connects this love with his obedience and self-sacrifice.[33] The concepts of union, of love, and of sacrifice are thus closely connected in Johannine moral theology.

To explicate this further, it will be helpful to refer to the account of love found in Thomas Aquinas, according to which love requires two interconnected desires: the desire for the good of the beloved, and the desire for union with the beloved. In the persuasive interpretation of this idea offered by Eleonore Stump,[34] to enjoy union with someone involves 'significant personal presence and mutual closeness',[35] and this in turn implies a certain mutual openness, where the parties involved are ready to stand before each other, as they are, with nothing concealed, dissimulated, or hidden. Such complex personal openness and closeness is difficult or impossible for the conflicted person, who has parts of himself that he would prefer to conceal from the other (and perhaps even from himself). So for two people to be truly and deeply united they must each be possessed of a certain wholeheartedness and integrity; and this, in the Thomistic way of thinking, entails a further connection with the good, since internal integration is ultimately possible only for someone who wholeheartedly desires the good.[36]

From all this it follows that Aquinas's conception of love is radically at odds with some popular conceptions of love, where one may be passionately attracted to someone, or desire to possess or be near them, without necessarily sharing their values, and without necessarily desiring their ultimate good. For Aquinas, love has a profoundly moral dimension: it has a deep connection with the good (and hence, ultimately with God). On this Thomistic view, therefore, people can, as Stump

---

33 John 10:17 and 14:31.
34 Eleonore Stump, *Wandering in Darkness*, ch. 5, p. 91. Stump's account is based on various theses of Aquinas: that the ultimate proper object of love is God (*Summa theologiae* [1266–73], Ia IIae, qu. 26, art. 1; that God is identical with his goodness (ST, Ia, qu. 3–6); and hence that the ultimate proper object of love is goodness (cf. ST Ia IIae, qu. 27).
35 Stump, *Wandering in Darkness*, p. 127.
36 Can one be integrated in the wholehearted pursuit of evil? This is a complex question that cannot be examined here; but there are good reasons (implicitly explored for example in Milton's portrayal of Satan (in *Paradise Lost*, 1668) or by C. S. Lewis in *The Screwtape Letters* [1942] (New York: HarperCollins, 2001)) for supposing that the pursuit of evil inherently carries with it a certain tension or internal dissonance. For Stump's arguments on this score, see *Wandering in Darkness*, pp. 125–126.

puts it, be 'ultimately and deeply united with each other only if they are united in goodness'.[37] Read in that light, the claim of Jesus to enjoy a reciprocal loving union with the Father is not just a 'psychological' (in the sense of a merely affective) claim about mutual desire or caring, but it has additional inherently moral implications about the goodness of the participants in the union, and the resulting convergence of ends. The picture that emerges from this is already one that is incompatible with the kind of tension or alienation envisaged in the model of bending one's desires to those of another, or submitting to an alien will. In loving the Father, and praying for his will to be fulfilled, Christ is orienting himself towards, and seeking to unite himself with, what is his own truest and deepest good.

The feature of the Aquinas-Stump account that is worth underlining as most salient and relevant for present purposes is the idea that *internal integration* is a vital requirement for two parties truly to love each other. If you desire union with someone, you desire to be intimately close and personally present to them; but such closeness is undermined if one of the parties suffers from internal conflict or psychic dissonance.[38] This is connected with the fact that love, on this Thomistic conception, cannot achieve its ends unless the good of the beloved person is realized; yet the good for a person requires internal integration, a whole-hearted and unconflicted desire for the good.[39] (This latter claim is one that in any case has a strong inherent plausibility, since to be internally divided or conflicted, or to be in doubt about what one truly and deeply wants, is self-evidently damaging to the equilibrium and tranquillity necessary for a fulfilled life.) The bearing of these points on the question of autonomy versus heteronomy should now be clear. Heteronomy is always the result of external force or manipulation, or internal conflict. The sense the agent has of not being in control arises from the fact that his rational perception of the good is counterbalanced or overridden either by an external power or, from the inside, by some sensual passion or contingent desire that is at odds with his rational perception. Hence, so far from rationally 'giving the law to himself', he is dictated to by the recalcitrant or disordered passion that draws him in an opposite

---

37 Stump, *Wandering in Darkness*, p. 95.
38 Stump, *Wandering in Darkness*, p. 130.
39 Compare Stump, *Wandering in Darkness*, p. 100.

direction to reason.[40] By contrast, the loving 'submission' to God, or the good, envisaged in the Johannine picture is Christ's self-orientation towards that wherein his own deepest good lies and that which he has supreme and unequivocal reason to seek; so he is able to say, even at the moment of his trial where he will be handed over to torture and death, 'for this I came into the world'.[41]

In the light of this we can see that the self-sacrificial actions of Christ are the very opposite of heteronomous or self-alienated, but are rather the actions of someone whose internal life is fully integrated around a wholehearted desire for, and union with, the good. None of this, of course, means that self-orientation towards the good is easy. The desperate struggle of Christ at Gethsemane tells us what we knew already, that for human beings – even for one whom we take to be a paradigm of goodness – pain and humiliation and death are things we instinctively dread and struggle to avoid. But can a life that is, in spite of these heavy costs, resolutely oriented to the good still be a meaningful life? The declaration of Jesus before Pilate just quoted ('for this I came into the world') is suggestive of a strong sense of purpose; and on any showing there is a strong link between a sense of purpose in life and a sense of its meaningfulness. The upshot is that the paradigm Christian virtue of obedience to the will of God turns out to be not obedience to an alien authority but orientation towards the good wherein lies the final goal and purpose of our lives.[42]

5. WHAT DIFFERENCE DOES ETERNITY MAKE?

To draw the threads of this chapter together, we need to return to the question of the afterlife and how far this aspect of the theistic worldview affects the question of human life and its meaning. We have already questioned the crude interpretation of the afterlife as a kind of exterior reward for good conduct that compensates for suffering. But what seems potentially much more relevant to the question of meaningfulness is the

---

40 See the references to Kant at notes 27 and 28 earlier.

41 John 18:37. The verse continues '...to bear witness to the truth'; but I take it that the kind of witness to the truth envisaged is not mere allegiance to certain correct propositional claims but implies a wholehearted orientation towards the goodness and truth that is at the heart of reality.

42 For more on this moral-teleological picture, see Chapter 4, section 4 this volume.

idea that the future life to be enjoyed by the blessed will be *eternal* – a life of endless communion with God.[43] The theist, of course, typically views the entire universe *sub specie aeternitatis* – under the form of eternity, or against the backdrop of an eternal creator. God himself is taken to be immortal and everlasting, either in the sense that he had no beginning in time and he will continue forever, or perhaps in the sense that he transcends time altogether (the difference between these two analyses of God's 'eternal' nature will not need to be unpacked for the purposes of the present inquiry).[44] God himself, then, is eternal: 'a thousand ages in thy sight are like an evening gone'.[45] In addition to this notion of *divine* eternity, many theistic faiths, such as Christianity and Islam, and some forms of Judaism,[46] hold that all or some humans will enter the 'life of the world to come' which is generally taken to mean eternal life after death.

Both these two ideas – that of the eternity of God, and that of our own possible eternal future existence – might be thought relevant to the meaningfulness of human life. Let us take the second first. The erosion of meaning in human life is by many people connected with the thought that in a thousand years, or certainly in ten thousand, all our struggles and achievements, such as they are, will be *as if they had never been*. The Roman poet Horace, in his celebrated poem *Exegi monumentum aere perennius* ('I have raised a monument more permanent than bronze')[47] sees meaning and value in his poetic achievement precisely insofar as it will not fade with the years, but will continue on into the remote future.

---

43 This section draws on Cottingham, 'Meaningfulness, Eternity and Theism', in Beatrix Himmelmann (ed.), *On Meaning in Life* (Berlin/Boston: De Gruyter, 2013), pp. 99–112.

44 'God is eternal. But this has been understood in two different senses: either as the claim that God is timeless (he does not exist in time, or at any rate in our time) or as the claim that God is everlasting (he existed at every moment of past time, exists now, and will exist at every moment of future time).' Richard Swinburne, *Was Jesus God?* (Oxford: Oxford University Press, 2008), p. 12. Swinburne favours the latter view.

45 From the hymn 'Abide with Me', by the Scottish Anglican Henry Francis Lyle (composed 1847).

46 The Jewish sacred texts do not appear to lay much stress on the notion of the afterlife, and it is often said that the main focus of the religion is on performing one's duties to God and one's fellow human beings in *this* life. Jewish sects during the lifetime of Christ were divided over the question of the Resurrection of the dead, the Pharisees (followed in later Rabbinical tradition) affirming it, and the Sadducees denying it (cf. Luke 20:27, Mark 20:18).

47 Horace, *Odes* [*Carmina*, 23 BC], Bk. III, no. 30.

But of course we know that even bronze, along with 'the cloud-capped towers, the gorgeous palaces, the solemn temples, the great globe itself',[48] will one day perish; and indeed the universe itself will descend into the ultimate stasis of heat-death. As William Lane Craig, an eloquent exponent of this theme, puts it,

Mankind is a doomed race in a dying universe. Because the human race will eventually cease to exist, it makes no ultimate difference whether it ever did exist. Mankind is thus no more significant than a swarm of mosquitoes or a barnyard of pigs, for their end is all the same. The same blind cosmic process that coughed them up in the first place will eventually swallow them all again.[49]

Would it help to dispel this futility (as Craig goes on to imply) if we live forever? As Bernard Williams pointedly argued in a celebrated paper, it seems not – indeed, to the contrary. For although it might initially seem nice to continue with our satisfying activities for many centuries without the fear of extinction, the lesson to be drawn from the Janáček opera *The Makropulos Case* is that an *indefinitely* prolonged future existence could only produce a sense of tedium.[50] Nor would an 'eternal recurrence', Nietzsche-style, seem to do much to help;[51] on the contrary, it might actually *detract* from meaningfulness, by the grinding cycle of everlasting repetition, which not only removes any hope of improvement but also erodes the uniqueness, and therefore the precarious preciousness, of our human struggles and choices here and now.

In the light of these difficulties, it seems that the better way of approaching the possible link between eternity and meaning will be to connect meaningfulness not so much with *our* eternal future existence, but with God's. If standard theism is true, then our actions will

---

48 William Shakespeare, *The Tempest* [1610], Act IV, scene 1.
49 William Lane Craig, 'The Absurdity of Life without God' [1984], in *Reasonable Faith, Christian Truth and Apologetics* rev. ed. (Wheaton, IL: Crossway Books, 1994), ch. 2, pp. 57–75, at p. 58.
50 Bernard Williams, 'The Makropulos Case: Reflections on the Tedium of Immortality', in *Problems of the Self* (Cambridge: Cambridge University Press, 1973), pp. 82–100.
51 See Friedrich Nietzsche, *The Joyful Science* [*Die fröhliche Wissenschaft*, 1882]. It should be added on Nietzsche's behalf that there are plausible interpretations of the eternal recurrence that construe this notion as essentially concerned with affirming the value of the present moment, experienced in its fullest intensity. For a pioneering example of this view, see Walter Kaufmann, *Nietzsche: Philosopher, Psychologist, Antichrist* (Princeton, NJ: Princeton University Press, 1950), Part III, §11.

be held forever, or are eternally present, in the mind of a supremely good and loving and wise God, and so will have ultimate significance.

On the naturalist picture as portrayed by Craig, there can be no such permanent significance, given that the universe is destined for total extinction. But it seems there could be an alternative, but still naturalist, picture in which the structure of the natural cosmos is one where (as it were) 'nothing ever goes away': each action is a permanent or timeless part of the complex web that is the space-time continuum.[52] But even were one to grant this, or something like it, it doesn't seem enough for meaningfulness, if the 'continuum' is taken to be simply an abstract web or impersonal matrix. What meaning is conferred by the permanent place my actions have in this blank space-time complex, along with every other event in the universe? But if, by contrast, reality is ultimately personal, and, in particular, if it is as envisaged on the theistic view, then our lives remain forever enfolded in the presence of a supremely loving God.

The poet Alfred Tennyson found his belief in such a benign cosmic order deeply shaken, when in the mid-nineteenth century he confronted the horror of the blank and purposeless processes of nature disclosed by the emerging fossil record – the long and brutal struggle for survival over vast millennia, in which countless individuals and species are wiped out. But he still clung 'faintly' to the theistic hope

> That nothing walks with aimless feet;
> That not one life shall be destroyed,
> Or cast as rubbish to the void,
> When God hath made the pile complete.[53]

His faltering but eventually (by the end of the poem) reaffirmed faith was in the possibility of individual survival in an afterlife, so that the poet would again be able to set eyes on the dear friend who is the subject of his agonized lament here in *In Memoriam*. But even if Tennyson was

---

52 The complexities of the views on this issue offered by contemporary theoretical physi-cists and philosophers of time are extremely difficult for the nonspecialist to follow, but a useful overview is provided in Stephen Savitt, 'Being and Becoming in Mod-ern Physics', *Stanford Encyclopedia of Philosophy*, http://plato.stanford.edu/entries/spacetime-bebecome/#2.1, accessed February 2013.

53 Alfred Lord Tennyson, *In Memoriam* [1850], stanza 54; in C. Ricks (ed.), *Tennyson, A Selected Edition* (London: Longman, 1989), p. 396.

wrong to 'faintly trust the larger hope',[54] even if we are indeed wholly mortal, our lives, on the theistic picture we are now considering, would still not be 'cast as rubbish to the void' when they end, since they would retain, eternally, their moral significance by being present to God.

In another of Tennyson's famous poems, 'Ulysses', the hero reflects on what remains of his own life and tries to encourage himself by referring to what good still remained to be sought on earth: 'every hour is saved from that eternal silence'.[55] That phrase clearly presupposes the bleaker view that meaning must slip away forever as our short existence ends and disappears into silence. But on the theistic view, instead of 'every hour is saved from that eternal silence' (which suggests a desperate clutching on to some transient spark of value and meaning in the face of our grim awareness of the eventual total extinction of everything), we would need to rewrite Tennyson and say something like 'every hour is saved in that eternal *presence*' – where 'saved' now means not 'temporarily salvaged', but something like 'preserved, protected, treasured'. Whatever of the good or meaningful we manage to achieve is, on this view, eternally stored and cherished in the loving presence of God.

6. PERSONAL IMMORTALITY AND AVERROEAN CONCERNS

A possible worry about the route to meaningfulness just sketched out is that it risks committing the 'Averroean heresy', named after the great twelfth-century Islamic philosopher and Aristotelian commentator Averroes (or Ibn Rushd), who denied that the individual soul survives death. Strictly speaking, of course, there are no necessary 'Averroean' implications in the argument we have been considering. The question of personal survival after death is left completely open; the point is simply that *even if* there is no personal immortality, there would still be a kind of ultimate metaphysical significance to our lives on the theistic view. Nevertheless, a qualm of an approximately 'Averroean' character may seem to remain. If the only meaning we can hope for is that our actions remain present in the divine mind after we die, then our lives perhaps have some 'cosmic' significance, but do not have ultimate personal significance *for us*, or from our point of view.

---

54 Tennyson, *In Memoriam*, stanza 55; in Ricks (ed.), p. 398.
55 Tennyson, 'Ulysses' [written 1833; published 1842], line 26; in Ricks (ed.), p. 143.

The frequent and fierce condemnations of Averroes by the Church in the middle ages were in part connected with the fear that without personal survival there could be no Last Judgment; and this was not just contrary to clear Christian doctrine, going right back to the Gospels, but was also felt to be subversive of morals. This continuing fear of the subversiveness of denying individual immortality was aptly summed up by Descartes, several centuries later: 'since in this life the rewards offered to vice are often greater than the rewards of virtue, few people would prefer what is right to what is expedient if they did not fear God or have the expectation of an afterlife.'[56] But the point at issue goes far beyond the crude idea of the afterlife as a means of keeping people on the straight and narrow, and has a direct impact on the question of meaning. The sense of responsibility, that we are truly accountable for our actions, is intimately bound up with the idea that they are morally significant, that they *matter*. But if the 'mattering' is something that fades over time, to that extent meaningfulness seems to be eroded. This is particularly apparent in the journalism-dominated culture of contemporary Western politics, where the 'story of the day' is frenziedly hyped up, only to disappear from view and be replaced by tomorrow's big news: politicians increasingly take advantage of this in a way that subtly but inexorably undermines the idea that personal moral conduct really matters. So when detected in corruption they will brazen things out, or if there is no other recourse, they will issue an 'apology' of transparent perfunctoriness and insincerity, trusting that in a few months' time the event will have been all but obliterated by the latest brouhaha.

Politicians are (for the most part) a particularly unappetising model to have in mind when we think about the value and meaningfulness of human lives. But for all of us there is the spectre of temporariness – the fading of memories, the steadily reduced impact of our actions, like the ripples in a pond slowly subsiding; all this does seem to threaten the idea of *enduring responsibility* that is one of the foundations of meaningfulness in our lives. But if it is true, as Christianity and other religions affirm (but as philosophical inquiry cannot determine one way

56 René Descartes, *Meditations on First Philosophy* [*Meditationes de prima philosophia*, 1641], Dedicatory Letter to the Sorbonne.

or the other) that there is personal survival, then this would function as a further 'bonus', as it were, as far as meaningfulness is concerned – a bonus to be added to the previous argument about the eternal presence of our actions in the mind of God. For if personal survival is true, then the eternal joy of God at the good deeds of his creatures would be a joy in which those who have lived well can somehow share.

But an important caveat to note here is that someone's continued personal existence, if it happens, could not *in itself* confer meaning on their life; that point is already clearly established by the Makropulos example. The imagined scenario instead is one of continuing joy that must arise in significant part out of the meaning-conferring achievements and actions of the human life as it was actually lived – or out of the fact that, though all the faults are acknowledged, life has found redemption. The religious believer might of course speculate about additional 'heavenly' joys not now conceivable; but on any plausible view of the continuing ultimate responsibility that is invoked by the idea of heaven, the joys would have to have a continuing personal connection with the former life and its character – just as indeed *any* joy, in ordinary earthly life, is laden with the past that has shaped the life up to that moment. The upshot of these points is that heavenly bliss, like earthly bliss, should not be thought of as *in itself* the generator of meaning; it must instead be thought of as having a somewhat similar status to pleasure on the account given in Aristotle's ethics: a kind of epiphenomenal fragrance or glow, like the bloom of youth, that sets the seal on, or is a sign of, the life well lived, or a life redeemed.[57]

In case all this seems to present too rosy and complacent an account of the religious conception of eternity, it is worth adding that the theistic idea that every single one of our actions on earth remains eternally present in the mind of God cuts both ways. Just as whatever we can achieve of genuine worth and meaningfulness somehow does not fade but endures forever, so whatever we do that undermines the value or meaning of our lives or the lives of others will also remain eternally present to the divine mind. That is indeed a terrible thought, and it

---

57 'Pleasure completes the activity as an end that supervenes, just as the bloom of youth does on those in the flower of their age.' Aristotle, *Nicomachean Ethics* [c. 325 BC], Bk. X, ch. 4.

becomes even more fearful when we add the further idea of individual survival of death; for this implies not just that our good and evil acts retain their significance forever but also that we shall be called to account for them. And although on the Judaeo-Christian picture (and perhaps most prominently in the Christianity of the Gospels) this insistence on responsibility is compatible with the possibility of divine forgiveness (cf. Luke 15:11–32; Matthew 18:22), there is nothing whatever in the tradition that suggests that that possibility can or should be taken for granted.[58]

But however that may be, the crucial point for present purposes is that the inescapability of ultimate judgement on our lives – that very prospect that is so unpalatable and even absurd in the eyes of those who hold strongly deterministic versions of a secularist or naturalist worldview – turns out to be an aspect of the theistic outlook that actually *adds* to meaning. The sense that our acts are eternally subject to divine evaluation, so far from detracting from their meaning, seems deeply to enhance their significance. The responsibility that we bear for every single act that we do or fail to do during our lives is not something that fades or slips away, but retains its ultimate significance. For on the theistic view, the cosmos is not just an indifferent backdrop to our fleeting lives; it is a cosmos shot through with meaning and value, where our contribution ultimately and eternally matters.

So the ultimate meaningfulness of our actions, on the view proposed here, comes from their taking their place, *sub specie aeternitatis*, as actions that eternally matter: where whatever sparks of good they contain is a source of joy to a being of supreme wisdom and love. This amplifies and confirms the meaningfulness that they already had on earth, and protects them against the erosions of time and contingency, shielding them against the backdrop of impermanence against which nothing in the long term matters very much. And if we add to this the doctrine of individual post-mortem survival, then the blessed who have led good lives, or received the grace of redemption, will share personally in that eternal meaningfulness and the joy that crowns it.

---

58 This incidentally explains why one feels there is something slightly rosy or sentimental in Tennyson's thought that from the perspective of eternity our lives will be viewed from a gently indulgent perspective: 'Be near us when we climb or fall:/Ye watch, like God, the rolling hours/With larger other eyes than ours,/To make allowance for us all.' *In Memoriam*, stanza 51.

7. MORTALITY, MEANING, AND HOPE

Some philosophical readers may feel that the considerations advanced in the last few paragraphs involve too many theological ideas whose acceptance is a matter of revelation or faith. It is no doubt true that the question of whether there is a future existence cannot be finally settled this side of death. But it would be a mistake to suppose that this takes the discussion outside the domain of rational discussion and philosophical evaluation. Part of our discussion has been about what religious claims about the existence of an eternal loving God, and of our own future existence, might coherently be supposed to contribute to the meaningfulness of our lives *if* they were true; and on any showing, that kind of analysis must be counted a legitimate matter for philosophical inquiry. But more important, by unpacking the implications of the theistic worldview as regards the meaningfulness of human life, we are able to see how far these implications resonate with our powerful pretheoretical intuitions about what makes for meaning and value in our lives. If, as has been suggested here, the theistic picture is strikingly hospitable to many of those intuitions, and if it is also true that those intuitions cannot be fully and satisfactorily accommodated within alternative naturalist pictures, then if we are disinclined to accept the theistic picture we face a stark choice. We could try to give up the search for ultimate meaning, and abandon the idea that our lives can be meaningful in any but a local and temporary sense: we could perhaps try to 'cure' ourselves of the idea, on the grounds that it is no more than a fantasy or an illusion born of our unwillingness to face the starkness of reality. But we may find that the yearning for ultimate meaning is an ineradicable part of our human nature, or that to try to abandon it would do too much violence to our fundamental human aspirations to be an option we can coherently pursue; and if that turns out to be the case, then this would, in itself, be a result of considerable philosophical importance. If nothing else, it might show that the boundaries between religious allegiance and philosophical conviction are more permeable than is often supposed.

But the final word on these questions must relate it to how they connect with the practical life and personal outlook of the believer. This chapter's opening epigraph from Rilke sees the poet looking out at the autumn fields, soon to be devastated by the icy blast of winter, which is a kind of allegory for the cycle of human life; the 'shadow' lengthening on the sundial is the impending shadow of our mortality. Yet the poet is able to accept this ('Lord, it is time!') and to keep in focus with gratitude the long summer days that are ending. In a way, despite the apostrophizing of the 'Lord' (who in the poem may in fact be less the God of traditional theism than a personification of the forces of Nature), there is nothing here that a secularist could not subscribe to: a glad awareness of the past goods that have been enjoyed, a wistful, willed acceptance of our mortality, and a sort of submission to the continuing cycle of the seasons that will endure after we are gone. There is a certain dignity in this position, and it would ill behove the theist to say it makes no sense without the promise of an afterlife. Yet for all that, by the final stanza of his poem, Rilke is plunged back into an existential horror at what awaits him in the cruel onslaught of winter:

> *Wer jetzt kein Haus hat, baut sich keines mehr.*
> *Wer jetzt allein ist, wird es lange bleiben...*
> *und wird durch den Alleen hin und her*
> *unruhig wandern, wenn die Blätter treiben*

> ('He who has no house cannot build one now.
> Who now is lonely, lonely long must stay...
> and up and down the empty streets will go
> restlessly roaming, as the dark leaves hound him')[59]

The lack of a house, of any final habitation or dwelling, symbolizes the impermanence of human life ('Here we have no abiding city'),[60] and the sense that we are all moving towards a dark end when all will be swept away. That possibility is one that most theists will find themselves from time to time confronting too, like everyone else. Religion emphatically does not present a 'toy world'[61] where everything is made easy; and we have been at pains to stress in this chapter that the theistic position is certainly *not* one of smug or complacent confidence that all will be fine before, or indeed after, death. But if the line of thought developed in the last few sections is accepted, then it will be possible, though not easy, for

59 Rainer Maria Rilke, *Herbsttag* ['Autumn Day', 1902], trans. J. C.
60 Hebrews 13:14.
61 See Richard Swinburne, *The Existence of God* (Oxford: Clarendon, 1979), p. 219; 2nd ed, p. 264.

the believer to press forward in hope, struggling, however imperfectly, towards that union with the good wherein the ultimate meaning and value of human life resides. Or as the early seventeenth-century poet Thomas Campion expressed it, as he contemplated his own end:

> View me, Lord, a work of thine!
> Shall I then lie downed in night?
> Might thy grace in me but shine,
> I should seem made all of light . . .
>
> In thy word, Lord, is my trust,
> To thy mercies fast I fly;
> Though I am but clay and dust,
> Yet thy grace can lift me high.[62]

---

62 Thomas Campion (1567–1620), 'View Me Lord, a Work of Thine!', c. 1600. A performance of a choral setting of the poem or hymn, composed by Richard Lloyd, may be heard at http://www.youtube.com/watch?v=HMW2rUCLvtk.

7

MATHESIS

Metamorphousthe tē anakainōsei tou noös
('Be transformed by the renewing of your mind.')
St Paul[1]

I. RELIGION AS A WAY OF LIFE AND THE NATURE OF PHILOSOPHY

Philosophical inquiry in any area has to be done in a way that is sensitive to the nature of the subject matter, and it should have become apparent at many points in the previous chapters that this is particularly true in the philosophy of religion. The habits of thought that philosophers develop inevitably predispose them to focus on the analysis and evaluation of propositions, the truth or falsity of beliefs, and the degree to which those beliefs are supported by argument and evidence. All this is perfectly valid, and valuable; but a proper philosophical understanding of religion requires us to take account of much more. To be religious is not just to espouse certain doctrines; it is to follow a certain way of life and to take up certain commitments. It is in part a project of *formation*, of forming or reforming the self, a process of *askēsis* (training) or of *mathēsis* (learning), to use two ancient Greek terms. The latter term when translated into Latin becomes *disciplina* (discipline), a word whose connotations are perhaps more informative for the modern reader. It suggests not just the theoretical acquisition of knowledge, but a structured programme supported by rules and practices.

---

1 *Letter to the Romans* [c. AD 56], 12:2.

This in turn connects with what is, for many people, a crucial part of religious adherence, namely, the disciplines of spirituality (which include prayer, fasting, meditation, and the like). The *learning* envisaged here is, of course, not merely intellectual but moral: the goal is to change, to set aside the spurious goals of self-aggrandisement, and to grow in wisdom and love of the good. And for this reason, the 'conversion' at which spiritual practices have traditionally been aimed is not conceived of as something that can be completed on a particular day, or even over a single season, but is thought of as a lifelong process. The Rule of St Benedict, for example, dating from the sixth century AD, speaks of a *conversatio morum*, often translated 'conversion of life', a continuous reshaping and renewal of one's whole character and way of life, which will often be a long and arduous process. Spirituality, its role in religion, and its relation to religious doctrine, will be a principal theme of the present chapter. But by way of preface, it may be useful to reflect for a moment on the nature of philosophy itself, and how if at all it is concerned with questions about spiritual praxis and the adoption of a 'way of life'.

Philosophy in its typical modern academic guise does not seem ideally adapted to address the 'spiritual dimension' of religious adherence, partly because of the focus on the analysis and evaluation of propositional knowledge noted earlier, and partly also because of the way in which the subject itself has developed in modern times. The predominant movement in today's anglophone philosophical culture is towards an increasing fragmentation of the subject into a set of highly professionalized specialisms: quasi-scientific and highly technical studies whose connection with a 'way of life' is virtually nil (except in the purely instrumental sense that achieving the relevant qualifications and mastering the relevant intellectual techniques is how their practitioners happen to earn their living). But it has not always been so. The French philosopher Pierre Hadot has persuasively argued that in its ancient Greek beginnings philosophy was a profoundly serious personal undertaking, concerned with nothing less than the art of living – a 'concrete attitude, a way of life and of seeing the world'.[2] For example, there were many Stoic treatises entitled 'On Exercises', and the central notion of *askesis*,

---

2 Pierre Hadot, *Philosophy as a Way of Life* (Oxford: Blackwell, 1995) [originally published as *Exercises spirituels et philosophie antique* [1987], p. 108.

found for example in Epictetus, implied not so much 'asceticism' in the modern sense as a practical programme of training, concerned with the 'art of living'.[3] For Hadot, it is a sign of the degeneration of philosophy that so much of it has ended up, in its modern academic guise, as 'mere fencing in front of a mirror',[4] in Schopenhauer's damning phrase – relegated to a purely abstract and theoretical discipline, cut off from the goal that gave it its very raison d'être in earlier times, the goal of achieving a vision of reality that would lead to self-understanding and self-transformation.[5]

One does not have to go all the way with Hadot here in order to believe that philosophy would suffer a serious impoverishment if it were ever to lose all touch with the grand 'synoptic' questions he discusses – questions about ways of living and understanding the world as a whole. And this point in turn has important implications for the methods, techniques, and modes of language that are appropriate in philosophy generally and in the philosophy of religion in particular. It will be clear to those who have read thus far in the present volume that there has been no shortage here of the standard logical techniques of argument and counterargument, objections and replies, analysis and clarification, which have always been part of philosophical inquiry from its earliest beginnings. But such standard techniques have not prevented other elements appearing – for example, scriptural examples, and poetic and literary references, which have been intermingled into the argument chapter by chapter. It would be a radical misunderstanding of the role played by such elements if one supposed them to be wholly extraneous to the main thread of the philosophizing. For on the view advanced here they are not just 'illustrations' but are an integral part of the way philosophy needs to conduct itself if it is to aspire to a synoptic vision of reality as a whole. The resonances and echoes heard from these literary and poetic materials are not mere surface noise, to be filtered out in order

---

3 Epictetus, *Discourses* [*Diatribae*, c. 100 AD], III, 12, 1–7; I, 4, 14ff; I, 15, 2. Cited in Hadot, *Philosophy as a Way of Life*, p. 110.

4 Arthur Schopenhauer, *Die Welt als Wille und Vorstellung* [1819], trans. as *The World as Will and Representation* by E. F. J. Payne (Indian Hills, CO: Falcon's Wing Press, 1958), Vol. 2, pp. 163–164; cited in Hadot, *Philosophy as a Way of Life*, p. 271.

5 See further J. Cottingham, 'Philosophy and Self-improvement: Continuity and Change in Philosophy's Self-conception from the Classical to the Early-modern Era', in Michael Chase, Stephen Clark, and Michael McGhee (eds.), *Philosophy as a Way of Life: Ancients and Moderns* (Oxford: Blackwell, 2013), pp. 148–166.

for the 'real' plain meaning to be seen more clearly. They are more like the 'hyperlinks' in a computerized text, which allow the reader to gain access to an entire network of connections, connotations, allusions and references. They may of course lead us astray (as the elements of any philosophical discussion are sometimes liable to); but at best they can nourish and deepen our philosophical understanding in ways that could never have been achieved by abstract analysis alone.

The metaphor of the network can perhaps be extended yet further. For if theism is true, the divine presence is itself like an ever present net of moral understanding and illumination that is there waiting for each of us to reach out and participate in it, albeit very haltingly and imperfectly. And if the moral core of theism is taken seriously, the understanding we achieve thereby is not just an explanatory or analytic kind of understanding, but is a growing response to an active power that changes us, so that we cease to be mere detached investigators and start to see reality in radically transformed ways. With this in mind, we may now turn to the task of looking at the role of spiritual praxis in the life of religious adherents, and what it contributes to the resulting transformations in their moral outlook and their perception of reality.

2. SPIRITUAL PRAXIS

Though the concept of spirituality as used today ranges over many different kinds of phenomena, there is some common ground. One is struck by the convergence in the forms of spiritual *practice* commonly found in the great world religions, and even in some types of secular spirituality, notwithstanding radical differences in the respective beliefs, doctrines and outlooks. For example, Buddhists, Christians, and practitioners of secular spiritual techniques may all from time to time seek periods of silence, stillness and meditation. This suggests that even if our primary interest is in theistic forms of spirituality it may be helpful to approach the phenomenon of spirituality in the first instance by looking at praxis rather than theory – that is to say, by looking at some of the practices religious people engage in, rather than by analysing the content of their theological commitments. So, let us provisionally include under the term 'spirituality' all the practical components of religious observance that come to mind when one is not specifically focusing on the doctrinal elements – in short, pretty much all the structured practices religious adherents engage in, qua religious adherents, when they are not actually asserting credal statements, or involved in theological analysis of the teachings of their faith. Ignatius of Loyola, in the sixteenth century, spoke of 'spiritual exercises', which is a convenient label for the various religious practices most religious adherents engage in from time to time, and which are undertaken in a more systematic and formal way in the kind of seven-day retreat that Ignatius had in mind.[6] This general category includes prayer, fasting, meditation, *lectio divina* (the attentive reading of Scripture), participating in communal worship, group activities such as singing psalms, individual self-examination and confession, and moments of prayer or reflective silence at key moments of the day (for example, before eating, or before retiring).

The first point to be made about such activities is that they are not exclusively intellectual. They may well have an intellectual component, but they are not characteristically directed towards the analysis of propositions or the evaluation of doctrines. Spiritual exercises are typically *polyvalent* – they operate on many different levels – emotional, physical, aesthetic, moral, pre-rational, subliminal, introspective and collaborative, to name but a few categories in a very heterogeneous list. The singing of psalms, to take one key example that is at the centre of the divine office in Benedictine spirituality and many subsequent monastic traditions, comprises the recitation of words learned by heart over a long period of weekly and monthly and yearly repetition. It involves a *formalized structure* of praxis – regulated patterns of observance assigned to set hours throughout each day. There is a *physical* component – prescribed movements of sitting and standing, in which the whole community participates, collectively as well as individually. It involves *music*, not just as an optional extra but essentially and integrally: there is a plainsong chant, again carefully regulated, with an antiphonal structure and other laid-down forms – for example the crucial two beats of silence at the colon or pause in the middle of each verse.

It is largely pointless to ask if the experience of a monk attending the divine office is an intellectual one, or an emotional one, or a religious one

---

6 Ignatius of Loyola, *Spiritual Exercises* [*Ejercicios espirituales, c.* 1525], trans. J. Munitz and P. Endean (Harmondsworth: Penguin, 1996). Ignatius's original Spanish text was first published posthumously in 1615, but a Latin translation (*Exercitia Spiritualia*) was published in Rome, with papal approval, in 1548.

or a moral one, or an aesthetic or musical one, since *all* these elements are involved, and not just involved as separate elements but interfused in a total act of devotion (and the same point clearly applies to many other liturgical traditions). The music, we may note in passing, is a part of this kind of spiritual praxis that can be thought of as a kind of icon or image of the whole; for the singing or chanting integrates all the aspects of the person – physical activity (of lungs, vocal cords, mouth, shoulders, diaphragm, and bodily posture), emotional expression and response, sensory appreciation, intellectual grasp, and, in the finest examples, more complex kinds of moral elevation and self-transcendence.

In the singing of psalms, as far as the cognitive or intellectual aspect goes there is of course a definite semantic content to the sentences that are chanted; but these sentences are typically not, or not very often, assertions about the truth of certain religious doctrines; they are cries of remorse, desperate pleas for help, shouts of praise, songs of thanksgiving, expressions of hope and trust, and so on. And their point is that they should work holistically, gradually transforming and perfecting the lives of those who participate; not just changing their intellectual outlook, but irradiating the very quality of their lived experience.

This very brief sketch of the features of a typical spiritual exercise may be thought to give support to the idea of the *primacy of praxis* when it comes to understanding spirituality.[7] This notion, however, must be employed with care. It may be that one can to some extent understand spirituality while bracketing off the doctrinal content, but it is important to note that *bracketing off is not the same as deleting*. It is dubious to claim (as did some of the noncognitivist philosophers of religion of the latter part of the twentieth century) that religious observance is entirely nondoxastic – that it does not involve any beliefs or truth-directed assertions about the nature of reality. Prominent amongst those who took this kind of line was the theologian Don Cupitt, who argued for a nonrealist account of religious spirituality, in which the God who is addressed in spiritual practices such as prayer has no independent reality but is simply 'the mythical embodiment of all one is concerned with in the spiritual life'.[8] One problem with this approach is that it is

---

7 See J. Cottingham, *The Spiritual Dimension* (Cambridge: Cambridge University Press, 2005), ch. 1, §1.
8 Don Cupitt, *Taking Leave of God* (London: SCM Press, 1981), p. 167.

very hard to deny that certain truth-claims are *presupposed* in the kinds of spiritual activity just mentioned; at the very least (to take an obvious point), the prayer and praise and thanksgiving expressed in a typical psalm presuppose the existence of a God, who is being thanked and praised and prayed to. That said, we need not suppose that the praxis in question depends for its authenticity on our being able to unpack the precise meaning of these presupposed truth-claims, let alone on our being in a position to provide definitive evidence to support the claims. As centuries of theological debate have shown, the very idea of God as conceived in the three great Abrahamic faiths, a creative power that transcends the natural world, is sufficiently outside the realm of ordinary human discourse as to generate a host of philosophical issues about the precise meaning of assertions about the deity, and their epistemic basis.[9] But this does not negate the validity of the praxis.

Why not? One clue to the answer may perhaps be seen in the part-for-whole analogy referred to previously, the case of music. Music would remain a valid human activity even if there were no musicologists, or even if (as is perhaps indeed the case) there is no clear metaphysical account available of what music is 'about'. One could go further: even if that which is expressed in a sublime work of music is utterly ineffable – that is, even if no cognitive or intellectual analysis were available that could pretend to capture what is expressed – this would not shake our confidence that music of this kind is amongst the most valuable and important enterprises that humans can undertake. The validity of the praxis survives the inadequacy of a theoretical account of it. It might even be claimed, drawing on the 'apophatic' tradition that has informed much Western spirituality,[10] that the very ineffability of what is expressed may be an indicator of its transcendent value. This line, to be sure, is not without its problems. The phenomenon of 'new age spirituality' (including everything from scented candles to magic gemstones and healing crystals) provides ample evidence that mystery and ineffability can be used as a cloak for a whole range of dubious activities, from the seemingly harmless to the more exploitative, whose authenticity is open to question. And this might suggest that any

9 See Chapter 3, this volume.
10 See Chapter 2, section 4, this volume.

approach to spirituality that accords primacy to praxis over theory risks shielding the domain of spirituality from critical evaluation. But here one may invoke the maxim 'by their fruits ye shall know them'. The evaluation of spiritual praxis is not a logical free-for-all, shrouded in the obfuscating mists of ineffability; it can be assessed, at least in part, by reference to the moral and psychological difference it makes in the lives of the practitioners.

3. CONVERSION

One result to emerge from our discussion so far is that one cannot understand spiritual praxis in isolation from what is taken to be its goal or purpose. And here, despite the points of convergence noted earlier between the spiritual practices of different faiths or none, certain crucial differences start to emerge. In the case of a secular meditation technique whose main purpose is simply to reduce stress or to lower blood pressure, even though such processes will of course involve mental as well as purely physical changes, there is no direct connection with the goal of moral change. In the case of the meditation techniques one finds in nontheistic faiths such as Buddhism and some other Eastern religions, the picture is more complex. Certainly Buddhism has a strong tradition of moral teaching, including the celebrated eightfold path of virtue (right understanding, thought, speech, conduct, livelihood, effort, mindfulness, and concentration);[11] but its final goal does not seem to be the salvation of the meditator in his unique particularity or selfhood so much as his or her liberation from the human world of involvement and attachment, aimed at an eventual state of enlightenment in which the very idea of individuality and selfhood will be seen as illusory. To say this is obviously to oversimplify matters somewhat; the idea of purging and leaving behind the cravings of the ego bears a great deal of similarity to what one finds in many theistic models of spirituality, and there is no doubt a case for inferring a great deal of overlap in the moral perspectives involved. But nevertheless, at the core of the theistic Abrahamic faiths we find something quite different – something

11 See further Peter Harvey, *An Introduction to Buddhist Ethics* (Cambridge: Cambridge University Press, 2000).

irreducibly individual and personal. God is seen as a personal being who calls each of us: in the Bible, there are many episodes where an individual is called by name (for example, Moses, Samuel, Saul/Paul), and the individual responds as one who is directly addressed – often the characteristic response is 'Here I am!' (Exodus 3:5; 1 Samuel 3:4; cf. Acts 9:4–5). Conversion, in this tradition, is a process initiated by a God who cares directly and individually for each of his creatures, and who calls them not to merge their individuality into some oceanic void, but to change their lives.

The literature on conversion makes it abundantly clear that such change cannot be understood as a purely cognitive or intellectual matter. In the Abrahamic religions, spirituality is closely bound up with *worship*, and this latter notion involves reverence, which has an irreducible emotional component. The philosopher Linda Zagzebski has plausibly argued that emotions like reverence are 'a more basic feature of religion than any belief'.[12]

Opinions may differ about the precise role of intellectual argument in moving someone towards a theistic outlook, but it seems clear that conversion, in any interesting sense of the term, is never about mere cognitive change. Clearly no one is converted, in the sense relevant to salvation, as a result of merely subscribing to or ceasing to subscribe to any given set of credal propositions. There is perhaps some confusion about this, both amongst religious supporters and their opponents, because of biblical pronouncements like 'He that believeth and is baptised shall be saved' (from the almost certainly spurious section added on to the final chapter of Mark's gospel (16:16)). But whatever this and similar passages elsewhere may mean, they cannot coherently be asserting that the mere fact of accepting a credal proposition is the key to salvation. The idea of a morally perfect God rewarding people or awarding salvation points merely on the grounds of doctrinal allegiance should, on reflection, appear manifestly absurd, not just to the opponents of religion but to its adherents as well. At least one reported pronouncement of Christ, incidentally, is very clear on this: in the parable of the last judgement, when the sheep are separated from the goats, it turns out that credal orthodoxy earns no points at all: those who sincerely say 'Lord, Lord', yet have failed to show moral transformation

---

12 Linda Zagzebski, *Philosophy of Religion* (Oxford: Blackwell, 2007), p. 3.

in their lives, are unequivocally condemned and thrust into outer darkness.[13]

These considerations suggest that the kind of change that is relevant to religious conversion is primarily to be understood as a *radical moral change*, a reorientation of one's life towards a new set of values. On the theistic worldview, this is something that cannot happen without divine help; though this does not logically entail that the action of God is necessarily always recognized as such by the individual in question. For example, the theologian Karl Rahner has argued that there can be 'anonymous Christians' – those who are in fact saved by the redeeming work of Christ, even though they lack explicit knowledge of the way God's grace has been manifested.[14] However that may be, someone who simply comes on reflection to a fundamental change of mind about some cluster of moral issues would not ordinarily be described as having undergone a conversion, except perhaps in a very loose sense of the term. Conversion typically has a certain characteristic phenomenology – there is, as it were, a *psycho-ethical dynamic* of conversion, which manifests itself to the subject in a very specific way.

How can we make this more precise? An initial suggestion might be that the change involved happens in a particularly quick and dramatic fashion. Such a suggestion, however, does not survive deeper scrutiny. Some conversion narratives, it is true, involve a very sudden event, a blinding light literally 'out of the blue', as in the most famous case of all, that of St Paul on the road to Damascus. Others, however, as in the intricately self-documented case of St Augustine, seem to have involved a protracted period of mental wrestling. But irrespective of the speed of the change, what seems common to both the sudden and the drawn-out conversion is the sense, phenomenologically speaking, of a *demand* for change: that is, conversion presents itself to the subject as something he is *called on* or *required* to undergo, resist as he might.

---

13 Matthew 7: 21–23; cf. 1 John 2:3, Revelation 22:14. See also J. Cottingham, 'Getting the Right Travel Papers. A Postscript to *The Spiritual Dimension*', *Philosophy* 83:326 (October 2008), 557–567.

14 See K. Rahner, 'Christianity and the Non-Christian Religions' [notes of a lecture delivered on 28 April 1961], in J. Hick and B. Hebblethwaite (eds.), *Christianity and Other Religions* (Philadelphia: Fortress Press, 1981), ch. 3, esp. p. 75; repr. in M. Peterson et al., *Philosophy of Religion: Selected Readings*, 2nd ed. (Oxford: Oxford University Press, 2001), pp. 549ff.

In a well-known sonnet of Rainer Maria Rilke, this idea, or something very like it, is expressed in aesthetic rather than religious terms, where the writer comes upon an ancient statue from the Classical world.[15] It happens to be a statue of Apollo, but Rilke does not invoke any specific doctrinal elements from the Greek polytheistic outlook. Rather, the salient point is a human and moral one: the poet, confronted by that headless torso, with its austere perfection of form, feels an acute sense of the inadequacy of his own life. Although the statue has no head, and hence of course no eyes, the poet as he stands in front of the statue feels himself nonetheless searchingly and uncompromisingly scrutinized, and he is somehow called upon to respond:

> *denn da ist keine Stelle,*
> *die dich nicht sieht. Du mußt dein Leben ändern.*
> for there no place is found
> that does not watch you. You must change your life.[16]

Being brought up against this uncompromising challenge may be something that happens only after a long and difficult struggle, as Augustine remarks in connection with his own conversion: 'The days had seemed long and many, because of my love of leisurely freedom, until at last I should sing from my inmost depths what my heart declared to you:

15 Rainer Maria Rilke, *Archaïscher Torso Apollos* [from *Der Neuen Gedichte anderer Teil*, 1908]. The significance of this poem is discussed further in J. Cottingham, 'The Self, the Good Life and the Transcendent', in N. Athanassoulis and S. Vice (eds.), *The Moral Life: Essays in Honour of John Cottingham* (London: Palgrave, 2008), pp. 228–271.
16 The quotation is from the last line and a half of the sonnet. The full poem, with an English translation I have provided to match the metre and rhyme-scheme of the original, runs as follows:

Wir kannten nicht sein unerhörtes Haupt,	We could not see his lost, unheard of head
darin die Augenäpfel reiften. Aber	where the eyes' berries ripened. Yet, despite,
sein Torso glüht noch wie ein Kandelaber,	his torso glows still, like a candle-light,
in dem sein Schauen, nur zurückgeschraubt,	his glance grown dimmer, but yet never dead:
sich hält und glänzt. Sonst könnte nicht der Bug	its gleam endures. Else could the subtle line
der Brust dich blenden, und im leisen Drehen	of the white chest not blind you, nor the curve
der Lenden könnte nicht ein Lächeln gehen	of those pale loins so smilingly down-swerve
zu jener Mitte, die die Zeugung trug.	to that dark core which held the seed divine.
Sonst stünde dieser Stein entstellt und kurz	Else would this marble not seem whole and tall
unter der Schultern durchsichtigem Sturz	beneath the shoulders' long, translucent fall
und flimmerte nicht so wie Raubtierfelle;	nor glisten so, like a wild creature's fleece;
und bräche nicht aus allen seinen Rändern	nor every edge burst forth like the bright blade
aus wie ein Stern: denn da ist keine Stelle,	of a star's point: of him, no single piece
die dich nicht sieht. Du mußt dein Leben ändern.	but looks you through. Your life must be remade.

I have sought your face; your face Lord I will seek.[17] But however it happens, authentic conversion involves a radical moral change, which arises as a result of a profound sense in the subject that his or her life has so far failed to measure up to certain objective ethical demands, which now require the whole direction of that life to be altered.

In short, the religious idea of conversion takes seriously both our 'wretchedness' and our 'redeemability' – the two poles of the human condition described by Pascal.[18] True moral and spiritual growth, on this picture, requires us to be shaken out of our ordinary complacency; it requires us to bring to the surface those 'reasons of the heart' which will open us to new ways of perceiving, and new possibilities for enriched awareness. Conversion, if this is right, is not a coercive process engineered by demonstrations of power, but is a response of the whole person, intellectual, emotional, moral, and spiritual, which enables what was hitherto hidden to come to light. The process is not one of being brought up short by new scientific evidence or paranormal events, but the working of an interior moral change that generates a new openness. Nothing can force acceptance unless we have 'ears to hear'.[19] And what is heard is not a barrage of confirmatory data, but a message that needs to be understood. It is, as the Second Epistle of Peter puts it, a *word* – one that must be 'heeded, as a light that shines in a dark place, until the day dawns and the morning star rises in your hearts'.[20]

4. DECONVERSION

The programme for a recent philosophical conference on 'conversion' included under this heading not just instances of converting *to* a religion but also the case of 'rejection of religion for a secular worldview';[21] this

---

17 *Longi et multi [dies] videbantur, prae amore libertatis otiosae, ad cantandum de medullis omnibus: tibi dixit cor meum, quaesivi vultum tuum; vultum tuum, domine, requiram.* Augustine, *Confessions*, Bk. IX, ch. 3; freely translated, JC. Augustine's closing quotation is from Psalm 27 [or 26 in the Vulgate Latin text], verse 8.

18 'Christian faith serves to establish virtually only two things: the corruption of our nature, and our redemption through Jesus Christ.' *Pensées*, ed. Lafuma, no. 427. Compare no 6: 'the wretchedness of man without God; the felicity of man with God.'

19 Matthew 11:15; Mark 4:9.

20 2 Peter 1:19.

21 Thirty-Second Annual Philosophy of Religion Conference, Claremont Graduate University, 2011.

implies that one can correctly speak of 'conversion' to atheism. As far as the actual usage of the term 'conversion' goes, it seems people's linguistic intuitions may vary as to whether conversion includes cases where religious commitment is abandoned. The *Oxford English Dictionary* suggests that the term always connotes a move *towards*, rather than away from, religious allegiance: it defines conversion as 'the bringing of anyone over *to* a specified religious faith, profession or party, especially to one regarded as true from what is regarded as falsehood or error'.[22] The latter clause does, however, hint that the term might be legitimately extended to the bringing of someone *away* from religious allegiance, if that were seen as an escape from a worldview taken to be false or erroneous. And it may well be that since this particular edition of the dictionary was compiled, the linguistic meaning of 'conversion' has indeed expanded to accommodate such cases – to accommodate the phenomenon of what we might call 'deconversion'.[23] Questions of linguistic usage aside, any philosophically balanced discussion of spiritual praxis and conversion needs to attend to the possibility, which appears to be increasingly actualized in our contemporary culture, of someone's turning away from long established habits of spirituality and religious observance and either suddenly or gradually leaving behind a theistic worldview.

A fairly typical modern account of what might be called a 'deconversion' to a naturalist or secularist position from previous religious allegiance can be found in a recent study by the French atheist philosopher André Comte-Sponville:

...not only was I raised a Christian, but I also believed in God. My faith, if occasionally laced with doubts, was powerful until around age eighteen. Then I lost it, and it felt like a liberation – everything suddenly seemed simpler, lighter, stronger and more open. It was as if I had left childhood behind me, with its fantasies and fears, its closeness and languorousness, and entered the real world at long last – the adult world, the world of action,

---

22 *Oxford English Dictionary* (Oxford: Oxford University Press, 1972), emphasis added.

23 The latest online edition of the complete OED (accessed October 2013) does not, however, include any such meaning; instead it merely lists the traditional theological sense of the term: 'the turning of sinners to God; a spiritual change from sinfulness, ungodliness, or worldliness to love of God and pursuit of holiness'.

the world of truth, unhampered by forgiveness or Providence. Such freedom! Such responsibility! Such joy![24]

One might suppose that such a scenario completely refutes the account put forward in the previous section of a distinctive phenomenology of conversion, structured round the sense of confrontation with an exterior moral demand. But it could be argued that this account is, paradoxically, reinforced by the scenario described by Comte-Sponville, since he offers us a kind of inverted mirror image, in which all the relevant features are reversed. In the religious cases cited earlier, the agent is made vividly aware of his own moral failure and presented with what seems an uncompromising exterior constraint – an absolute demand for moral change or reform. In Comte-Sponville's description of his 'deconversion', by contrast, it is the exact opposite. There is a sense of *liberation*, of the constraints or 'closeness' of the previous structure falling away, and of the subject's 'freedom' to do as he wishes. 'Such freedom!'

It is true that Comte-Sponville immediately adds 'such responsibility!' – thereby bolstering what turns out to be his repeated insistence in the book that deconversion to atheism does not at all imply abandoning morality. This latter claim is of course indisputable: despite Dostoevsky's 'without God everything is permitted',[25] it would be absurd to suggest that those who have come to atheism after previous religious allegiance feel themselves thereby to be freed from moral constraints. But it is nonetheless significant that Comte-Sponville goes on to declare that his liberation from the religious worldview has led him to see that the 'absolutization of ethics', as he terms it, is in the end 'illusory'. There are, in Comte-Sponville's new naturalist worldview, no truly absolute or unconditional moral demands; rather, he construes moral imperatives as 'projection on to Nature' of 'what only exists within ourselves'.[26]

Now there may be alternative versions of secularism that somehow preserve the normative character of morality in the strong sense of an absolute or unconditional demand.[27] But at least from the particular case under discussion, together with the religious cases referred to

24 André Comte-Sponville *The Book of Atheist Spirituality* [originally published as *L'esprit de l'athéisme*, 2006] (London: Bantam, 2008), pp. 5–6.
25 Fyodor Dostoevsky, *The Brothers Karamazov* [*Brat'ya Karamazovy*, 1880], Bk XI, ch. 4.
26 Comte-Sponville, *Atheist Spirituality*, p. 178.
27 See Chapter 3, sections 3–5, this volume.

earlier, the position seems clear enough: conversion in the original and strict sense of being brought *to* a religious faith is characteristically experienced in terms of a phenomenology of being brought up against an uncompromising moral demand. Conversion in the opposite sense of moving away from a religious allegiance – what I have called 'deconversion' – is experienced as a liberation from absolute demands, and a sense of the subject's freedom to determine the course of his own life as he sees fit. Comte-Sponville's conclusion, at any rate, is that once one comes to see the 'illusion' of absolute moral demands, morality becomes a function of the agent's wholly autonomous decision about how he chooses to live his life: 'Should I rob or rape or murder?', Comte-Sponville asks; and he quotes admiringly from the answer given by the philosopher Alain: 'No, because it would be unworthy of what I am, and what I wish to be'.[28] The phenomenology of submission to an absolute external demand is replaced by that of the liberation of the ego as autonomous creator and determiner of what is worthwhile. As to whether this inverted image of religious conversion is an authentic mode of moral growth for human beings, or else a kind of temptation, a distorting fantasy of the human agent as creator and determiner of value – this is a question with too many complex moral, theological and psychological ramifications to be embarked on within the framework of the present volume.[29] What can be said here is that the attempt to replace the theistic grounding for morality with the individual's own autonomously chosen 'projects', which then become the supposed source of normativity, has become a characteristic signature of much contemporary secular moral philosophy.[30]

5. SPIRITUALITY, MORAL GROWTH, AND THE PSYCHOTHERAPEUTIC FRAMEWORK

In pursuing our investigation into the more practical and personal aspects of religious allegiance and how they relate to an individual's

---

28 Comte-Sponville, *Atheist Spirituality*, p. 42. Alain was the pseudonym of Émile Chartier (1869–1951).

29 See further J. Cottingham, 'Impartiality and Ethical Formation', in B. Feltham and J. Cottingham (eds.), *Partiality and Impartiality: Morality, Special Relationships and the Wider World* (Oxford: Oxford University Press, 2010), pp. 65–83, esp. section 4.

30 See Chapter 4, section 5, this volume.

journey through life, we have implicitly identified certain factors as playing a key role in someone's turning to religion. These include emotional response, moral crisis, interior descent, and radical psycho-ethical change. To reflect on these a little further, I want in this concluding section of the chapter to introduce an analogy between the domain of spiritual conversion and the seemingly very different domain of psychotherapy. The latter domain is one about which many philosophers as well as theologians have serious reservations, but if these can be put on one side just for the moment, I think the comparison between the religious and the psychoanalytic journeys will turn out to be an illuminating one in several respects.

A first and immediately obvious point of comparison is that self-reflection and self-examination are integral to both projects. St Augustine describes his religious quest as proceeding via a descent into the 'interior' of the human psyche 'in which truth dwells';[31] and we have already noted the importance in the religious life of the structured disciplines of reflection and interior meditation, which have always been taken to be a crucial element in a spiritual praxis.

A second striking point of comparison between the religious and the psychoanalytic journey is that both are in a certain way directed towards the goal of self-purification. The aim of the psychotherapeutic process can be thought of as a kind of rebirth (some describe the process as a kind of re-parenting): the aim is to help liberate us from infantile projections, from fantasies of control and domination, so that we may begin live openly and freely, in a way that acknowledges our own vulnerability and respects the vulnerability of others. The teleology of religious or spiritual conversion, I would suggest, has to be understood in a broadly similar way. The image repeatedly used by St Paul is that of coming out of darkness into light – into a state, in other words, where there is no room for projection or evasion, but where one is seen as one truly is. And to see oneself in this way has automatic implications for one's relation to others. The ideal of 'brotherly love', which Paul enjoins on his fellow converts, involves ceasing to treat others as objects to be used or defrauded or despised, and seeing them instead

---

31 *Noli foras ire, in teipsum redi; in interiore homine habitat veritas.* ('Go not outside, but return within thyself; in the inward man dwelleth the truth.') Augustine, *De vera religione* [391] XXXIX, 72.

as just as deserving of love and respect as one would wish to be one-self.[32]

A third similarity between the structure of the religious way of life and the psychoanalytic project is that the ultimate object posited in each domain is what may be called *anomalous*. In the psychoanalytic case the object is what is termed 'the unconscious', while in the religious case it is God; and the anomaly lies in the fact that neither object can be brought entirely within the arena of ordinary human understanding. The unconscious is, by its nature, that which is opaque to conscious apprehension – a fact that led some early philosophical critics of Freud to declare that the very idea of the unconscious mind was incoherent, since what could not be brought within the domain of mental awareness could not, by definition, count as a mental phenomenon. Yet in truth the fact that the unconscious is anomalous, outside the framework of ordinary mentation, need not be a fatal objection to positing it; for what cannot be fully encompassed may nonetheless be something we can reach towards. The 'shadowy presentations' of the unconscious mind, as Jung termed them,[33] while remaining beneath the threshold of what is consciously registered, can nevertheless leave their *traces* in the faint forgotten memories of childhood, or the weird and only partly recoverable deliverances of dreams; and they can make sense, as Freud showed, of a whole range of similar phenomena, thereby illuminating and transforming aspects of our affective life that would otherwise be wholly baffling.

There is a close analogy here with what the religious adherent holds with regard to God – the elusive and mysterious source of being who, as Augustine declared, can never be brought fully within the grasp of the human mind. This resistance to being mentally encompassed is in the very nature of the divine: *si comprehendis, non est Deus*, wrote Augustine – if you grasp him, he is not God.[34] For the very fact of

32 Compare 1 Thessalonians, 4:3–9, and 5:4. See also Acts 26:18; Colossians 4:13; cf. 1 Peter 2:9.
33 Carl Jung, *Modern Man in Search of a Soul* (London: Routledge, 1933), p. 40. For further discussion of Jung's position, see J. Cottingham, *Philosophy and the Good Life: Reason and the Passions in Greek, Cartesian and Psychoanalytic Ethics* (Cambridge: Cambridge University Press, 1998), ch. 4.
34 Augustine of Hippo, *Sermons* [*Sermones*, 392–430], 52, vi, 16 and 117, iii, 5. See Chapter 2, section 2, this volume.

our encompassing him, bringing him entirely within the horizon of our human understanding, would be the best evidence that what was so grasped was not God but a mere idol of our own construction. Hence, to use a striking image from Descartes, discussed earlier in Chapter 2, God is like the mountain which we can never comprehend or grasp, never put our arms round, but which we can nevertheless touch; we can somehow reach towards him in our thought.[35] This anomalous aspect, which applies both to God and to the unconscious – their resistance to the encompassing grasp of human inquiry – is only an obstacle to their acceptance for those who make the mistake of equating the limits our conscious apprehension with the limits of reality. And just as with the mysterious 'traces' left by the unconscious, so (as we saw earlier, in discussing our human 'intimations of the transcendent') the divine reality that we cannot fully grasp or describe may be thought of as leaving *traces* that are manifest in the beauty of the natural world and the compelling power of our moral sensibilities.[36]

This leads us to a fourth and final parallel between the psychoanalytic and the religious domains, which brings us back to the theme broached earlier in this chapter, that of the primacy of the practical and moral dimension over the theoretical and metaphysical when it comes to understanding the nature of the phenomena in question. Like religion, psychoanalysis has, to be sure, a theoretical or doctrinal component; and just as we find in the religious case, that component can be the subject of fierce intellectual controversies and convoluted debates (the precise structure and dynamics of the unconscious mind calling forth almost as much furious factionalism as one finds in the long history of denominational schisms and heresies in the Church). But as in the case of the religious journey, so in the psychoanalytic case one can to a large extent understand the process while bracketing off the theoretical and doctrinal content. Psychoanalytic theorists may debate the precise role of the pleasure principle, or the depressive position, just as theologians will continue to thrash out the niceties of the monophysite versus Nestorian views of the Incarnation. But the healing work of psychotherapy, like the salvific work of religious conversion, depends not

---

35 René Descartes, letter to Mersenne of 27 May 1630, discussed in Chapter 2, section 2, this volume.
36 Chapter 3, section 4.

so much on intellectual discussion of metaphysical doctrines (which in any case, let us remember, concern what cannot ultimately be brought within the grasp of complete human cognition) as on the *psycho-ethical dynamics of the praxis*. The underlying nature of the process involved must remain partly opaque, and no amount of intellectual theorizing will capture it completely. For although real hidden entities and processes are surely at work, what must occur in order for the required healing and self-understanding to take place is the requisite effort on the part of the subject, a willingness to relinquish the narcissistic fantasy of self-sufficiency, and the humility to accept the need for change. The framework that makes sense of it all, in the therapeutic as in the spiritual case, is inescapably a practical and a moral one; and it is one that must be activated on the level of each individual psyche or soul.

Like all analogies, the one we are considering must not be pressed too far, and the points of comparison we have been exploring are certainly not supposed to entail any strong conceptual or causal link between the religious and the psychoanalytic domains, let alone to imply that embarking on one necessarily requires one to become involved in the other. But once these caveats are acknowledged, there is no good reason to deny ourselves the partial illumination that the analogy does provide in the various ways just explored. And what above all it seems to shed light on is something that is seldom brought to the fore in philosophical discussions of religion, namely, that the whole process of religious involvement and commitment has a *purpose*: the aim is to cast off the old self and learn to live 'more abundantly' (John 10:10). There are many dimensions to this 'more abundant life', but one feature that emerges in several of the Gospel stories is that the call to such a life comes about through a direct face-to-face encounter: 'Jesus looked at him' (John 1:42; Mark 10:21; Luke 18:24). The psychoanalytic encounter is of course vastly different from this in countless respects, but there is one crucial point of comparison: what the analysand learns, if all goes well, is to confront the therapist without evasion, or projection, and to be able to return that gaze not in anger or confusion, but in trust and hope. The goal of the process is to allow oneself to be seen, exactly as one is, without concealment, without trying to manipulate or extort a response, simply as a human being amongst others, weak and dependent, desperately needing to transcend one's confused and conflicted self, yet for all that, deserving of equal respect. Psychological and ethical integrity, in short, implies the ability to stand before the wise and compassionate and discerning gaze of another person, one who cares, but not in a needy or demanding way, who knows one's failings and weaknesses, and yet is prepared to offer support in the continued endeavour to trust and to grow.

For the believer, the encounter with the divine, which can never be grasped by intellectual analysis alone, may perhaps be understood in something like this way. God, as conceived in religious tradition, is the compassionate Other, before whom one must present oneself in wholeness of being, without concealment or manipulation or dissembling. Before that gaze, there is no room for evasion. In brief, having one's life held up to the presence of God, precisely the phenomenological core of the conversion experience, becomes part of the psycho-ethical framework for what every human being, if they are honest, must acknowledge that they aspire to: the continued growth of the morally maturing individual in his or her entirety. Believing that one's life is presented in its entirety to such a being can be a powerful vehicle for continued moral growth and integration. And perhaps most important, it can bring with it the growing resolve to move away from preoccupation with the self and its flaws and conflicts, and to turn outwards in love and compassion towards one's fellow creatures and fellow sufferers. For the scrutiny to which one's life is presented is the scrutiny of one who has compassion on all alike, 'as a Father has compassion on his children' (Psalms 103:13).

Philosophical reason alone, as we have seen in early chapters, may not be able settle the question of whether or not there is such a transcendent divine being, but that does not mean that the belief in question is without rational support. Part of the support derives from the phenomenology of our encounter with the undeniable requirements of morality, as explored earlier in Chapter 3,[37] and vividly dramatized in the kind of personal encounter described in the Gospel passages just referred to: the individual feels himself or herself to be confronted by a loving yet implacable gaze that 'sees right through us'. The demand is

37 Chapter 3, sections 4 and 5.

presented, phenomenologically, as one that is not of our own making, as one that exerts a call upon us whether we like it or not. And whatever the details of the imagery, the moral content of the demand remains constant; in its simplest form, to come back to last line of Rilke's *Apollo* poem, it tells us *du mußt dein Leben ändern* – you must change your life.

8

CONCLUSION: HUMANE PHILOSOPHIZING ABOUT RELIGION

Do you see yon wicket gate?
John Bunyan[1]

To bring our discussion to a close, let us draw together some of the threads of the last chapter and indeed of the book as a whole. Ancient religious imagery, going right back to the Gospels, speaks of the road to salvation as a journey that has to be entered upon by first passing through a gate – the 'wicket gate', as it appears in John Bunyan's famous seventeenth-century allegory, *The Pilgrim's Progress*. In Christian symbolism, of course, Christ himself is the gate, or 'door' (*thura*) to salvation: the entrance the flock must pass through to find 'pasture' (John 10:9). Like many symbols, the gate image contains many layers of meaning. But the idea of a *transition* that needs to be made, or a change that needs to be undergone, in order for certain possibilities to become actual turns out to be a linking thread that ties together many of the themes in this book.

We began by suggesting that the special nature of religious understanding requires a certain methodology if it is to be approached in a philosophically appropriate way. An epistemology of detachment, so far from being the paradigm of proper philosophizing that it is often supposed to be, may be a way of hardening oneself against the porousness and receptivity that is a necessary condition for certain kinds of evidence to become salient (Chapter 1). As we have just seen in Chapter 7, the disciplines of spiritual praxis can be interpreted as a training process that facilitates just the kind of interior moral transformation that will

---

1 John Bunyan, *The Pilgrim's Progress* [1678], §17.

generate the required receptivity, as envisaged in the conversion process as traditionally understood.

An important implication of this is that we cannot force the evidence for the truth of religion into a scientific template; for the most important evidence is of a kind that may only be accessed by passing through the 'gateway' to new and transformed modes of understanding. None of this means that once that door has been entered all will miraculously become clear and transparent. The ancient theme of the mystery and hiddenness of the divine, particularly prominent in the apophatic tradition of theology, places limits on our human ability to theorize about the divine reality that the believer takes himself to be seeking by entering through the gate (Chapter 2). But the underlying reality that is 'unknown' is nevertheless manifest, for the theist, in terms of a personal address that is individually directed. What is more, this personal call to allegiance is one that is addressed not to the analytic mind but to the heart – to the emotions and the will (Chapter 2).

Philosophy of religion needs to take account of this if it proposes to pronounce on the acceptability or otherwise of the theistic outlook. Verification, or evaluation of truth, was taken to be the key to understanding any statement or set of statements on the positivist model that ruled philosophy around the middle of the twentieth century; the slogan was 'the meaning of a proposition is its method of verification',[2] and verification was taken to be empirical confirmation by scientific procedures. While most philosophers working today have long since abandoned verificationism, the spirit of positivism in a certain way still lives on, especially in the 'naturalism' that dominates our contemporary philosophical climate, which outlaws from acceptable discourse whatever is not 'empirically grounded' through the methods of science.[3] Perhaps this partly explains how the central questions of philosophy of religion have often been presented in a way that makes paramount the evaluation of the truth or otherwise of the metaphysical claims of religion and the empirical evidence that is supposed to support them. But our discussion in the previous chapter of spiritual *mathēsis*, the actual processes whereby an individual grows into a religious outlook, and the

---

2 See A. J. Ayer, *Logical Positivism* (New York: Free Press, 1959), p. 13.
3 See John Dupré, 'Review of Nagel's *Mind and Cosmos*', *Notre Dame Philosophical Reviews*, 29 October 2012.

slow development of moral and spiritual understanding that defines the process, suggests a rather different approach. It suggests that there can be no question of reaching a final verdict on the relevant truth-claims from outside the forms of practical and affective engagement through which alone genuine understanding flourishes.

This can of course lead to a standoff in the philosophy of religion, which in some ways resembles what one finds in the philosophy of psychoanalysis; in the latter case we find on the one side a baffled disdain that any serious and rational philosopher can be attracted to such an 'unscientific' domain, and on the other a community of 'disciples' who are committed to the value of psychotherapeutic methods, often as a result of the moral and psychological changes they have experienced in their own case as a result of undergoing the process. As with any impasse of this kind, there is no way to resolve it from a 'neutral' standpoint of detached rationality; for the question of whether detachment is the appropriate stance is itself part of what is at stake, whether in the psychotherapeutic or the religious case.

The analogy between religious and psychoanalytic domains (explored in the final section of Chapter 7) might in one way be misleading, since it might suggest that both domains take us beyond the realm of rational evaluation and into a subjective realm where everything depends on our personal perspective. If one restricts oneself to a methodology that takes scientific inquiry as its model, that is perhaps how it must seem. But part of the 'humane' or humanistic turn in philosophy of religion which this book has been advocating involves a move away from the science-based model towards a model that *prioritizes understanding over verification*. Reversing the slogan of the positivists, according to which meaning depends on verification, this more humane model insists that in order to evaluate something you must first understand it properly. And in the present context, proper understanding has to be construed not in a detached analytic way but in an involved and experiential way. This is a model of understanding that insists that we need to some extent to try to enter into a form of life before we presume to dissect and judge it.

Entering into a form of life is personally risky, in the way scientific investigation or purely intellectual analysis is not. For one has to be prepared to give up certain things, to abandon sources of respect and gratification that our entrenched habits incline us to cling to, especially if we pride ourselves on our supposed academic detachment and intellectual autonomy. Yet as the image of the wicket gate in Bunyan's *The Pilgrim's Progress* reminds us, there may be gates, difficult to find and hard to enter because of the sacrifice required, which nonetheless open the way to new and transforming kinds of experience. These kinds of experience are not, however, something wholly beyond the reach of impartial evaluation, as might perhaps be the case if there were no continuity between the lives of those who are wary of entering the 'gate' and those who have sought to pass through it. For even from outside the gate, there will, in the lives of most if not all human beings, be 'intimations of the transcendent': there are moments in every life when we have glimpses of the compelling and authoritative power of beauty and moral goodness that call us to transcend ourselves and reach forward to something we are not yet, but might yet become (Chapter 3).

The authoritative character of morality takes us to a key point of difference between a theistic and a nontheistic outlook that forms a central battle ground in the philosophy of religion (Chapter 4). The main issues here, as we saw, will hinge on whether we can accept a deflationary account of morality, as no more than a projection of our human preferences or inclinations, or, if the idea of the objective authority and 'normativity' of morality is retained, whether there are viable ways to account for it in purely secular terms. The theist too faces challenges about how exactly God functions as the source of normativity, and intellectual analysis alone cannot finally settle the questions of whether morality is best accommodated within a naturalist or a theistic cosmos.

Nothing in either story compels rational assent. One may yearn for probabilistic or deductive proofs of the theistic outlook, and either think one has found them, as some religious philosophers do, or conclude from their shortcomings that theism is untenable, as many contemporary philosophers do. But to say these issues are not finally decidable is not to say there are no considerations that tend to tip the scales one way or the other. The suffering and evil found in the world is one important consideration that has seemed to many to tip the scales against theism. But here again, the moral transformations that many believers undergo, even in the midst of suffering, are also relevant evidence (Chapter 5).

Some of our deepest intuitions about what makes a human life worthwhile are also relevant here. It does not require explicit adherence to the Judaeo-Christian or indeed any religious worldview to subscribe to the Socratic dictum that it is better to suffer wrong than to do wrong.[4] But if we take this dictum seriously, then some important consequences follow. Who, for example, will we want to say had a better, more flourishing life: Cain, who murdered his brother, or Abel, whose life was cut off in his prime? The answer must surely be the latter. Abel unquestionably suffered a terrible tragedy – his life, and therefore his capacity for human flourishing, was cut short through no fault of his own. But he lived a good life: his offering, we are told, 'found favour with the Lord', which we may take for present purposes to mean that he achieved an acceptable degree of righteousness. His life, though cruelly ended, was a good life, a flourishing human life. Cain, on the other hand, irrevocably ruined his own life. He gave way to poisonous envy and did irreparable evil; and however long he may have lived, he remained a 'restless wanderer upon earth' – his peace was destroyed.[5]

If there is a message that emerges from this and many such stories in the Hebrew Bible and the Christian New Testament it is that our task as human beings is to strive to do what is right, and to live in love and peace with our neighbours. What the Judaeo-Christian outlook affirms, and it is an affirmation that many nonbelievers may well also subscribe to, is that addressing this task is the key to true human flourishing: it is the right way to use the precious gift of life, the way we can make an 'acceptable offering'. There is no guarantee, whether one is a religious believer or not, that such commitment to the good will stop terrible things from happening to us, which may erode or truncate our continued flourishing; and there is even a likelihood that if we live long enough we may risk such erosion creeping up on us anyway through the characteristic maladies and eventual decay that beset any mortal organism. But a life so eroded or truncated can still have been a flourishing life. And even if illness or misfortune is so heavy as to undermine entirely the continued capacity for moral action or sensibility, then, to be sure, the sufferers may be pitied, and may need the care and compassion of

---

4 Plato, *Gorgias* [c. 390 BC], 473–475.
5 For the story, and the phrases quoted, see Genesis, ch. 4.

others, but they will not, in virtue of that condition, have turned away from the good and blighted their lives, as Cain did.

This brings us back to the *primacy of the moral dimension* in understanding the religious outlook, and to the questions about mortality and meaningfulness that are so closely bound up with such an outlook (Chapter 6). Such questions are explored with painful vividness in a text written in 2010 by a seventy-six-year-old patient, at a time when his wife was undergoing treatment for cancer, and when he, having himself recovered from cancer, was now battling with the fast-progressing motor neurone disease that was to end his life later that same year:

I see life as a continuous learning process. I learn how to live in the process of living. The learning is lifelong, and continues until the end.... The speed of these changes is turning our lives upside down. The rules of the game are changing faster than we can adapt. And in the midst of this chaos, some patterns are becoming clear. One is to do with time. I am getting a sense that there is no limit to the depth of now; no limit to the journey into the deep. We are being drawn to live more deeply in the here and now. And as we live more deeply in the here and now, we come closer to one another and closer to God.... To live more deeply in the here and now is to make the journey into the depths of the human heart where God is always here now.... And for some the journey passes through hell.[6]

The passage links several of the ideas that have emerged in our last three chapters: the idea discussed in Chapter 7 of the religious life as continuous process of learning; the conclusion of Chapter 5, that a religious framework for interpreting these things is very far from a matter of turning glibly away from our human sufferings; and the suggestion in Chapter 6 that the religious outlook is certainly not a matter of denying our vulnerability or subsuming it entirely under the framework of the post-mortem consolation, which is so often assumed by critics to be the main focus of attention.

Traditional spiritual exercises (of the kind discussed in Chapter 7) are aimed at an interior purification that will enable us to live worthwhile and meaningful lives *despite* our human weakness and vulnerability. How might this work? The theistic answer will of course refer to the grace of God at work in human life while the atheist will perforce deny

---

6 Philip Sheppard, 'Conclusion of a Life's Journey', *Douai Magazine* 173 (2011), 16–17.

the reality of any such process. But what cannot be ignored or denied on any interpretation is the praxis, the daily and weekly and monthly habits of spirituality that sustain the life of the religious adherent. These may include, for example, an assigned time near the start of each day to collect one's thoughts. This will be a time of silence and meditation. It will be a time to reflect with gratitude on the gift of life and the blessing of another day. It will be a time to recall the mistakes of the previous day, and summon the strength to improve. It will be a time of focused contemplation of the tasks to be done this day and of awareness of the need for grace in performing and accomplishing them. It will be a time of recalling the needs of others, both of loved ones and in the wider world, and of resolving to respond to those needs in one's actions and behaviour. For the religious adherent such patterns of thought and action are so integrated into the fabric of life, and so closely bound up with a continuing affirmation of its value and meaning, as to make religious allegiance something vastly more profound and pervasive than a matter of mere intellectual assent.

At the core of such spirituality is *focused and morally oriented reflection*. But for the religious adherent this will not be just a free-floating individual enterprise that could peter out at any time, but will be incorporated into *formalized structure*, one that has been developed and refined through centuries of religious tradition and continued practice, and which is aimed at nurturing the integration of the self and fostering moral maturity and orientation towards an objective source of goodness. Reinforced by daily habit, the relevant structure will also be available in moments of special stress and difficulty such as arise in the crises of every life. And it will also be strengthened by weekly rhythms of communal observance and by the organized patterns of collective worship that mark the regular seasons of the liturgical year.

But here the theoretical and the practical components of religion come together; for it is clear that the theistic framework within which the practices just described take place is what gives them shape and significance. There is a kind of mutual reinforcing here, where the credal or doxastic elements of the religious life inform the practical structures of spirituality and give them meaning and purpose, and conversely the practices have a transformative function that opens the practitioner, cognitively, imaginatively and affectively, to experiences that seem to reinforce the validity of the worldview. And this in turn has implications for the philosophizing about religion: it is no longer possible to see it as an exercise in detached intellectual scrutiny of a belief system, since the phenomenon to be studied is one whose meaning is integrally bound up with the interior transformations that condition the life of the believer. Whatever conclusions we finally draw about these complex questions, one underlying theme throughout our discussion has been that we should be prepared to investigate them in a humanistic way, that is to say, by opening ourselves to all the resources of human experience that are relevant to the shaping of a philosophically rounded worldview. These will accord logical analysis a central place; but they will also include the resources of poetry, music, scriptural and other literature, and also of our own experience as we undergo psychological and moral change; and these latter resources will be used not in an uncritical or irrational way, but in such a way as to allow the insights arrived at to work on our imagination and enrich our understanding. There is nothing question-begging about such a procedure; for it remains possible, even when all these avenues are explored, that one may decide to reject a theistic interpretation of the reality that underlies them. But the question of whether acceptance or rejection is the more philosophically defensible position will not be something that can be decided on intellectual grounds alone. For it is partly a moral decision: a decision about whether, in the light of one's own experience and a sincere willingness to open oneself to all the dimensions of that experience, a certain interpretation of what reality is like can be with integrity accepted, or with integrity rejected. Engaging in the philosophy of religion may not be a way of settling this matter definitively – few if any branches of philosophy could claim to establish final answers to the questions they raise. But if the argument of this book has been on the right lines, a properly enriched philosophy of religion can help us to see more clearly what is at stake.

BIBLIOGRAPHY

Adams, Robert M., *Finite and Infinite Goods* (Oxford: Oxford University Press, 1999).

Alston, W. P., *Divine Nature and Human Language* (Ithaca, NY: Cornell University Press, 1989).

Anselm of Canterbury, St, *Proslogion* [1077], in Anselm, *The Major Works*, ed. B. Davies and G. R. Evans (Oxford: Oxford University Press, 1998).

Aquinas, Thomas, *Summa contra Gentiles* [1259–65], trans. A. C. Pegis (Notre Dame, IN: Notre Dame University Press, 1975).

Aquinas, Thomas, *Summa theologiae* [1266–73], trans. Fathers of the English Dominican Province (London: Burns, Oates and Washbourne, 1911).

Aristotle, *De Anima* [c. 320 BC], ed. and trans. D. W. Hamlyn (Oxford: Clarendon, 1968).

Aristotle, *Nicomachean Ethics* [c. 325 BC], ed. T. Irwin (Indianapolis, IN: Hackett, 1985). Also in *The Ethics of Aristotle*, trans. J. Thomson, rev. H. Tredennick (Harmondsworth: Penguin, 1976).

Augustine of Hippo, *Confessions* [*Confessiones*, 397–401], trans. W. Watts (Cambridge, MA: Harvard University Press, 1912).

Augustine of Hippo, *Sermons* [*Sermones*, 392–430], in J. Migne (ed.), *Patrologia Latina* (Paris, 1857–66).

Augustine of Hippo, *Against Faustus the Manichaean* [*Contra Faustum Manichaeum*, 400], in J. Migne (ed.), *Patrologia Latina* (Paris, 1857–66).

Austin, John, *The Province of Jurisprudence Determined* [1832] (Cambridge: Cambridge University Press, 1995).

Ayer, A. J., *Language, Truth and Logic* [1939] 2nd ed. (London: Gollancz, 1946).

Ayer, A. J., *Logical Positivism* (New York: Free Press, 1959).

Baggett, David, and J. L. Walls, *Good God: The Theistic Foundations of Morality* (Oxford: Oxford University Press, 2010).

Barth, Karl, *Epistle to the Romans* [*Romerbrief*, 1919], trans. E. C. Hoskins (Oxford: Oxford University Press, 1968).

Barth, Karl, *Nein!* [1934], trans. in Emil Brunner and Karl Barth, *Natural Theology* (Eugene, OR: Wipf and Stock, 2002).

Blackburn, Simon, *Ruling Passions* (Oxford: Clarendon Press, 1998).

Boghossian, Paul, *Fear of Knowledge: Against Relativism and Constructivism* (Oxford: Oxford University Press, 2009).

Bonaventure, St, *Itinerarium mentis in Deum* [1259] ('Journey of the Mind towards God'), in *Opera Omnia* (Collegium S. Bonaventurae: Quaracchi, 1891).

Bunyan, John, *The Pilgrim's Progress* (London: Penguin, 2008).

Comte-Sponville, André, *The Book of Atheist Spirituality* [originally published as *L'esprit de l'athéisme*, 2006] (London: Bantam, 2008).

Conway, Anne, *The Principles of the Most Ancient and Modern Philosophy* [1690], repr. in C. Taliaferro and A. J. Teply (eds.), *Cambridge Platonist Spirituality* (Mahwah, NJ: Paulist Press, 2004).

Cottingham, John, 'The Desecularization of Descartes', in Nathan Jacobs and Chris Firestone (eds.), *The Persistence of the Sacred in Modern Thought* (Notre Dame, IN: Notre Dame University Press, 2012), pp. 15–37.

Cottingham, John, 'Confronting the Cosmos: Scientific Rationality and Human Understanding', *Proceedings of the ACPA* (Philosophy Documentation Center), Vol. 85 (2011), pp. 27–42. DOI: 10.5840/acpaproc 2011854.

Cottingham, John, 'Getting the Right Travel Papers: A Postscript to *The Spiritual Dimension*', *Philosophy* 83:326 (October 2008), pp. 557–567.

Cottingham, John, 'Human Nature and the Transcendent', in Constantine Sandis and M. J. Cain (eds.), *Human Nature*, Royal Institute of Philosophy supplement 70 (Cambridge: Cambridge University Press, 2012), pp. 233–254.

Cottingham, John, 'Impartiality and Ethical Formation', in B. Feltham and J. Cottingham (eds.), *Partiality and Impartiality: Morality, Special Relationships and the Wider World* (Oxford: Oxford University Press, 2010), pp. 65–83.

Cottingham, John, 'Meaningful Life', in Paul K. Moser and Michael T. McFall (eds.), *The Wisdom of the Christian Faith* (Cambridge: Cambridge University Press, 2012), pp. 175–196.

Cottingham, John, 'Meaningfulness, Eternity and Theism', in Beatrix Himmelmann (ed.), *On Meaning in Life* (Berlin/Boston: De Gruyter, 2013), pp. 99–112.

Cottingham, John, 'Philosophy and Self-improvement: Continuity and Change in Philosophy's Self-conception from the Classical to the Early-modern Era', in Michael Chase, Stephen Clark, and Michael McGhee (eds.), *Philosophy as a Way of Life: Ancients and Moderns* (Oxford: Blackwell, 2013), pp. 148–166.

Cottingham, John, 'Sceptical Detachment or Loving Submission to the Good: Reason, Faith and the Passions in Descartes', *Faith and Philosophy* 28:1 (January 2011), pp. 44–53.

Cottingham, John, 'Spirituality', in C. Taliaferro, V. S. Harrison, and S. Goetz (eds.), *The Routledge Companion to Theism* (New York: Routledge, 2013), pp. 654–665.

Cottingham, John, 'The Good Life and the "Radical Contingency of the Ethical"', in D. Callcut (ed.), *Reading Bernard Williams* (London: Routledge, 2008), pp. 25–43.

Cottingham, John, 'The Self, the Good Life and the Transcendent', in N. Athanassoulis and S. Vice (eds.), *The Moral Life: Essays in Honour of John Cottingham* (London: Palgrave, 2008), pp. 228–271.

Cottingham, John, 'What Difference Does It Make? The Nature and Significance of Theistic Belief', *Ratio* 19:4 (December 2006), pp. 401–420.

Cottingham, John, 'What Is Humane Philosophy and Why Is It at Risk?', in A. O'Hear (ed.), *Conceptions of Philosophy* (Cambridge: Cambridge University Press, 2009).

Cottingham, John, 'Wittgenstein's Philosophy of Religion', in H.-J. Glock and J. Hyman (eds.), *A Companion to Wittgenstein* (Oxford: Wiley, forthcoming).

Cottingham, John, *Philosophy and the Good Life: Reason and the Passions in Greek, Cartesian and Psychoanalytic Ethics* (Cambridge: Cambridge University Press, 1998).

Cottingham, John, *The Spiritual Dimension* (Cambridge: Cambridge University Press, 2005).

Cottingham, John, *Why Believe?* (London: Continuum, 2009).

Cox, Brian, *The Wonders of Life*, BBC television series, first broadcast January 2013.

Craig, William Lane and James D. Sinclair, 'The Kalam Cosmological Argument', in W. L. Craig and J. P. Moreland (eds.), *The Blackwell Companion to Natural Theology* (Oxford: Wiley-Blackwell, 2012), Ch. 3.

Craig, William Lane, 'The Absurdity of Life without God' [1984], in *Reasonable Faith, Christian Truth and Apologetics, rev. ed.* (Wheaton, IL: Crossway Books, 1994), pp. 57–75.

Cupitt, Don, *The Fountain: A Secular Theology* (London: SCM Press, 2010).

Cupitt, Don, *Taking Leave of God* (London: SCM Press, 1981).

Dante Alighieri, *The Divine Comedy: Paradise* [*La Divina Comedia: Paradiso*, c. 1320], ed. G. Bickersteth (Oxford: Blackwell, 1981).

Darwin, Charles, *The Origin of Species by Means of Natural Selection* [1859], ed. G. Beer (Oxford University Press, 2008).

Davies, Brian, 'Is God beyond Reason?', *Philosophical Investigations* 32:4 (October 2009), pp. 338–359.

Davies, Brian, *Aquinas* (London: Continuum, 2002).

Dawkins, Richard, *Rivers Out of Eden* (New York: Basic Books, 1995).

Dawkins, Richard, *The God Delusion* (London: Bantam, 2006).

Dawkins, Richard, *The Blind Watchmaker* (London: Penguin, 1986).

De Vries, Hent, ' "Winke": Divine Topoi in Hölderlin, Heidegger, Nancy', in A. Rioretos (ed.), *The Solid Letter: New Readings of Friedrich Hölderlin* (Stanford, CA: Stanford University Press, 1999), pp. 112–131.

Dennett, Daniel, *Intuition Pumps* (London: Allen Lane, 2013).

Descartes, René, *The Philosophical Writings of Descartes*, ed. J. Cottingham, R. Stoothoff, and D. Murdoch, Vols. I and II (Cambridge: Cambridge University Press, 1985) (referred to as 'CSM'), and Vol. III, The Correspondence, by the same translators and A. Kenny (Cambridge: Cambridge University Press, 1991) (referred to as 'CSMK').

Dostoevsky, Fyodor, *The Brothers Karamazov* [*Brat'ya Karamazovy*, 1880], (Harmondsworth: Penguin, 1958).

Dougherty, Trent, and Jerry L. Wells, 'Arguments from Evil', in C. Taliaferro, V. Harrison, and S. Goetz (eds.), *The Routledge Companion to Theism* (London: Routledge, 2013), pp. 370ff.

Dupré, John, 'Review of Thomas Nagel's *Mind and Cosmos*', *Notre Dame Philosophical Reviews*, 29 (October 2012), pp. 50–55.

Eliot, Thomas Stearns, 'Little Gidding' [1942], in *Four Quartets* (London: Faber, 1959).

Ellis, Fiona, *God, Value, and Nature* (Oxford: Oxford University Press, forthcoming).

Epictetus, *Discourses* [*Diatribae*, c. AD 100].

Evans, C. Stephen, *God and Moral Obligation* (Oxford: Oxford University Press, 2013).

Evans, C. Stephen, *Natural Signs and Knowledge of God* (Oxford: Oxford University Press, 2010).

First Vatican Council, Dogmatic Constitution on the Catholic Faith (*Dei Filius*) [1870].

Fraassen, Bas van, *The Scientific Image* (Oxford: Oxford University Press, 1980).

Frank, Anne, *Diary* [*Dagboekbrieven 14 juni 1942 – 1 augustus 1944*], trans. S. Massotty (London: Puffin, 2007), entry for 23 February 1944.

Frege, Gottlob, *The Basic Laws of Arithmetic* [*Die Grundgesetze der Arithmetik*, Vol. I, 1893], trans. M. Furth (Berkeley: University of California Press, 1964).

Freud, Sigmund, *Civilization and Its Discontents* [*Das Unbehagen in der Kultur*, 1929] (London: Penguin, 1991).

Hadot, Pierre, *Philosophy as a Way of Life* (Oxford: Blackwell, 1995) [originally published as *Exercises spirituels et philosophie antique* (1987)].

Hampson, Daphne, *After Christianity* (London: SCM Press 1996; 2nd ed. 2002).

Harvey, Peter, *An Introduction to Buddhist Ethics* (Cambridge: Cambridge University Press, 2000).

Heidegger, Martin, *Being and Time* [*Sein und Zeit*, 1927], trans. J. Macquarrie and E. Robinson (New York: Harper and Row, 1962).

Helm, Paul, *Faith and Understanding* (Edinburgh: Edinburgh University Press, 1997).

Hobbes, Thomas, *The Questions concerning Liberty and Necessity and Chance* [1654], in *English Works of Thomas Hobbes*, ed. W. Molesworth (London: Bohn, 1841), Vol. V.

Hoff, Johannes, 'Mystagogy beyond Onto-theology. Looking back to Postmodernity with Nicholas of Cusa', in J. Hoff, *The Analogical Turn. Rethinking Modernity with Nicholas of Cusa* (Eerdmans, MI: Grand Rapids, 2013), ch. 1.

Hölderlin, Friedrich, *Hymnische Entwürfe* (Sketches for Hymns), 1800–1805, in *Selected Poems* (London: Penguin, 1998).

Hopkins, Gerard Manley, *Note-books and Papers*, ed. H. House (Oxford: Oxford University Press, 1937).

Hopkins, Gerard Manley, *Poems (1876–1889)*, ed. W. H. Gardner (Harmondsworth: Penguin, 1953).

Housman, A. E., *Last Poems* [1922], repr. in *Collected Poems* (Harmondsworth: Penguin, 1956).

Howard-Snyder, Daniel, and Paul Moser (eds.), *Divine Hiddenness* (Cambridge: Cambridge University Press, 2002).

Hume, David, 'The Sceptic', in *Essays Moral and Political*, Vol. 2 [1742], repr. in Hume, *Selected Essays*, ed. S. Copley and A. Edgar (Oxford: Oxford University Press, 1993).

Hume, David, *An Enquiry concerning Human Understanding* [1748], ed. T. Beauchamp (Oxford: Oxford University Press, 1999).

Hume, David, *An Enquiry concerning the Principles of Morals* [1751], ed. T. L. Beauchamp (Oxford: Oxford University Press, 1998).

Hume, David, *Dialogues concerning Natural Religion* [c. 1755], ed. H. D. Aiken (New York: Haffner, 1948).

Ignatius of Loyola, *Spiritual Exercises* [*Ejercicios espirituales*, c. 1525], trans. J. Munitz and P. Endean (Harmondsworth: Penguin, 1996).

Inwagen, Peter van, 'Metaphysics', in Adrian Hastings et al. (eds.), *The Oxford Companion to Christian Thought* (Oxford: Oxford University Press, 2000).

James, William, *The Will to Believe* [1896] (Cranston, RI: Anglenook, 2012).

James, William, *Varieties of Religious Experience* [1902] (London: Fontana, 1960).

Johnston, Mark, *Saving God: Religion after Idolatry* (Princeton, NJ: Princeton University Press, 2009).

Johnston, Mark, *Surviving Death* (Princeton, NJ: Princeton University Press, 2010).

Jones, Ward E., 'Religious Conversion, Self-Deception and Pascal's Wager', *Journal of the History of Philosophy* 36:2 (April 1998), pp. 167–188.

Jones, Ward E., 'Being Moved by a Way the World Is Not', *Synthèse* (DOI 10.1007/s11229-009-9522-z), published online 9 April 2009.

Jonkers, Peter, and Marcel Sarot (eds.), *Embodied Religion. Ars Disputandi: The Online Journal for Philosophy of Religion*, Supplement, series 6 (2013).

Jung, Carl G., *Collected Works*, rev. ed. (London: Routledge, 1967–77).

Jung, Carl G., *Modern Man in Search of a Soul* (London: Routledge, 1933).

Kant, Immanuel, *Groundwork for the Metaphysic of Morals* [*Grundlegung zur Metaphysik der Sitten*, 1785], Akademie edition (Berlin: Reimer/De Gruyter, 1900–), Vol. IV, trans. T. E. Hill Jr. and A. Zweig (Oxford: Oxford University Press, 2003).

Kant, Immanuel, *Prolegomena to any Future Metaphysic that will be able to present itself as a Science* [*Prolegomena zu einer jeden künftigen Metaphysik die als Wissenschaft wird auftreten können*, 1783], ed. G. Zöller (Oxford: Oxford University Press, 2004).

Kant, Immanuel, *Critique of Practical Reason* [*Kritik der Practischen Vernunft*, 1788], trans. T. K. Abbott (London: Longmans, 1873; 6th ed. 1909).

Kant, Immanuel, *Critique of Pure Reason* [*Kritik der reinen Vernunft*, 1781–87], trans. N. Kemp Smith (New York: St. Martin's Press, 1965).

Kaufmann, Walter, *Nietzsche: Philosopher, Psychologist, Antichrist* (Princeton, NJ: Princeton University Press, 1950).

Kekes, John, *The Human Condition* (Oxford: Oxford University Press, 2010).

Kenny, Anthony, *What I Believe* (London: Continuum, 2006).

Kierkegaard, Søren, *Concluding Unscientific Postscript* [*Afsluttende Uviden-skabelig Efterskrift*, 1846], trans. D. F. Swenson (Princeton, NJ: Princeton University Press, 1941).

Korsgaard, Christine, *Self-Constitution* (Oxford: Oxford University Press, 2009).

Korsgaard, Christine, *The Sources of Normativity* (Cambridge: Cambridge University Press, 1996).

Kuhn, Thomas S., *The Structure of Scientific Revolutions* [1962], 2nd ed. (Chicago: University of Chicago Press, 1970).

Leibniz, Gottfried Wilhelm, *Philosophical Writings*, ed. G. H. R. Parkinson (London: Dent, 1973).

Leibniz, Gottfried Wilhelm, *Theodicy* [*Essais de théodicée*, 1710], trans. E. M. Huggard (London: Routledge, 1951).

Leiter, Brian, *The Future for Philosophy* (Oxford: Clarendon Press, 2004).

Levinas, Emmanuel, *Ethique et infini* [1982], trans. as *Ethics and Infinity* (Pittsburgh, PA: Duquesne University Press, 1985).

Lewis, C. S., *The Screwtape Letters* [1942] (New York: HarperCollins, 2001).

Løgstrup, Knud E., *The Ethical Demand* [*Den Etiske Fordring*, 1956], ed. H. Fink and A. MacIntyre (Notre Dame, IN: University of Notre Dame Press, 1997).

Lothrop, S. K., *The Consolations of Old Age* (Boston: Eastburn's Press, 1846).

Louth, Andrew, *Discerning the Mystery* (Oxford: Clarendon Press, 1983).

Lowe, Jonathan, *A Survey of Metaphysics* (Oxford: Oxford University Press, 2002).

Mackie, John, *The Miracle of Theism* (Oxford: Clarendon, 1982).

Marion, Jean-Luc, 'In the Name: How to Avoid Speaking of "Negative Theology"', in J. D. Caputo and M. J. Scanlon (eds.), *God, the Gift, and Post-modernism* (Bloomington, IN: Indiana University Press, 1999).

Marx, Karl, *Critique of Hegel's Philosophy of Right* [*Zur Kritik der Hegelschen Rechtsphilosophie* 1843], trans. A. Jolin and J. O'Malley (Cambridge: Cambridge University Press, 1970).

McCabe, Herbert, *God and Evil in the Philosophy of Thomas Aquinas* [1957] (London: Continuum, 2010).

McDowell, John, *Mind and World* (Cambridge, MA: Harvard University Press, 1994).

McGilchrist, Iain, *The Master and His Emissary* (New Haven, CT: Yale University Press, 2009).

McPherson, David, 'Cosmic Outlooks and Neo-Aristotelian Virtue Ethics', *International Philosophical Quarterly*, forthcoming June 2015.

Meyer, Stephen C., *Signature in the Cell* (New York: HarperCollins, 2009).

Moser, Paul, *The Elusive God: Reorienting Religious Epistemology* (Cambridge: Cambridge University Press, 2008).

Moser, Paul, *The Evidence for God* (Cambridge: Cambridge University Press, 2010).

Nagel, Thomas, *Mind and Cosmos* (Oxford: Oxford University Press, 2012).

Nagel, Thomas, *The Last Word* (Oxford: Oxford University Press, 1997).

Nancy, Jean-Luc, *Des lieux divins* (Mauvezin: Editions Trans-Europe Repress, 1987), trans. as *The Inopererative Community* (Minneapolis: University of Minnesota Press, 1991).

Nietzsche, Friedrich, *Beyond Good and Evil* [*Jenseits von Gut und Böse*, 1886] transl. W. Kaufmann (New York: Random House, 1966).

Nietzsche, Friedrich, *On the Genealogy of Morals* [*Zur Genealogie der Moral*, 1887] ed. D. Smith (Oxford: Oxford University Press, 1996).

Nietzsche, Friedrich, *The Joyful Science* [*Die fröhliche Wissenschaft*, 1882] trans. W. Kaufmann as *The Gay Science* (New York: Vintage, 1974).

Nozick, Robert, *Philosophical Explanations* (Oxford: Oxford University Press, 1981).

Nussbaum, Martha, *Love's Knowledge* (Oxford: Oxford University Press, 1990).

Owens, Joseph, 'Aristotle and Aquinas', in N. Kretzmann and E. Stump (eds.), *The Cambridge Companion to Aquinas* (Cambridge: Cambridge University Press, 1993), ch. 2.

Palmer, Michael, *Freud and Jung on Religion* (London: Routledge, 1977).

Parfit, Derek, *On What Matters* (Oxford: Oxford University Press, 2011).

Parfit, Derek, *Reasons and Persons* (Oxford: Oxford University Press, 1984).

Pascal, Blaise, *Pensées* ('Thoughts') [1670], ed. L. Lafuma (Paris: Seuil, 1962).

Phillips, D. Z. (ed.), *Religion and Understanding* (Oxford: Blackwell, 1967).

Plantinga, Alvin, 'Reason and Belief in God', in A. Plantinga and N. Wolterstorff (eds.), *Faith and Rationality* (Notre Dame, IN: University of Notre Dame Press, 1983), pp. 16–93.

Plath, Sylvia, *The Bell Jar* [1963] (London: Faber, 1966).

Putnam, Hilary, 'Levinas and Judaism', in S, Critchley and R. Bernasconi (eds.), *The Cambridge Companion to Levinas* (Cambridge: Cambridge University Press, 1986).

Radcliffe, Timothy, *What Is the Point of Being a Christian?* (London: Continuum, 2005).

Rahner, Karl, 'Christianity and the Non-Christian Religions' [notes of a lecture delivered on 28 April 1961], in J. Hick and B. Hebblethwaite (eds.), *Christianity and Other Religions* (Philadelphia, PA: Fortress Press, 1981), ch. 3, repr. in M. Peterson et al., *Philosophy of Religion: Selected Readings*, 2nd ed. (Oxford: Oxford University Press, 2001), pp. 549ff.

Rajchman, J., *Truth and Eros: Foucault, Lacan, and the Question of Ethics* (New York: Routledge, 1991).

Rees, Martin, *Our Cosmic Habitat* (London: Weidenfeld & Nicolson, 2002).

Rilke, Rainer Maria, *Der Neuen Gedichte anderer Teil* [1908]. Several editions and translations available including *Neue Gedichte/New Poems* (Manchester: Carcanet, 1997).

Ritchie, Angus, *From Morality to Metaphysics* (Oxford: Oxford University Press, 2012).

Rorty, Richard, *Philosophy and the Mirror of Nature* (Princeton, NJ: Princeton University Press, 1981).

Sartre, Jean-Paul, *Existentialism Is a Humanism (L'existentialisme est un humanisme)* [1946].

Scanlon, Tim, *What We Owe to Each Other* (Cambridge, MA: Belknap, 1998).

Schopenhauer, Arthur, *The World as Will and Representation* [*Die Welt als Wille und Vorstellung* 1819], trans. E. F. J. Payne (Indian Hills, CO: Falcon's Wing Press, 1958).

Scruton, Roger, 'The Sacred and the Human' [2010] http://www.st-andrews.ac.uk/gifford/2010/the-sacred-and-the-human/, accessed 30 March 2010.

Scruton, Roger, *The Face of God* (London: Continuum, 2012).

Sheppard, Philip, 'Conclusion of a Life's Journey', *Douai Magazine* 173 (2011), 16–17.

Sidgwick E. M. and A. Sidgwick (eds.), *Henry Sidgwick, A Memoir* (London: Macmillan, 1906).

Sidgwick, Henry, *Methods of Ethics* [1874], 7th ed. (London: Macmillan, 1907).

Soskice, Janet Martin, 'Theological Realism', in W. Abraham and S. Holtzer, *The Rationality of Religious Belief* (Oxford: Clarendon, 1987).

Steiner, George, *Heidegger*, 2nd ed. (London: Fontana Press, 1992).

Sterry, Peter, *A Discourse of the Freedom of the Will* [1675]; repr. in C. Taliaferro and A. J. Teply (eds.), *Cambridge Platonist Spirituality* (Mahwah, NJ: Paulist Press, 2004).

Stratton-Lake, P. J., *Ethical Intuitionism* (Oxford: Clarendon Press, 2002).

Strawson, Galen, 'Religion is a sin', *London Review of Books* 33:11 (June 2011), pp. 26–28.

Stump, Eleonore, 'Dante's Hell, Aquinas's Moral Theory, and the Love of God', *Canadian Journal of Philosophy* 16 (1986), pp. 181–198.

Stump, Eleonore, *Wandering in Darkness* (Oxford: Oxford University Press, 2010).

Swinburne, Richard, *The Evolution of the Soul* [1986] (Oxford: Clarendon, 2005).

Swinburne, Richard, 'God as the Simplest Explanation of the Universe', in Anthony O'Hear (ed.), *Philosophy and Religion*, Royal Institute of Philosophy Supplement 68 (Cambridge: Cambridge University Press, 2011), pp. 3–24.

Swinburne, Richard, *The Existence of God* [1979], 2nd ed. (Oxford: Oxford University Press, 2004).

Swinburne, Richard, *Was Jesus God?* (Oxford: Oxford University Press, 2008).

Taliaferro, Charles, 'Religious Rites', in C. Taliaferro and C. Meister (eds.), *The Cambridge Companion to Christian Philosophical Theology* (New York: Cambridge University Press, 2010), pp. 183–200.

Thomas, R. S., *Laboratories of the Spirit* (London: Macmillan, 1975).

Thomas, R. S., *Mass for Hard Times* (Newcastle: Bloodaxe Books, 1992).

Turner, Denys, *The Darkness of God* (Cambridge: Cambridge University Press, 1995).

White, Roger M., *Talking about God: The Concept of Analogy and the Problem of Religious Language* (Farnham: Ashgate, 2010).

Williams, Bernard, 'The Makropulos Case: Reflections on the Tedium of Immortality', in *Problems of the Self* (Cambridge: Cambridge University Press, 1973), pp. 82–100.

Williams, Bernard, 'Replies', in J. Altham and R. Harrison (eds.), *World, Mind, and Ethics* (Cambridge: Cambridge University Press, 1995).

Williams, Bernard, *Ethics and the Limits of Philosophy* (London: Collins, 1985).

Williams, Bernard, *Making Sense of Humanity* (Cambridge: Cambridge University Press, 1995).

Williams, Bernard, *Shame and Necessity* (Berkeley: University of California Press, 1993).

Williams, Bernard, *Truth and Truthfulness* (Princeton, NJ: Princeton University Press, 2002).

Williamson, Tim, 'Past the Linguistic Turn', in B. Leiter (ed.), *The Future for Philosophy* (Oxford: Clarendon Press, 2004), pp. 109–110.

Wittgenstein, Ludwig, 'A Lecture on Ethics' [1929], in *Philosophical Occasions*, ed. J. Klagge and A. Nordmann (Indianapolis, IN: Hackett, 1993).

Wittgenstein, Ludwig, *Philosophical Investigations* [*Philosophische Untersuchungen*, 1953], trans. G. E. M. Anscombe (New York: Macmillan, 1958).

Wittgenstein, Ludwig, *Tractatus Logico-Philosophicus* [1921], trans. D. F. Pears and B. F. McGuinness (London: Routledge, 1961).

Wolterstorff, Nicolas, *Justice: Rights and Wrongs* (Princeton, NJ: Princeton University Press, 2008).

Wordsworth, William, *A Critical Edition of the Major Works*, ed. S. Gill (Oxford: Oxford University Press, 2010).

Wright, N. T., *The Resurrection of the Son of God* (London: SPCK, 2003).

Wynn, Mark, *Emotional Experience and Religious Understanding* (Cambridge: Cambridge University Press, 2005).

Zagzebski, Linda, *Philosophy of Religion* (Oxford: Blackwell, 2007).

INDEX